Feminism and Empire

Feminism and Empire establishes the foundational impact that Britain's position as leading imperial power had on the origins of modern western feminism. Based on extensive new research, this study exposes the intimate links between debates on the 'woman question' and the constitution of 'colonial discourse' in order to highlight the centrality of empire to white middle-class women's activism in Britain.

The book begins by exploring the relationship between the construction of new knowledge about colonised others and the framing of debates on the 'woman question' among advocates of women's rights and their evangelical opponents. Moving on to examine white middle-class women's activism on imperial issues in Britain, topics include the anti-slavery boycott of Caribbean sugar, the campaign against widow-burning in colonial India, and women's role in the foreign missionary movement prior to direct employment by the major missionary societies. Finally, Clare Midgley highlights how the organised feminist movement which emerged in the late 1850s linked promotion of female emigration to Britain's white settler colonies to a new ideal of independent English womanhood. Through this she shows how middle-class women's involvement in empire-focussed campaigns was crucial in enabling them to find opportunities to participate in life beyond the domestic sphere. In turn, British women had a distinctive impact in shaping the reform of empire.

This original work throws fascinating new light on the roots of later 'imperial feminism' and contemporary debates concerning women's rights in an era of globalisation and neo-imperialism.

Clare Midgley is Research Professor in History at Sheffield Hallam University. Her publications include *Women Against Slavery: The British Campaigns, 1780–1870* (Routledge, 1995) and *Gender and Imperialism* (1998).

Feminism and Empire

Women Activists in Imperial Britain, 1790–1865

Clare Midgley

Routledge
Taylor & Francis Group

LONDON AND NEW YORK

First published 2007
by Routledge
2 Park Square, Milton Park Abingdon, Oxon, OX14 4RN

Simultaneously published in the USA and Canada
by Routledge
270 Madison Avenue, New York, NY 10016

Routledge is an imprint of the Taylor & Francis Group, an informa business

Typeset in Garamond by Keyword Group Ltd
Printed and bound in Great Britain by Antony Rowe Ltd,
Chippenham, Wiltshire

British Library Cataloguing in Publication Data
A catalogue record for this book is available from the British Library

Library of Congress Cataloging in Publication Data
Midgley, Clare, 1955–
    Feminism and empire: women activists in Imperial Britain,
1790–1865/
Clare Midgley.
        p. cm
    Includes bibliographical references.
    1. Women–Great Britain–Political activity–History–
18th century. 2. Women–Great Britain–Political activity–History–
19th century. 3. Feminism–Great Britain–History–18th century.
4. Feminism–Great Britain–History–19th century. 5. Women–Great
Britain–Social conditions. I. Title.
    HQ1593.M53 2007
    305.4209171'24109034–dc22   2007013243

ISBN 10: 0-415-25014-5 (hbk)
ISBN 10: 0-415-25015-3 (pbk)
ISBN 10: 0-203-08949-9 (ebk)

ISBN 13: 978-0-415-25014-6 (hbk)
ISBN 13: 978-0-415-25015-3 (pbk)
ISBN 13: 978-0-203-08949-1 (ebk)

In memory of my father, John Winwood Midgley

Contents

Acknowledgements

Over 10 years have passed between the initial conception of this book as an overview of the shifting historical relationship between feminism and Empire in Britain between the 1790s and the 1930s and its eventual completion as a more focused research-based study. In the process, I have tried out my developing ideas at numerous seminars and conferences in Britain, Australia, Canada, Finland and the USA: my sincere thanks to all those who have invited me to speak and who have read and commented on work in progress, and thus helped me to clarify, modify and develop my ideas. Early versions of some of the material in this book have appeared in published form as: 'Slave sugar boycotts, female activism and the domestic base of British anti-slavery culture', *Slavery and Abolition*, 1996, vol. 17, pp. 137–62 (journal website: http://www.informaworld.com); 'Female emancipation in an imperial frame: English women and the campaign against sati (widow-burning) in India, 1813–30, *Women's History Review*, 2000, vol. 9, pp. 95–121 (journal website: http://www.informaworld.com); 'From supporting missions to petitioning Parliament: British women and the Evangelical campaign against *sati* in India, 1813–30', in K. Gleadle and S. Richardson (eds), *Women in British Politics, 1760–1860*, Basingstoke, Macmillan, 2000, pp. 74–92; 'Can women be missionaries? Envisioning female agency in the early nineteenth-century British Empire', *Journal of British Studies*, 2006, vol. 45, pp. 335–58. I am grateful to these publishers for allowing me to reprint material from these articles. Thanks, too, to the staff of the British Library, where much of the work of researching and writing this book was undertaken, to Liz O'Reilly for her efficient work on transforming endless endnotes into a bibliography and to Eve Setch, my very helpful editor.

I also wish to acknowledge the following: the financial support of the Leverhulme Trust, whose award of a Research Fellowship in 1998–9 enabled me to get the research for this project under way; the Arts and Humanities Research Council for their Research Leave Award in 2002–3 and London Metropolitan University for matching study leave, which helped forward it; and I am particularly grateful to my new employers, Sheffield Hallam

University, for granting me research leave last year, which finally enabled me to complete the manuscript.

The intellectual stimulus of the 'Reconfiguring the British' seminar at the Institute of Historical Research in London, that I convene with Catherine Hall, Keith McClelland and Zoë Laidlaw, has been vital in maintaining my enthusiasm for rewriting the history of Empire, while a rigorous writing schedule over the past year has been maintained with wonderful support from fellow members of the 'history girls' writing group, Lucy Bland, Alison Oram, Krisztina Roberts, Katharina Rowold and Cornelie Usborne. Thanks, too, for their inspiration and engagement, to my former colleagues at London Guildhall (now London Metropolitan) University, especially the staff of the Women's Library, and students on the MA in Modern British Women's History.

This book has been researched and written through some challenging times, and among many who have offered friendship, inspiration and support, in addition to those named above, I would particularly like to thank Anne Alwis, Kelly Boyd, Anna Clark, Shani D'Cruze, Leonore Davidoff, Kathryn Gleadle, Kate Goslett, Rohan McWilliam, John Mackenzie, Amanda Sackur, Megan Smitley, Laura Tabili and Susan Thorne. June Cox Smith's sustaining friendship, and her company on wonderful days out, has helped keep me reasonably sane – here's to our 40 years of friendship! Finally, my sincere appreciation to my partner, Norris Saakwa-Mante: without him I would not be quite the same person, or have written quite the same book, and it thus seems very appropriate that I should have completed the manuscript today, the 50th anniversary of Ghana's independence from British colonial rule.

Introduction

'The true history of the Women's Movement is the whole history of the nineteenth century'. Thus wrote British feminist activist Ray Strachey in the preface to *The Cause. A Short History of the Women's Movement in Great Britain*, published in 1928, the year British women finally gained the vote on the same terms as men. Explaining her meaning, Strachey elaborated:

> I have not referred to such events as the Indian Mutiny, the Franco-Prussian War, the Home Rule Agitation, or the Parliament Act, and yet I know that these things undoubtedly had a bearing on the problem and did their part, along with the whole progress of the world, in shaping this special development.[1]

In this book I focus on this wider context to the history of feminism in Britain, looking specifically at the relationship between the development of British imperialism and the origins of modern feminism in Britain in the period between the 1790s, when Mary Wollstonecraft's *Vindication of the Rights of Woman* was published, and the mid-1860s, when a concerted campaign for women's suffrage was launched. My aim is to explore the influence that Britain's position as a leading imperial power had on the formulation of discussions of the 'woman question', and to examine the openings that campaigns around Empire offered for assertions of feminine agency and power both in relation to British men and in relation to colonised peoples, particularly women. In the process, I aim also to draw out the ways in which women were actively involved in shaping colonial discourse, debates on Empire, and projects of imperial reform.

The link which Strachey made between women's rights and the idea of world progress continued a central theme in discussions of the position of women that, as will be discussed in Chapter 1, can be traced back to the development of Enlightenment thought in the context of European overseas exploration and imperial expansion. Her awareness that the historical development of feminism in Britain was influenced not only by domestic political developments, but also by Britain's involvement in international, and particularly imperial, affairs was not surprising, given the context within which she was writing. The interwar period was a turning point in the relationship between female activists and Empire, as British women entered the political sphere and Britain fought to strengthen its Empire in the face of the rise of anti-colonial movements. The conservative pro-imperialism of the Primrose League and the Victoria League and the 'imperial feminism' of one of the first female members of Parliament, Eleanor Rathbone, both came under challenge from 'commonwealth feminism' with its roots in white settler colonies and from female supporters of Indian and Irish nationalism, pan-Africanism and anti-racism.[2] Strachey was close friends with Millicent Garrett Fawcett (1847–1929), best known today as leader of the constitutionalist wing of the women's suffrage movement, but also prominent as a liberal imperialist who headed the ladies' commission set up by the government in response to the concentration camps controversy during the South African War, and who was an outspoken opponent of Irish Home Rule.[3]

Succeeding generations of British feminist activists and scholars did not, however, show the same awareness as Strachey of the interrelationship between feminism and Empire. In the 1970s and 1980s, writing after the demise of the British Empire, feminist historians were preoccupied with the relation of gender to class rather than to race or ethnicity, and concerned to write women into left-leaning social history rather than imperial history, which remained a bastion of conservative scholarship.[4] When women's involvement in the British Empire was addressed, it was in popular histories of white women in the colonies: stories of the lives of memsahibs linked to the 'Raj nostalgia' of the 1980s, and tales of plucky women travellers, republished as inspirational tracts by the new feminist publishing house, Virago (which was also responsible for reprinting Strachey's *The Cause* in 1978).[5] The scholarly studies which did appear, often written by cultural anthropologists rather than historians, tended to be recuperative in tone, downplaying women's imperial power and privileges in an effort to combat misogynist imperial stereotypes of white women as racists who disrupted supposedly hitherto good relations between coloniser and colonised and were, in the words of Percival Spear, a leading historian of the British Raj, the 'ruin of empire'.[6]

In the last 15 years, however, a rich array of historical scholarship has been produced which develops more critical analytical perspectives on the relationship between the history of Western, European and British feminisms and the history of racism and imperialism. The emergence of this literature in the early 1990s, including my own work on British women anti-slavery campaigners, was strongly influenced by the searing critiques of the racism and Euro-centrism of the contemporary Western women's movement mounted throughout the 1980s by women of colour based in the United States and Britain. Their interventions held to account feminists who took white middle-class Western women's experiences as the norm, and who stereotyped Third World women as passive victims, seeking to 'save' them rather than to offer them solidarity.[7] Attempting to respond to this challenge, the new scholarship on white women and Empire explored the historical roots of this 'imperial feminism'. It sought to clarify the spectrum of Western feminist engagements with imperialism, from complicity to resistance; it explored the intersecting politics of gender and race in the anti-slavery movement, the relationship between abolitionism and feminism, and the links between black and white women anti-racist campaigners in Britain and the United States; it exposed the 'imperial feminism' of British women's suffrage campaigners who claimed a role for themselves in the imperial Parliament as saviours of Indian women; and it began to develop new readings of literary texts from a feminist postcolonial perspective.[8]

This book builds both on these studies of the links between feminism and imperialism and on scholarship in the overlapping field of the 'new imperial history', a term coined to signal its distinction from, and opposition to, the traditional field of Imperial History. The latter, as postcolonial critics have emphasised, developed as an intrinsic part of the imperial enterprise and, even if no longer generally written from an overtly pro-imperial perspective, has continued to favour the top-down approach focused on the ideas and actions of male imperial elites while presenting Empire as something that happened 'out there', with little connection to domestic British history. One challenge to this approach has been the production of new histories written from the perspectives of the colonised, exploring slave resistance, anti-colonial nationalisms, and the agency of 'subaltern' groups such as peasants and women under colonialism. Another, and one to which this book seeks to contribute, has been the attempt to draw out the links between the domestic histories of imperial nations and the histories of their empires, and to place metropole and colony within one analytic frame.[9] The beginnings of the process of writing Empire into the history of Britain can be traced to the 1970s and 1980s in the pioneering work of John Mackenzie on imperialism and popular culture, in studies of Victorian attitudes to race, and in attempts to root the history of anti-slavery into British social history, and to recover the historical experiences of black and Asian peoples in Britain.[10] However, a new impetus was provided by the development of postcolonial studies, the growth of interdisciplinary approaches and the 'cultural turn' in history.[11] With the accumulation of a rich new body of historical and literary scholarship (far too substantial to list here), it has become clear that Empire has had a strong impact on society, culture, politics and economic development within the Britain Isles from the beginnings of Empire in the sixteenth century onwards, despite the attempts of some historians to continue to deny that this is the case.[12]

The 'new imperial history' is particularly concerned with questions of identity and the gendered operations of imperial power. Katherine Wilson's *The Island Race* explores eighteenth-century understandings of national identity developed in Britain in the context of exploration and colonization. It shows how Britishness and Englishness were 'sites of struggle' rather than fixed entities, 'understood, performed and consumed in a variety of ways by different groups'. Wilson's insights into the ways in which 'the nation and the empire were gendered, as well as racialized locations that shaped the under-standing of difference in the metropole' have informed my understanding of the shaping of British feminist identities.[13] Catherine Hall's *Civilising Subjects*, exploring the place of metropole and colony in the English imagination through a study of Baptist missionary and abolitionist men in the 'imperial metropolis' of Birmingham between 1830 and 1867, provides an in-depth case study of the ways in which 'the identity of the coloniser is a constitutive part of Englishness' and racial thinking is 'deeply rooted in English culture'. Hall's stress on links between Jamaica and England as complex 'relations of power', as not simply 'mutually constitutive' but inherently 'hierarchical', and her positioning of herself in relation to the history she writes, makes her study an inspiring model for radical scholarship on Empire.[14]

Such scholarship is beginning to render redundant Robert Young's caution that 'one Bertha Mason does not make an imperial summer': his warning that it is dangerous to base generalisations about the impact of Empire on British culture from the texts of a small number of canonical novels such as Charlotte Bronte's *Jane Eyre* (1847).[15] Nevertheless, the impact of Empire on the origins of modern feminism in Britain over the period between 1790 and 1865 has remained underexamined, and one of the key purposes of this book is to explore the historical relationship between 'nascent feminist individualism' and 'imperial social mission' beyond the confines of the literary creation of *Jane Eyre*.[16]

Jane Eyre was in fact one of my favourite novels as a teenager, and rereading *Jane Eyre* in the light of feminist postcolonial studies of the text has led me to think about what it means for me to have identified – indeed, to continue to identify – with the English heroine of the title, giving me insights into my own constitution as a feminist and my own relationship to Empire. Like many British-born girls of my generation, my family background and childhood were marked by Empire. My mother was born in Calcutta to an English mother, who was working as live-in nurse and nanny for a Scottish jute merchant's family, and an Irish father, a seaman. Both my maternal grandparents, in characteris-tically gendered ways, were playing a part in sustaining the British Empire, but they were among the mass of ordinary white colonial workers who rarely feature in standard histories of Empire. Born in 1888, my grandmother was also among the first generations of British women able to exercise the right to vote in elections for Britain's imperial Parliament. The year 1924, significant for me as the year of my mother's birth, was also a significant one in the public history of Empire: Indian nationalist leader Mahatma Gandhi and Irish nation-alist leader Eamon de Valera were released from jail by the British, the British Empire Exhibition was held at Wembley, and E.M. Forster's *Passage to India* was published. The following year my grandmother and her baby made the passage back to England, meeting on the long sea voyage a woman missionary who was instrumental in finding my grandmother a job back home.

I was born in 1955, at the beginnings of the end of the British Empire and in the build-up to the Suez Crisis. As a girl I attended Glen Preparatory

School, a school which (my parents later told me) had been transplanted into the English Midlands from Egypt, in reaction (as I later found out) to the rise of Arab nationalism, opposed to British imperial control of the country. Reading leading postcolonial critic Edward Said's autobiography *Out of Place*, I was amazed to realise that Gezira Preparatory School, the school he had attended in a large villa in colonial Cairo, was the forerunner of the school I had attended 20 years later in a spacious country house near Leicester. He describes the school as giving him 'my first experience of an organized system set up as a colonial business by the British': the 'lessons in English glory' and regimented regime seemed to have changed little with the passage of time and shift from colony to metropole between his education and mine.[17] I am only now coming to recognise how the hidden imperial histories of this female-run institution and of my maternal family line have surfaced in my own academic preoccupation with the history of British women's engagements with empire. The explorations in this book of women's involvement in colonial education, in missionary activity, and in colonial emigration, I realise, all intersect with aspects of my personal history.

This study is also fuelled by contemporary political concerns. In the long process of conceiving, researching and writing this book, a wonderful array of new scholarship has appeared identifying the impacts of globalisation and neo-imperialism on women as key issues for contemporary feminist activists, attempting to rethink and reorient Western feminism in the light of different forms of feminism, and critically examining the racialised origins of feminism. Together, this has helped sustain my motivation and develop my approaches to tracing to some of the historical connections between feminism and imperialism.[18] The link between imperial feminism past and present was brought home to me in 2002 when Tessa Jowell, Culture Secretary in the Labour government, opened the new Women's Library at my university. She used her speech to justify the British Labour government's military support for the US invasion of Afghanistan in the name of saving Afghan women from the *Burka*. The library might no longer be called the Fawcett Library, but it seems that the liberal imperialism espoused by the women's suffrage leader Millicent Garrett Fawcett, after whom the library had originally been named, is still very much alive. Jowell's speech provides an example of the way in which Western women have been implicated in the justification of imperialism in the name of saving women, a process that, as I discuss in Chapter 3, can be dated back to the British campaign against *sati*, or widow burning, in colonial India in the early nineteenth century. While speaking out against this 'imperial feminism', I am uneasily aware of how, at the same time, my own habits as a Western consumer implicate me in another form of neo-imperialism, whereby women in the South are exploited as cheap labour by trans-national corporations producing cheaply priced clothing for the North. Calls for ethical consumer responsibility by contemporary anti-globalisation activists echo earlier women campaigners' calls for a boycott of sugar produced by African slaves, a campaign which forms the focus of Chapter 2.

Joan Scott has usefully identified two kinds of histories of feminism. The first involves the creation of a feminist tradition, what might be labelled a teleological history, seeking the origins of the present in the past. The second is a history of how what comes to be seen as 'feminism' is formulated in the specific context of its times and is 'strategically fashioned to exploit inconsistencies, contradictions and possibilities inherent in the politics of the moment': feminism understood in terms of 'discontinuous political strategies' and as a 'process of formation of collective identifies among differently positioned females'.[19] Here, I try to hold these two approaches in creative tension. My main aim is to interpret debates on the women question and women's public activism on imperial issues within the specific historical contexts of Britain and its Empire in the period between 1790 and 1865. Building on Jane Rendall's germinal 1985 study of 'the origins of modern feminism',[20] I also seek to clarify the origins of a feminism that was self-consciously modern and Western in its formulation, and to excavate the roots of the 'imperial feminism' so characteristic of the later nineteenth century. In the process I also hope to provide richer historical understandings to inform contemporary attempts to create more meaningful and productive forms of global solidarity among women.

The period on which this book focuses is identified in traditional accounts of British imperial history as the era of the 'second British Empire', between the loss of Britain's Thirteen Colonies in North America in 1783 and the 'new imperialism' and 'scramble for Africa' of the late nineteenth century. It was a period of imperial expansion when Britain became Europe's preeminent imperial power, shifted from protectionist 'mercantile' to 'free trade' imperialism, consolidated its control over the Indian subcontinent, cemented union with Ireland, and began to grant the white inhabitants of its settler colonies increasing control over their own affairs.[21]

The period was also, of course, a dramatic and pivotal one in the domestic history of Britain, as it became the world's dominant economy and transformed from a commercial into an industrial nation, a process associated with the birth of new forms of class consciousness and major challenges to the social, cultural and political status quo.[22] Boyd Hilton has described the period as 'the age of atonement' to emphasise the immense impact of the evangelical religious revival on social and cultural thought. Both gender and imperial relations were central to evangelicals' programme of moral reform of the nation, and here I explore the relationship between their shaping of hegemonic ideas about women's proper social place through the ideology of 'separate spheres' and their concept of 'women's mission', and their reshaping of the public image of imperialism from that of military conquest and economic exploitation to that of a social mission spreading Christianity and civilisation.[23] Alternative designations of the period as the 'age of improvement' or the 'age of reform' usefully point to the optimistic faith in human progress that informed middle-class liberal ideology and shaped both feminism and imperial reform.[24] However, they perhaps give too tranquil an impression of the politics of an era when the politics of gender occupied a central place in clashes between political radicals and the forces of conservative reaction, and in crises of imperial authority. In the 1790s, Mary Wollstonecraft's call for the extension of the 'rights of man' to women was inspired by the American, French and Haitian Revolutions, while conservative evangelicals led by Hannah More stressed women's duties in reaction to the perceived threat of social disorder in Britain and its Empire. At the other end of the period, during the Indian Rebellion of 1857–8, a serious threat to the security of the Empire was presented in the British media as a threat to the bodies of white English women, increasing support for more virulently racist ideologies in Britain.

The period between the 1790s and the early 1860s as a whole was marked by heated debates on the 'woman question', on the value and purpose of Empire and on the appropriate treatment of the colonised. However, the connections between the history of imperialism and the history of feminism and female activism over this period have hitherto received far less attention than the equivalent links during the late Victorian and Edwardian periods, the period of 'high' or 'new' imperialism when Empire is more widely accepted to have had a major impact on the British public. Antoinette Burton, in the fullest attempt to date to historicise 'imperial feminism', has shown that many British liberal feminists promoted their own right to vote in the imperial Parliament through claiming a role as social reformers of Empire, and in particular as saviours of supposedly victimised Indian women.[25] Julia Bush, in turn, has revealed the complex relationship between 'imperialist' and the 'feminist' women's movements.[26] One of this book's aims is thus to explore to what extent the developments of this later period can be traced to roots in the first half of the 'long' nineteenth century: Did 'imperial feminism' and pro-Empire women's organisations have antecedents in the earlier period, or were they outgrowths of the 'new' imperialism? To what extent were perspectives critical of Empire and racism present among female activists in the period prior to the emergence of anti-colonial nationalist movements?

In using the term 'feminism' in the title to this book I am, of course, using an anachronism: the term was not used in Britain until the end of the nineteenth century.[27] However, anachronism, in the sense of applying the conceptual tools of the present to the study of the past, is inevitable; we need to use it critically, rather than attempt to avoid or discard it: as Katherine Wilson has so pithily put it, 'history itself is but a higher form of anachronism'.[28] Setting this problem aside, we are still faced with the problem of coming up with a definition of 'feminism' that does justice to its diversity across time, across cultures and even at a particular time and in a particular place. As Robert Young has noted, 'the drawback for any name that ends in an "ism" is that it will be taken to imply a set of shared ideas, and a single, homogeneous ideology. Such a characterization will of necessity be a broad generalization, produced after the event'.[29] This is particularly the case with feminism, which, unlike Marxism, is not founded on the thought of one particular individual. Scholars now tend to speak of 'feminisms' rather than a unitary 'feminism'. What these feminisms have in common, whether manifested in written analyses, organised activism or the practices of everyday life, is resistance to male domination over women, promotion of women's freedom to determine their own destinies, and a stress on the importance of solidarity among women. Some feminisms, however, downplay gender distinctions and emphasise women's equality with men, while others place more stress on the positive evaluation of women's differences from men.[30]

In the context of women in early nineteenth-century Britain, the women who form the focus of this book, the complexity of identifying feminism historically is thrown into sharp relief. As Jane Rendall has pointed out, 'equality' was used by these women to signal their equal moral and rational worth with men, but not necessarily a claim to equal political, civic or economic rights.[31] In addition, women activists of the period, in common with later feminists, combined arguments based on equality, variously defined, with those based on difference – their moral superiority to men or the importance of women's role as mothers, for example – in asserting claims to fuller participation in the life of the nation.[32] Political radicalism provided the context for Mary Wollstonecraft's articulation of a feminism stressing the rights of women. However, the relationship between feminism and evangelicalism is more difficult to interpret: some have labelled Hannah More an anti-feminist, others a counter-revolutionary or conservative feminist.[33] While, in my view, evangelical women's stress on the social subordination of women renders a feminist label inappropriate, it is clear that, despite their own protestations, their views on women were not simply the diametric opposite of those of feminist radicals. In addition, as we will see in the following chapters, evangelicalism, while promoting the ideology of 'separate spheres', in practice opened up an intermediate social sphere of organised philanthropic work for women that could stretch to public promotion of social reform and even interventions in the political sphere. It is thus impossible to understand the origins of modern feminism without considering the evangelical movement in which More played such a leading role.

The term 'feminism' in the title to this book is thus convenient shorthand signalling my interest in exploring a range of positions on the 'woman question', and a variety of forms of activism through which women collectively asserted agency and power over the period between 1790 and 1865. It was a period when definitions of female emancipation and understandings of the roots of women's oppression and the sources of women's liberation were highly contested. Until the mid-1850s, too, it was one in which organised female activism often subverted the boundaries of 'separate spheres' while rarely explicitly challenging male domination. The white middle-class women activists who form the focus of the central chapters of this study organised collectively, intervened in public life and politics, and sought to push their own local, national and imperial agendas, laying the grounds for the emergence of an organised feminist movement among middle-class women, the earliest phase of which is discussed in the final chapter of the book. They tended, however, not to press explicitly for their own rights. Rather, they focused on their duty to help those whom they saw as less privileged than themselves by virtue of their class, race, ethnicity or religion.[34]

This book thus focuses on the ideas and actions of a section of the population whose identities as white Protestant middle-class women were constituted in an imperially expansionist nation. These were not, of course, the only group of women who articulated feminist ideas or became involved in public activism in Britain over this period. Any comprehensive history of the origins of British feminism would, for example, need to include Chartist women, who organised in support of working-class men's demands for the vote as a way of improving their own lives, who were the first to call for women's suffrage, and who sought to remould male working-class culture through a militant domesticity targeting male drunkenness and wife-beating.[35] It would also need to include women of African descent, whose fight for emancipation as women was inseparable from their struggle for emancipation from slavery, a struggle that took place within Britain as well as within its Empire.[36] However, it was among white middle-class women that a self-consciously modern and Western feminist movement emerged from the mid-nineteenth century in an imperial nation, and in this book I am concerned to explore the roots of that movement and the origins of a hegemonic feminist discourse which privileged the white middle-class woman as the norm of womanhood, and developed an analysis of gender oppression and a programme for change based around their specific experiences, but claiming a universal validity.[37]

In examining the self-conscious modernity of this emergent feminism I follow Kathleen Wilson in exploring modernity not as an objective stage in economic, social and political development, but rather as a 'discursive and cultural construct'.[38] Paul Gilroy has drawn attention to how modernity begins 'in the constitutive relationships with outsiders that both found and temper a self-conscious sense of western civilisation'.[39] Here, I seek to explore the 'constitutive relationships' that white middle-class women in Britain entered into with those 'outsiders', particularly women in colonised lands, and examine how these helped shape their own sense of themselves as modern women, inhabitants of a country they deemed to be the most progressive and civilised nation in the world.

An awareness of the historical presence of alternative feminisms in Britain and its Empire during the early nineteenth century helps us to understand the limits to the vision of this strand of feminism and female activism. It also makes us alert to the ways in which the empowerment of this group of women might involve the disempowerment of women identified as unequal and different on the grounds of race, ethnicity and class, even, or perhaps especially, through campaigns in which activists claimed to speak on behalf of the 'other'. The relationship between the politics of class and the politics of race and ethnicity was, however, a complex one: white middle-class women attempted to draw white working-class women into support for foreign missionary and anti-slavery movements in a way which kept class hierarchies in place while positioning all white Christians as superior to the heathen or the black slave. The historical construction of white working-class identities in imperial Britain lies beyond the scope of this book, but it is a subject deserving future historical attention.

A number of key questions are addressed in the course of this book. In what ways did Britain's position in the world as a leading imperial power impact on national debate on the 'woman question'? To what extent were feminist and colonial discourses mutually constitutive? What was the significance of women's activism on imperial issues, both in shaping the lives of British women and in shaping imperialism? How did British women's engagements with Empire, and particularly with colonised women, contribute to constituting the identities of the white English woman and the modern Western feminist? How far can the roots of the imperial feminism of the later nineteenth century be traced into this earlier period? How can an examination of the origins of modern Western feminism inform contemporary debates on women's rights in an era of neo-imperial globalization?

My focus, as I have explained, is on the 'Empire at home', on the impact of Empire on women in Britain, and the impact of women in Britain on the Empire. This makes sense given my central aims of exploring the origins of modern Western feminism and the roots of imperial feminism within Britain, contributing to our understanding of the impact of Empire on British society, and elucidating the nature and extent of involvement by women in Britain in imperial affairs. However, the Empire 'out there' must not be lost sight of, and this study, which examines how the imperial world looked through the eyes of British-based activists and how they attempted to shape that world from their bases in the imperial metropole, needs to be read alongside those which focus on the interactions between British women, colonial authorities and indigenous peoples in colonial contexts. Missionary women in the field or emigrant women in settler societies did not necessarily act in accordance with the objectives and approaches prescribed by campaigners in Britain, neither was the range of their lives and experiences fully reflected in the carefully selected and edited accounts published for a British readership.

In this study, influenced by a general shift in historians' preoccupations over the past decade from social to cultural history, I am particularly interested in exploring the meanings women attached to their actions, the ways they saw and understood the imperial world in which they lived, and the discursive spaces they created for female agency and power.[40] I am attempting, primarily, to elucidate the development of public discourses rather than private patterns of thought, and thus I have drawn my primary source material almost entirely from publications rather than manuscripts: from tracts, pamphlets, published reports, periodicals, newspapers and memoirs and, to a lesser extent, literary texts, visual images and material culture.

This book begins with a consideration of the nature of debates on the 'woman question' in imperial Britain between the 1790s and the 1850s, looking at how both liberal feminist radicals and evangelicals discussed the position of British women within a broad cross-cultural framework informed by knowledge created in the process of Britain's global expansion and marked by the emergence of anti-slavery and foreign missionary movements. Chapters 2, 3 and 4 then explore the nature of British women's collective activism on imperial issues over the period, highlighting the imperial dimensions of female philanthropy and female social reform. Chapter 2, developing on my earlier work on women anti-slavery campaigners, examines the relationship between women's domestic power as imperial consumers and the politics of anti-slavery, exploring the link between women's promotion of a boycott of slave-grown sugar and their radical challenge to male authority in the abolitionist movement. Chapter 3 examines British women's contributions to the campaign against *sati,* or widow burning, in colonial India, exploring the significance both to imperial politics and to the development of feminism of white women adopting the role of saviours of brown women from indigenous patriarchy, petitioning Parliament and beginning to participate actively in the foreign missionary enterprise. Chapter 4 explores how women built on these missionary initiatives, looking at the development of an imperial dimension to female philanthropy focused on the project of 'native' female education, and exploring the openings which evangelicalism offered for female missionary agency in the foreign field. Chapter 5 offers a fresh perspective on the emergence of an organised feminist movement in Britain, highlighting how the Langham Place Circle's construction of a new model of educated and independent English womanhood was rooted in the promotion of female emigration to the white settler colonies. The book is structured in such a way that each chapter is fairly self-contained and can be read on its own; however, read consecutively, the chapters are intended to build up into a multifaceted picture of the origins of modern feminism in an imperial nation.

1 The 'woman question' in imperial Britain

Despite the lack of an organised feminist movement in Britain between the 1790s and the mid 1850s, there was a rich debate throughout the period concerning the position of women in British society. Were British women oppressed or privileged? Did women's biological differences from men imply differences in their mental capacities or emotional qualities? What were the appropriate social roles for women, and what type of education would best fit them for these roles? Should women be treated as men's equals or as their social subordinates? Should they be encouraged to focus on their domestic duties or urged to assert their civic rights? Positions were often very polarised, particularly in the late 1790s, when conservative evangelicals were at pains to distance themselves publicly from radical advocates of the 'rights of woman'. However, across the political spectrum, writers on the 'woman question' shared a reformist zeal, a conviction of the important role of women in the nation, and a belief that women exerted a strong influence on society, for good or for ill.[1]

While the debate on the woman question in Britain between the 1790s and the 1850s has attracted considerable attention from historians, the implications of this debate taking place within an imperial nation have not been fully examined. This chapter seeks to clarify the ways in which analyses of the condition of British women over the period were influenced by Britain's position as an expansionist imperial nation and leading world power. It will examine how these texts encouraged British women to consider their own social position in relation to the position of women in non-Western societies and to colonised peoples, particularly enslaved Africans.

Writing on the 'woman question' was shaped by understandings of the world developed in the contexts of British overseas exploration and imperial expansion, in particular by eighteenth-century Enlightenment stadial theory, which used the position of women as a key marker of the level of civilization in particular societies. In addition, campaigns to improve the position of women in Britain were influenced by new popular movements that arose in the late eighteenth century: the campaigns against the slave trade and colonial slavery, and the foreign missionary movement, with its global aspirations and complex relationship to British imperialism. Writers on British women drew on abolitionist and missionary discourses in comparing or contrasting the position of British women with that of colonial slaves, women in the 'oriental' harem, women in African, Pacific Islander or North American 'savage' societies, and Hindu women who committed *sati*, burning on the funeral pyres of their husbands.

The chapter begins by discussing a set of key feminist tracts that highlighted the oppression of women in Britain through making analogies between women and slaves, and which advocated the 'rights of woman' through developing a discourse of women's progress from savage to civilised societies. It then moves on to discuss tracts from the opposing evangelical tradition, which contrasted the position of women in Protestant Britain with that of women in 'heathen' lands, drawing on Enlightenment stadial theory but stressing Christian religion rather than socio-economic development as the source of women's privileges. The later sections of the chapter examine texts by two authors who approached the 'woman question' from rather different angles: Elizabeth Hamilton, who used the fictional correspondence of a 'Hindu rajah' to provide an outsider perspective on women's position in Britain, and Henry Lawrence, who imagined a matrilineal Utopia located in India.

Civilisation, slavery and women's rights

In analysing British women's oppression and calling for women's rights, feminist tracts drew critically on eighteenth-century European Enlightenment stadial theory. In the 1770s, French and Scottish theorists created conjectural histories of the world that linked stages of economic development, from an original state of nature through hunter–gatherer, pastoral, agricultural and then commercial stages, to levels of social and cultural development from savagery to civilisation, and levels of political development from despotism to liberty. The treatment of women by men was taken as an index of the stage of progress. Indeed, women formed the central focus of Scottish writer William Alexander's 1779 history which was, the advertisement claimed, written specifically for a female readership. Central to Enlightenment stadial theory was a belief that women had been reduced to a state of slaves and drudges to men in savage societies, that political despotism was associated with men's despotic rule over women, and that in contemporary European commercial society women that become the companions of men rather than their slaves. Indeed, Barbara Taylor has described the view that women's positions had gradually improved with the advance of civilisation and political liberty as 'a veritable *idée fixe* among educated Britons' of the late eighteenth century.[2]

Stadial theory drew on knowledge of non-European peoples created in the process of European exploration and colonisation overseas from the late fifteenth century onwards. By the 1770s, the two nations within which conjectural histories were written, France and Britain, were the two leading European colonial powers, and a new phase of British exploration and exploitation in the Pacific was being initiated by the voyages of Captain James Cook between 1768 and 1779.[3] Britain's imperial expansion during the eighteenth century and her rivalry with France on the global stage had a profound impact both on the forging of an overarching sense of British Protestant national identity and on the emergence of a new sense of English ethnic selfhood.[4] The commercial society that stadial theorists placed at the apex of civilisational progress was one heavily reliant both economically and socially on imperial commerce. As will be discussed in Chapter 2, a central component of this was the trade in African slaves and in slave-grown Caribbean sugar.[5] With European colonial expansion, the creation of forms of knowledge about non-European peoples, as Edward Said so influentially pointed out in *Orientalism*, became a key part of the assertion of colonial power, 'a Western style for dominating, restructuring, and having authority' over those defined as 'other'.[6] However, Enlightenment thinking was diverse, and included a strand critical of European imperialism.[7]

While some Enlightenment thinkers adopted a culturally relativist approach that questioned the superiority of Western civilisation, stadial theorists, as G.S. Rousseau and Roy Porter have discussed, constructed a history of world within which 'the peoples and stages of civilisation of the European past were readily mapped onto the tribes contemporaries encountered in Africa or America', with such contemporary societies seen as living relics of earlier, less civilised, eras.[8] Savage man was taken to be the mirror image of the primitive ancestor of the civilised European. This, as Silvia Sebastiani has suggested, 'broke open the universalistic discourse on progress' present in stadial theory to a 'hierarchical discourse contrasting the stasis of non-European peoples and the dynamism of Europe'. This hierarchical discourse was associated with a new 'science of man' that constructed racial difference through naturalising cultural characteristics 'by rendering them innate and inscribing them on the body', with women assigned an important role in the formation of these distinct races.[9]

Just as Enlightenment thinkers' belief in natural equality was in tension with their construction of contemporary hierarchies of cultural and racial difference, so their stress on the social malleability of human nature and the shifting social position of women was in tension with their emphasis on natural differences between the sexes. Depictions of women as a civilising and progressive influence, and indeed women's actual contributions to Enlightenment culture as writers and as hostesses of intellectual *salons*, sat uncomfortably alongside the association of women with nature, the idea of historical progress as the assertion of masculine reason over female irrationality, and fears of the corrupting influence of ignorant and frivolous women on contemporary commercial society. In Jean-Jacques Rousseau, the emphasis on women's unique physiology was seen to necessitate the circumscribing of her social role to that of wife and mother within the patriarchal rural family, her ability to exert a good moral influence dependent on her seclusion.[10]

It was partly through engaging with the tensions and inconsistencies in Enlightenment thought, and through directly challenging those 'men of reason' who postulated women's natural inferiority, that modern feminist discourse emerged. The relationship of this discourse to European colonialism was complex. On the one hand, feminists drew on stereotyped and often negative views of non-European peoples forged in the process of the expansion of European colonial power. On the other hand, like their fellow political radicals and religious dissenters, they drew inspiration from anti-colonial and anti-slavery movements. The immediate sparks for the emergence of modern feminism in the 1790s Britain were the dramatic political developments of the late eighteenth century, when Enlightenment ideas of natural rights were translated into a political agenda promoting the 'rights of man' by Americans in revolt against British colonial control, French revolutionaries and 'Black Jacobins' in France's richest Caribbean sugar colony of San Domingue.[11]

This complex set of influences is very evident in the work of Catherine Macaulay, whose writings span the period from the American Revolution to the French Revolution and who was one of the leading female intellectuals of the late eighteenth century. Macaulay gained fame as the author of an eight-volume *History of England* (1763–1783), an Enlightenment history of the progressive acquisition of liberty by the English written from a republican perspective. Her attitudes to British imperialism were complex: her support for the American Revolution, based on her belief that legitimate government must be based on a contract between the ruler and ruled, was combined with enthusiasm for Britain's commercial development based on her sea empire, tempered by an opposition to colonial slavery.[12]

In her *Letters on Education* (1790), Macaulay's assertion of natural equality between the sexes is linked to a broader assertion of the 'the natural equality of man' that encompasses an attack on those who claim the natural superiority of Europeans over Asians or Africans. She acknowledges that there are some positive aspects to non-European societies and argues that while 'most European states have at this day an apparent superiority in government, in arts, and in arms', this is an accident of history, and European history itself shows periods of achievement followed by periods of decline.[13] When it comes to the position of women, however, Macaulay sees nothing positive in non-Western societies. She states that 'the situation of women in modern Europe ..., when compared with that condition of abject slavery in which they have always been held in the east, may be considered as brilliant', thus locating Europe as the site of progress towards female emancipation, while simultaneously acknowledging that 'if we withhold comparison ... we shall have no great reason of boast of our privileges'.[14] Macaulay's image of the unchangingly oppressive east, which reiterates a commonplace of European eighteenth-century Enlightenment thought, reappears in her call for equality in the education of boys and girls. She condemns the inferior state of female education in Europe as resulting from 'a prejudice, which ought ever to have been confined to the regions of the east, because it accords with the state of slavery to which female nature in that part of the world has been ever subjected'.[15]

This presentation of female subjection as anomalous to Western society is reinforced by Macaulay's critique of Rousseau's views on female education, which she characterises as Eastern,[16] and contrasts with her own programme of female education in these terms: 'I intend to breed my pupils up to act a rational part in the world, and not to fill up a niche in the seraglio of a sultan'.[17] Macaulay, while calling into question the assumption of an automatic link between the development of enlightened culture in Europe and the liberation of women, thus promotes female emancipation as Western progress away from a negatively imagined East, with the woman of reason replacing man's sexual slave. This marks an early appearance of what Joyce Zonana has labelled 'feminist orientalism', which shares with other Orientalist discourse a dominant association of the East with the harem, an image that linked the sexual enslavement of women with political despotism.[18]

Mary Wollstonecraft's *A Vindication of the Rights of Woman* (1792), the most famous foundational text of modern Western feminism, was influenced by Macaulay's work but went beyond her in seeking to extend radical calls for the 'rights of man' to women. Like Macaulay, Wollstonecraft critiques Rousseau's views on natural female inferiority and his associated views of female education. She is sympathetic with Rousseau's disillusionment with the frivolity and corruption of current European society.[19] She disagrees, however, with what she interpreted as Rousseau's belief that 'a state of nature is preferable to civilization, in all its possible perfection'.[20] She argues that he was mistaken in assuming that the existing ills of European societies were 'the consequence of civilization' rather than 'the vestiges of barbarism'.[21] The problem, as she stated at the opening of the *Vindication*, is that 'the civilization which has hitherto taken place in the world has been very partial'.[22] Here, Wollstonecraft distanced herself from what Barbara Taylor has described as the 'bourgeois-triumphalist' strand in British Enlightenment readings of history, which saw contemporary commercial society as the apex of civilisational achievement.[23] However, she argues that 'the perfection of man' should be sought 'in the establishment of true civilization' rather than a 'ferocious flight back to the nights of sensual ignorance'.[24]

Wollstonecraft, as Jane Rendall has noted with reference to her *Historical and Moral View of the French Revolution* (1794), followed Enlightenment stadial thought in using the presence of slavery and the oppression of women as markers of how supposedly civilised societies fell short of full civilisation.[25] She was also clearly influenced by the emergence of the British campaign against the slave trade: in the *Vindication* she compares her countrywomen to colonial slaves in a passage which aligns her with the contemporary campaign for abstention from slave-grown sugar, in which British women played a key role, as will be discussed in the Chapter 2. Wollstonecraft questions: 'Is sugar always to be produced by vital blood? Is one half of the human species, like poor African slaves, to be subject to prejudices that brutalize them, when principles would be a surer guarantee only to sweeten the cup of man?'[26] Here, calling attention to the discriminatory and degrading treatment of both African slaves and European women that underlay the 'polite and commercial society' of eighteenth-century Britain, Wollstonecraft aligns the cause of women's rights with the anti-slavery cause, assuming an abolitionist stance on the part of her readers.[27]

Wollstonecraft's use of the woman–slave analogy, however, also problematically obscures the differences between the experiences of (black) slaves and (middle-class white) women, and rests for its effectiveness on an erasure of the specific sufferings of black women under slavery. In addition, it is tied to a negative view of indigenous African societies. In contrast to the authors of sentimental anti-slavery poetry and tales of the period, Wollstonecraft is no idealiser of the 'noble savage'.[28] Comparing fashionable European women's vanity and fondness for dress to the 'strong inclination for external ornaments' which 'ever appears in barbarous states' where 'the mind is not sufficiently opened to the pleasure in reflection', she argues that the fact that 'all the hardly earned savings of a slave are commonly expended on a little tawdry finery' provides evidence of 'the savage desire of admiration which the black heroes inherit from both their parents' and which 'even the hellish yoke of slavery cannot stifle'.[29] Here, the presentation of African men is highly ambivalent. On the one hand, their description as 'black heroes' signals her support for the slave rebellion in San Dominigue and places a positive emphasis on their masculinity. On the other hand, African men are associated with Western feminine vices, and labelled as uncultivated savages. Savages, she claims, do not have full powers of reasoning or the ability to act from principle, the very qualities that she wishes to cultivate in European women: they are 'uncivilized beings who have not yet extended the dominion of the mind, or even learned to think with the energy necessary to concatenate that abstract train of thought which produces principles'. The fact that European women have 'an immoderate fondness of dress, and for sway' is thus a mark of the distance still to be travelled in the progress from savagery to civilisation: at present 'their education and the present state of civilized life, are in the same condition' as savages.[30] While her purpose is thus to call for improvement in the position of British women, her text also implies that 'savages' would benefit from civilising along the model of the European Enlightenment ideal.

Wollstonecraft also reiterates the standard Enlightenment association of the East with the despotic treatment of women as a way of effectively undermining Rousseau's agenda for female education as out of place in a civilised European nation. She argues that inadequately educated (European) women are 'in worse than Egyptian bondage'. The attempt to make women virtuous by the assertion of male authority over them 'is a contradiction in terms' which would necessitate them being treated like Eastern women: 'immured in seraglios and watched with a jealous eye' and 'educated only to excite emotions in men'.[31] The way to instil 'private and public virtue' in women is thus not to subject them 'to a severe restraint', that of 'blind propriety'. Rather, the approach should be to 'cultivate their understandings, in order to plant virtue in their hearts'. European women should thus be educated to become rational human beings like their menfolk; in the process, she implies, they will not only become less like colonial slaves, but also less like African 'savages' and 'Oriental' women. The *Vindication* ends with the following rousing exhortation appealing for men of reason to distinguish themselves from oriental despots in their treatment of women: 'allow her the privileges of ignorance, to whom ye deny the rights of reason, or ye will be worse than Egyptian task-masters, expecting virtue where nature has not given understanding'.[32] It is only by European men acting less like Egyptian men that, Wollstonecraft argues, her main objective can be achieved: that of creating women whose independence of mind informs their virtue and who can thus fulfil their duty to themselves as well as their duties as mothers and as citizens.

The rhetorical power of Wollstonecraft's arguments thus stemmed in good part from her ability to harness to a feminist bandwagon both the anti-slavery sentiment of the 1790s and the negative stereotypes of non-Western societies deployed by Enlightenment stadial theorists of the 1770s. This helped position her radical assertion of women's rights within the respectable cultural mainstream. Reaction against her work came less because of its content than because of the scandal caused by revelations about her unconventional personal life with the publication in 1798 of her husband William Godwin's biography of his wife.[33] More broadly, in the context of war with revolutionary France, government clampdown on radical activism in Britain, and alarm caused by the attempted uprising against British rule in Ireland in 1798, any assertion of the rights of woman was viewed as politically subversive. Mary Hays, another controversial feminist writer of the period, defended intellectual women through the use of stadial theory in her own short 'life' of her friend Wollstonecraft: 'In the intellectual advancement of women, and their consequent privileges in society, is to be traced the progress of civilization, or knowledge gradually superseding the dominion of brute-force'.[34] Anti-Jacobins, however, launched a series of attacks on her reputation, using her private life and support for the French Revolution to discredit her feminist ideas as unpatriotic and 'destructive of domestic, civil, and political society' rather than heralding the next stage of civilisational progress.[35]

Not all radical women were deterred from speaking out. The other major feminist ally of Wollstonecraft in the 1790s was Mary Darby Robinson (1758–1800) whose *A Letter to the Women of England, on the Injustice of Mental Subordination* (1799) was first published under the pseudonym of Anne Frances Randall. An actress notorious for her adulterous affair with the Prince of Wales, Robinson's popular novels drew on her own experiences of ill-treatment by men, questioned conventional notions of sexual propriety and played with characters who crossed gender boundaries. After terminating her long relationship with Banastre Tarleton, a pro-slavery MP and hero of the colonial war in North America, she articulated an increasingly radical, feminist and abolitionist political position, and in *A Letter* she openly declares herself a disciple of Wollstonecraft. Like her role model, she draws on stadial theory and analogies with slavery in asserting the intellectual equality of women and call for improvements in their education.[36] She claims that 'the barbarity of custom's law in this *enlightened* country, had long been exercised to the prejudice of woman' and informs men that women 'will not be your slaves; they will be your associates, your equals in the extensive scale of civilized society; and in the indisputable rights of nature'.[37] Her footnote, stating that while Muslims are claimed to believe that women have no souls, British husbands treat them as if they have no sense, challenged evangelical Christian writers who, as will be discussed in the following section, asserted women's spiritual equality while promoting their social subordination. Given that it is asserted that 'the best test of civilization, is the respect that is shewn to women', then 'heaven forbid that the criterion of this national and necessary good, should be drawn from the conduct of mankind towards British women'.[38] Indeed, Robinson suggested that, rather than becoming progressively more civilised, European society was in danger of going backwards in its treatment of women: of becoming more, rather than less, 'Oriental'. She comments that 'I should not be surprized, if the present system of mental subordination continues to gain strength, if, in a few years, European husbands were to imitate those beyond the Ganges. There, wives are to be purchased like slaves, and every man has as many as he pleases. The husbands and even fathers are so far from being zealous, that they frequently offer their wives and daughters to foreigners'.[39]

Robinson argues uncontroversially that women are the creators of civilized society: 'every good which cements the bonds of civilized society, originates wholly in the forbearance, and conscientiousness of woman'. However, rather than accepting that women's civilising influence should be exercised exclusively from a domestic base, she questions women's exclusion from politics. Here, she breaks with Wollstonecraft's unequivocally negative representation of 'savage' societies in order to establish that women's active engagement in politics is not without precedent. In a footnote she draws out a similarity between some contemporary 'savage' societies and Britain's own Anglo-Saxon past: 'many of the American tribes admit women into their public councils, and allow them the privileges of giving their opinions, first, on every subject of deliberation', while ancient Britons 'allowed the female sex the same right'.[40]

In making such a positive association between Western and non-Western cultures, Robinson reinforces the challenge in her text to the nationalistic patriotism that characterised the period of the wars with France and which infused much writing by and about women at the period.[41] She expresses the hope that 'in proportion as women are acquainted with the languages they will become citizens of the world' rather than patriots. She presents a Utopian vision of a world in which 'the laws, customs and inhabitants of different nations will be their kindred in the propinquity of nature', linking a future in which 'prejudice will be palsied, if not receive its death blow, by the expansion of intellect' with one in which 'woman being permitted to feel her own importance in the scale of society, will be tenacious of maintaining it'.[42]

Lucy Aikin's *Epistles on Women* (1810) is, in contrast, representative of the cautious approach that many of those wishing to improve the position of British women adopted at a time of counter-revolutionary reaction against Wollstonecraftian feminism. Writing in the midst of the Napoleonic Wars, she focuses on a reformed domesticity rather than a public role for women, positioning herself as an English patriot rather than a citizen of the world, adopting a tone of appeal rather than assertion, and couching her reformist agenda in the form of letters in verse addressed to her sister rather than as a political tract, Aikin is at pains to distance herself from Wollstonecraft. In her introduction she disclaims 'the absurd idea that the two sexes ever can be, or ever ought to be, placed in all respects on a footing of equality'. She links men's greater bodily strength to a public, active and authoritative role in society, women's lesser strength to a domestic, private and to 'a certain degree' subordinate role. Nevertheless, she asserts women's intellectual equality with men and echoes Wollstonecraft in criticising Rousseau for failing to 'consult the interests of the weaker sex in his preference of savage life to civilised'.[43]

Aikin's epistles are in effect an exposition in verse form of stadial theory, designed to demonstrate the wider social benefits of improvements in the condition of women. As she explains in her introduction, her text seeks to 'mark the effect of various codes, institutions, and states of manners, on the virtue and happiness of man, and the concomitant and proportional elevation or depression of woman in the scale of existence' in order to draw the moral that 'that it is impossible for man to degrade his companion without degrading himself, or to elevate her without receiving a proportional accession of dignity and happiness'.[44] Her account, in addition to the standard condemnations of 'savage' and 'oriental' societies for their treatment of women, incorporates examples that update Enlightenment texts by drawing on new colonial constructions of non-European others, complete with footnotes providing references that give a learned authority to her text. Her condemnation of the treatment of women by 'savage man' draws on a missionary account of infanticide in Tahiti, where, following Captain Cook's 'discovery' of the Pacific island, members of the London Missionary Society had been active since 1797.[45] Her condemnation of 'Hottentots' for keeping their women in servitude was horribly ironic, given that her text was published in the same year that abolitionists brought a charge of involuntary servitude against a white South African man who was publicly exhibiting his black servant Saartje Baartman as the 'Hottentot Venus' to a voyeuristic public in Britain.[46] Her description of the 'self-dissembling' Hindu 'victim-widow' who commits *sati* in order 'not to live with shame' highlighted a practice that evangelicals were increasingly pressurising the British imperial government to ban in India, as will be explored in Chapter 4.[47]

Aikin turns her attention to Europe in the final sections of her *Epistle*, positioning improvements in the position of women as a patriotic national project. She laments the fact that, in France, high hopes had given way to tyranny and then turns to England, which she presents as a land of 'domestic virtue'. Presenting herself as a patriot who will 'trace English manners with an English heart', she praises heroic and educated women of the English past. She then addresses 'sons of fair Albion' urging them to recognize that God formed women as intelligent beings and urging them 'Be generous then, unbind/Your barbarous shackles, loose the female mind'. Finally, she turns to address the 'bright daughters' of this free land, urging them to rise and be free through embracing both domesticity and the world of knowledge, thus becoming the full partners of man, sharing his ideas and virtues, guiding his conduct, and soothing his cares.[48] Aikin's stress on female reason as a single standard of virtue for men and women echoes Wollstonecraft, but her linking of domesticity with English patriotism rather than a transnational ideal of republican motherhood distances her from the feminists of the 1790s.[49] If Wollstonecraft wants European men as a whole to be less 'oriental' in their treatment of women, Aikin wants English men to be more English.

With the end of the Napoleonic Wars in 1815 and the consolidation of Britain's unrivalled position as leading industrial and imperial power, openings for radical writing and public political activism gradually began to reappear. However, feminists writing in the 1820s articulated their ideas in relation to new intellectual currents, including the rise of Utilitarian philosophy, and new imperial developments, including the consolidation of British rule in India and the launching of the campaign for the emancipation of colonial slaves. These new developments influenced Irish landowner and Owenite economist William Thompson's socialist-feminist tract, *Appeal of One Half of the Human Race* (1825), written in collaboration with his partner, Anna Doyle Wheeler. Thompson, like earlier feminists, argues that female equality is essential to the social progress of both men and women.[50] However, his vision of a 'new moral world' moved beyond feminist radical tracts of the 1790s in associating the liberation of women with the abolition of private property, cooperative living and the complete transformation of family life.[51]

The *Appeal* makes extensive comparisons between the position of the British wife and that of Africans under colonial slavery in order to highlight Thompson's opposition to women being treated like private property and denied legal rights in marriage. He condemns the 'law-supported, literally existing slavery of wives', and likens the marriage contract to slave-codes.[52] Writing in the year that the first female anti-slavery societies were formed in Britain, Thompson linked women's liberation to an active role for women in the overthrow of colonial slavery. He calls on women to 'awake, arise, shake off these fetters', and to 'make the most certain step towards the regeneration of degraded humanity' by freeing the world of both colonial and female slavery: 'opening a free course for justice and benevolence, for intellectual and social enjoyments, by no colour, by no sex restrained'.[53]

While earlier feminists attacked Rousseau's influential views on women and their appropriate education, Thompson positions his tract as a feminist critique of leading Utilitarian philosopher James Mill's renowned 'Essay on Government', published in the 1824 supplement to the *Encyclopaedia Britannica*.[54] Thompson, a friend of Jeremy Bentham, who was strongly influenced by his Utilitarian philosophy, sought to apply Bentham's central objective of promoting the 'greatest happiness of the greatest number' to gender relations, arguing in the *Appeal* that sexual inequality is a source of unhappiness for both men and women. Thompson was outraged by Mill's exclusion of women from his call for men to have the right to represent their own interests politically, an exclusion based on the argument that women could be adequately represented by their husbands or fathers. Mill, Thompson argues, had constructed a system of liberty built on continued 'political, civil, and, therefore, the social and domestic, slavery' of one half of the human race.[55]

While Thompson's direct critique of Mill's 'Essay on Government' has been discussed by a number of scholars, his indirect engagement with another highly influential text by Mill, his *History of British India* (1817), has hitherto gone unremarked. Mill's *History* sought to measure the place of Hindus in the scale of civilisation through using the yardstick of utility and, as Jennifer Pitt has noted, transformed the 'comparatively subtle developmental gradations' posited by eighteenth-century Scottish conjectural historians into 'crude dichotomy between civilization and rudeness'.[56] Presenting an unremittingly negative picture of Indian culture and society, Mill also argued that the best way of raising India on the scale of civilisation was not the introduction of representative democracy on the lines he proposed for Britain but, rather, the imposition of legal reforms through authoritarian British imperial rule.[57] In his introduction, Thompson positions Mill, the supposedly modern and progressive thinker, as putting forward arguments for the exclusion of women from democratic participation which represent 'the inroad of barbarism, under the guise of philosophy, into the nineteenth century'. British marriage laws, which deny women any rights, are condemned as a 'disgrace to civilisation' which 'represents the remnants of the barbarous customs of our ignorant ancestors'.[58] Thompson argues that while the 'favorable tendencies of civilization' had 'mitigated the abuses of savage strength despotically used by man over woman', Mill was seeking to reverse this progressive trend.[59] This called into question Britain's claim to be 'the most enlightened' and civilised country in the world.[60] Mill is then condemned by Thompson for having acted 'in true Eastern style' when he explicitly excluded women from his distribution of rights.[61] Thus, while Thompson makes no explicit critique of Mill's views on India and promotion of British imperial rule through his role as a leading member of the East India Company's executive Council, his advocacy of despotic rule over Indians in the name of progress and civilisation is implicitly called into question, pointing to what Eric Stokes has referred to in his study of British utilitarians and India as 'the paradox in utilitarianism between the principle of liberty and the principle of authority'.[62]

Thompson also draws two specific comparisons between the position of British and Eastern wives. First, British women suffer from a double standard of sexual morality, whereby women are punished for adultery whereas men's attachments may be 'as extensive and public as those of any Eastern despot'.[63] Second, like Aikin before him, he refers to *sati*, but in his text the reference is used to draw a parallel rather than make a distinction between the position of British women and that of Indian women. When her husband dies, he states, a wife is left in poverty; but, when his wife dies, a husband can simply select 'the next willing victim trained like the self-immolating widow of Hindostan'.[64]

While Utopian socialists desire to create a 'new moral world' in Western countries was based on strong condemnation and rejection of existing social norms, and a questioning of supposed Western progress in the position of women, many early nineteenth-century feminists adopted a more reformist approach. They were keen to present female emancipation as the logical end product of social progress during an age of reform and to find ways of reconciling women's domestic duties with their achievement of social, legal and political equality in modern society. In her widely circulated *A Plea for Woman* (1843), Scottish writer Marion Reid, like many earlier feminists, takes Enlightenment stadial theory as a starting point.[65] Her argument is a radical one: women, who had been explicitly excluded from the extension of the franchise in 1832, have the right to participate in politics because they 'possess of the same rational and responsible nature as man'. Opening her text with quotes from both Utilitarian philosopher Jeremy Bentham and evangelical poet of domesticity William Cowper, she seeks to combat evangelical advocates of 'separate' spheres' by demonstrating that women's possession of political privileges was compatible with 'the right performance of the home duties of the sex' and, indeed, would 'ennoble' their influence over their husbands.[66] Britain's abolition of colonial slavery following the Emancipation Act of 1833 provides her with the opportunity to argue that this is an auspicious time to call attention to women's 'degraded rank': the present age is one of progressive breaking with 'oppressive and tyrannical' social institutions previously revered as 'precedent and ancient custom'.[67] It also provides her with a way of refuting the argument that women's intellectual capacities were unsuited for full citizenship: it is not necessary or possible, she argued, first to establish women's complete natural equality with men before giving them civil rights because, though 'negroes' have often been seen as an 'inferior race of men', this is no longer considered a moral justification for enslaving them.[68]

In London, too, a group of feminist thinkers emerged in the reformist atmosphere of the 1830s and 1840s. Labelled 'radical unitarians' by Kathryn Gleadle, the group broke with the Unitarian mainstream, which adopted a cautious approach to the 'woman question', favouring improved female education but not female independence. The radicals centred around William Johnson Fox, minister of South Place Chapel in London and promoted their ideas through the magazine the *Monthly Repository*. Gleadle has drawn attention both to their critical engagement with Enlightenment stadial theory and to their close links with William Lovett, leader of the wing of the Chartist movement that was most sympathetic to feminist demands and most willing to form alliances with middle-class reformers. However, as she points out, the differing approaches to the woman question among radical unitarians and Chartists was exemplified by their differing use of the woman–slave analogy. While among working-class activists the analogy was used to highlight the drudgery, hardship, low status and low pay of women's labour and was associated with demands for a 'family wage' for men so that their wives could focus on their domestic roles, the analogy was used among middle-class intellectuals to draw attention to women's cultural oppression and was associated with demands for greater employment opportunities for women.[69]

Emerging from this radical Unitarian milieu, Harriet Taylor attacked Chartist petitioners for excluding women from their call for the vote in her essay on 'The Enfranchisement of Women' which appeared in the *Westminster Review* in 1851. The essay was published in the same year that Quaker feminist and anti-slavery campaigner Anne Knight was involved in helping organise Chartist women in Sheffield to set up a Female Reform Association, which petitioned parliament for the inclusion of adult women in the suffrage.[70] The year 1851 was also the year after the passage of the Fugitive Slave Act in America, and a time when the attention of many British radical women, like Anne Knight and her fellow anti-slavery activist and Chartist sympathiser Elizabeth Pease, was focused on developments in the abolitionist movement in the United States and their links with the radical abolitionist-feminists there.[71]

Writing in this political context, Taylor, like prominent Unitarian writer Harriet Martineau before her in *Society in America* (1837), highlights the contradiction between the principles of the American Declaration of Independence and the practice of excluding both women and black people from rights. She also aligns herself with the radical Garrisonian wing of American abolitionism by stressing that it is fitting that those associated with the extirpation of 'the aristocracy of colour' should be among the originators of 'the first collective protest against the aristocracy of sex', which she described as 'a distinction as accidental as that of colour, and fully as irrelevant to all questions of government'.[72]

Elsewhere in her text, however, Taylor's references to slavery focus on the enslavement of women in non-European cultures. Arguing that female emancipation should be promoted as part of 'human improvement in the widest sense',[73] she describes the Australian 'savage' and the American Indian as treating women as 'slaves of men for purposes of toil', whereas Asians treat women as 'slaves of men for purposes of sensuality'. She contrasts this with Europe, where, she asserts, progressive 'improvement in the moral sentiments of mankind' has rendered women the companions of men though full progress has not yet been achieved because marriage remains a companionship between unequals.[74]

In attempting to address the fact that many women in England seemed content with their subordinate position, Taylor positions herself as a free-thinking woman, part of a feminist vanguard, and in the process suggests that she knows what is best not only for English women and non-European peoples. The fact that some English women do not desire their emancipation, she claims, does not mean that they should not get it: Asiatic women accept their seclusion and veiling, Asians do not desire political liberty, the 'savages of the forest' do not want civilisation – but the fact that habits of submission make people servile-minded 'does not prove that either of those things is undesirable for them, or that they will not, at some future time, enjoy it'.[75] Thus, while Taylor's use of stadial theory and the woman–slave analogy reiterated commonplaces of feminist argument from the 1790s onwards, her adoption of this self-confident and culturally arrogant tone marked a new departure for feminist discourse. It echoed the approach of her partner, the leading liberal thinker John Stuart Mill, who, like his father James Mill, justified despotic British rule in India in the name of civilisation.[76] Mill's own influential essay on *The Subjection of Women* (1869) was strongly influenced by Taylor and made similar use of stadial theory and analogies with slavery.[77]

Christianity and women's privileges and influence

A second, and often conflicting, approach to the 'woman question' in late eighteenth- and early nineteenth-century Britain was promoted by writers influenced by the evangelical religious revival. Evangelical Protestants, both within and without the established church, promoted active Christianity rather than nominal adherence to institutionalised religion and linked this with a broader agenda of moral and social reform. Between the 1790s and 1830s the influential Evangelical Anglican 'Clapham Sect' around William Wilberforce led this push for the transformation of nation and Empire, aiming not only to combat political radicalism among the working class, but also to reform the corrupt upper class and moralise the Empire through the abolition of slavery and the spread of Christian missionary activity. All these arenas were ones in which women were seen as having the potential to make vitally important contributions: evangelicalism promoted a feminised religion of the heart in which family life lay at the heart of their project for the regeneration of the world, and women were assigned a key role as moral guardians of the nation from a domestic base.[78]

Evangelicalism, as Jane Rendall has noted, had 'a complex and ambiguous effect on the position of women'. On the one hand, it was associated with an outburst of sermons and prescriptive literature by men and women stressing women's domestic duties rather than their rights. On the other hand, women such as Hannah More, while supporting women's social subordination to their husbands, developed an ambitious agenda for the reform of female education that had similarities with that of Mary Wollstonecraft and other feminist radicals and which aimed to enable women to play a fuller part in improving the nation.[79]

Evangelicals discussing the position of women drew, like feminist radicals, on Enlightenment thought. However, they drew on those thinkers who stressed domesticity within companionate marriage as the ideal condition for women, and interpreted woman's bodily difference from man as the sign of natural differences between male and female minds. Evangelicals also rewrote the secular discourse of stadial theory to link the progress of civilisation with the spread of Christianity, which was credited as the main source of the improved treatment of women.

Leading evangelical clergymen and ministers, concerned to combat feminist calls for women's rights, used this reworked stadial theory to assert a rather complacent view of the current position of British women, one that emphasised their privileged position. Thomas Gisborne (1758–1846), an Evangelical Anglican clergyman who was part of the circle of 'Clapham Sect' reformers around William Wilberforce, is a good example. He followed his *Inquiry into the Duties of Men in the Higher Ranks and Middle Classes* (1794) by *An Enquiry into the Duties of the Female Sex* (1797). The difference in the titles of the two works is itself indicative of Gisborne's views: men are identified by their social status, women by their biological sex. He devotes a whole chapter to delineating 'the peculiar features by which the character of the female mind is naturally discriminated from that of the other sex'. This combines a stress on natural difference between the sexes with a story of social progress measured not by material improvements in the social position of women, as common in feminist uses of stadial theory, but rather by shifts in men's views of women. He claims that 'In different countries, and at different periods, female excellence has been estimated by very different standards'. In barbarous nations it is rated 'by the scale of servile fear and capacity for toil'; but, as nations become more refined, women are treated more gently and held in 'more reasonable estimation'. Such improvement 'prepares the way for additional progress in civilization'. Gisborne expresses approval of the fact that the custom until recently in Britain of measuring female perfection solely by their skills in domestic duties has now been expanded to praise of female 'genius, taste, and learning'.[80]

Gisborne then launches into an attack on those 'bold assertors of the rights of the weaker sex' who went so far as to claim the 'perfect equality of injured woman and usurping man'. These advocates of women's rights and female equality were, he argued, going against the God-given natural order: God has designed men and women with different bodily frames and 'mental powers and dispositions', fitting them for different tasks. The endowments which 'form the glory of the female sex' are 'the dispositions and feelings of the heart': 'of modesty, of delicacy, of sympathizing sensibility, of prompt and active benevolence, of warmth and tenderness of attachment'. These natural feminine attributes are not confined to any particular stage of civilisational development.

Rather, they 'shine amidst the darkness of uncultivated barbarism; they give to civilized society its brightest and most attractive lustre'. Here he includes a long footnote on writers who have described the 'conjugal and parental affection of the women among the North American Indian', an interesting contrast to Robinson's 1799 feminist tract, which, as we have seen, high-lights the rights to full participation in public affairs enjoyed by some native American women. Helpfulness and generosity to travellers, he argues, is shown by women, whether savage or civilised. These, then, are the natural feminine qualities which need to be cultivated in women through education.[81]

Gisborne's positive evaluation of the current condition of women in 1790s Britain contrasts with the critical and urgent tone adopted by Hannah More in her *Strictures on the Modern System of Female Education* (1799), a highly influential text that went though nine editions in two years. More, the leading female member of the Clapham Sect, had earlier been part of Elizabeth Montagu's blue-stocking literary circle, but by the 1790s she had switched focus to the promotion of evangelical religion and a conservative reform agenda designed to combat political radicalism.[82] Calling for the reform of the education of women of 'rank and fortune', she warned against the complacency that might be induced by cross-cultural comparison of the type present in Gisborne's text: 'The character of British ladies, with all the unparalled [*sic*] advantages they possess, must never be determined by a comparison with the women of other nations, but by what they themselves might be if all their talents and unrivalled opportunities were turned to the best account'.[83] More begins by reiterating the standard Enlightenment argument linking the condition of women and the state of society in order to emphasise the vital importance of the condition of women to the state of the nation: 'The general state of civilized society depends more than those are aware …. On the prevailing sentiments and habits of women, and on the nature and degree of the estimation in which they are held'. This condition, she claims, is far from ideal. In words that are almost indistinguishable from those of Mary Wollstonecraft, she attacks women who 'use their boasted power over mankind to no higher purpose than the gratification of vanity or the indulgence of pleasure'. Like her feminist opponent, she likens such Western women to women who are sexual slaves in the Eastern harem. However, whereas feminists linked 'oriental' ill-treatment of women to political despotism, More attributes it to Muslim religion: Eastern women are describes as 'those fair victims to luxury, caprice, and despotism, whom the laws and the religion of the voluptuous prophet of Arabia exclude from light, and liberty, and knowledge'.[84]

In the next part of her argument, More clearly distinguishes her message from that of Wollstonecraft through stressing Christian women's privileges. She paints a much more positive picture of the current condition of women in Britain, which, she claims, offers 'the bright reverse of this mortifying scene': it is a civilized Christian country 'where our sex enjoys the blessings of liberal instruction, of reasonable laws, of a pure religion, and all the enduring pleasures of an equal, social, virtuous, and delightful intercourse'. Writing in the context of war with revolutionary France, she expresses the hope that British women, will, at this moment of terrible danger, 'come forward with a patriotism as once firm and feminine for the general good!' However, this should not be as female warriors or politicians, but through promoting public morality, religious principle and active piety.[85]

Later in the first volume of the *Strictures* More attacks cultural relativism and religious toleration in language that seems to be a direct riposte to Robinson's call for women to become 'citizens of the world' in her feminist tract published in the same year. Linking British patriotism with Christian conviction, she urges: 'let us teach the youth to hug his prejudices rather than to acquire that versatile and accommodating citizenship of the world, by which he may be an Infidel in Paris, a Papist in Rome, and a Mussulman at Cairo'. Christianity, she goes on to argue, should not tolerate other religions. Making an implicit distinction between the Christian British Empire and the heathen Roman Empire, she states that, unlike the Roman Emperor, who ordered that the image of Christ be set up in the Pantheon and worshipped alongside heathen gods, 'Christianity not only rejects all … partnerships with other religions, but it pulls down their images, defaces their temples, founds its own existence on the ruins of specious religions and spurious virtues, and will be every thing when it is admitted to be any thing'. There is no space for Enlightenment cultural relativism in this militant, intolerant assertion of imperial Christian mission.[86]

In the *Strictures*, More's anti-feminism becomes clear when she positions advocates of women's rights as un-Christian, stressing the need to preserve 'the original marks of difference stamped by the hand of the Creator'. She argues that differences in the roles of the sexes are rooted in nature: 'women have equal parts, but are inferior in wholeness of mind in the integral understanding'. This results in narrowness of vision: 'A woman sees the world, as it were, from a little elevation in her own garden, whence she takes an exact survey of home scenes, but takes not in that wider range of distant prospects, which he who stands on a loftier eminence demands'. Women would thus be wise to follow the path that Providence has marked out for them as 'the lawful possessors of a lesser domestic territory', rather than 'the turbulent usurpers of a wider foreign empire'.[87] The ambivalence she felt about her own prescriptions is, however, suggested when, returning to cross-cultural comparison, and drawing on her own engagements with Empire, she undermines this confident assertion of a natural difference between men's and women's minds. Until women are better educated, she argues, 'we have no juster ground for pronouncing that their understanding has already attained its highest attainable perfections, than the Chinese would have for affirming that their women have attained to the greatest possible perfection in walking, while the first care is, during their infancy, to cripple their feet', just as 'the shades of distinction' between the 'native powers' of blacks and whites can 'never be fairly ascertained' until 'Africans and Europeans are put nearer on a par in the cultivation of their minds'.[88] More attempts to reconcile the inconsistencies in her argument by reasserting Christian women's privileges.

Whatever the actual degree of women's mental or physical inferiority might be, and whatever the extent of her social subordination, she argues 'there is one great and leading circumstance which raises her importance, and even establishes her equality. *Christianity* has exalted woman to true and undisputed dignity'. Spiritual equality is more important, she argued, than social equality: 'in Christ Jesus, there is neither "rich nor poor", "bond nor free", so there is neither "male not female"'.[89]

As evangelicals became increasingly preoccupied with the promotion of foreign missionary activity following the opening of Britain's Indian Empire to Protestant missionary activity in 1813, they began to emphasise British women's privileges by deploying cross-cultural comparisons with women in the societies on which missionary efforts were now becoming focused. The Baptist promoter of missions, Francis Augustus Cox, for example, opened the second volume of his *Female Scripture Biography* (1817) with an 'essay on what Christianity has done for women'. This presented a 'picture of female degradation' in pagan, Jewish, and Muslim nations and included a section on 'Hindostan' that reproduced accounts of *sati* by Dr Carey, one of the first Baptist missionaries active in India. This picture was contrasted with Christianity, which 'assigns to women their proper place in society' as the respected helpmeets of men.[90]

From the 1820s such comparisons between Christian and 'heathen' women increasingly took place within appeals for women to support the foreign mission movement, as will be discussed in Chapters 3 and 4. In these texts the evangelical reformist agenda for women articulated by More is focused away from British women and onto 'heathen' women. Evangelical women authors of prescriptive tracts and conduct books that did focus on the lives of British women at this period tend to adopt a more insular approach, perhaps concerned that cross-cultural comparison was being used in some missionary appeals to encourage women to move beyond the domestic sphere and become missionary agents in their own right. Sarah Lewis's influential *Women's Mission* (1839) offers a vision of women as moral regenerators of the world, but stresses that this should be from an exclusively domestic and local community base, a message whose inherent contradictions are discussed further in Chapter 4. Sarah Stickney Ellis's popular 1840s series of conduct books addressed to the women of England promotes a similarly self-contained English domesticity, in which women's sphere is separated from the wider world, despite her marriage to a man who had been a pioneering missionary in the Pacific Islands and who had written a memoir celebrating his first wife's role as an active missionary agent.[91]

Birmingham Independent minister John Angell James, while strongly influenced by Ellis's views on women's sphere, returned to cross-cultural comparison in his *Female Piety* (1852).[92] A highly influential tract, which had gone into ten editions by 1864, *Female Piety* reproduced a set of 12 monthly sermons directed at young women. The first sermon is on 'the influence of Christianity on the condition of women' and begins rather in the style of Hannah More with a powerful statement about the tremendous power of women to influence for good or for ill. James then moves into a consideration of 'the condition of the sex beyond the boundaries of Christendom'. Drawing on evangelical missionary discourse, he incorporated an unattributed quote that contains a long litany of horrors about the position of women in India. He also refers to the details about the condition of women in Pagan and Mohammedan countries in Cox's *Female Scripture Biography*, adopting a strong anti-Muslim position. Like Cox and More, James argues that it is to Christianity that 'woman owes her true elevation' and 'her proper place and influence in the family and in society'. While acknowledging that early Christian society did not give women full freedom, he argues that most polished nations of the globe are Christian and there the condition of female sex is improved. The situation in contemporary Britain, where Christianity is married to economic progress, is presented as the most favourable: 'it was reserved for that glorious and gracious economy under which we are placed to raise the female sex into their just position and influence in society'. Where there has been improvement in the position of women outside Europe and America is because of Christian missionary work: 'It has abolished the Suttee in India …. It has stopped the suicidal prostration before the idol's car in Ceylon – the drudgery of the wives of all savage tribes – the incarcerating seclusion of Mohammedan and Pagan nations – the polygamy, the infanticide, and the concubinage of all countries whither it has gone'. In this way Christianity has, 'in modern times proved itself woman's emancipator and friend'. Even in 'this Christian and Protestant nation' it has elevated women by changing men's hearts and making them into better husbands. Christianity fits women to be 'the friend and companion of man'.[93]

James uses this cross-cultural comparison of the effect of different religions on the position of women as a way of attacking 'modern infidels' such as William Godwin, Robert Owen and the French revolutionaries. Arguing that infidelity corrupts and degrades the female sex and 'a female infidel is the most dangerous and destructive of the furies', he urges British women to 'look around upon your condition in society, and especially as often as you contrast your situation with that of women in Pagan countries, let a glow of gratitude warm your heart'. The Bible protects women 'from the sad effects which would arise from an assumption of prerogatives which do not belong to her'. Rather than becoming political radicals or advocates of women's rights, British women should 'seek to extend that benign system to others which has exerted so beneficial an influence upon herself' through zealous support for missionary schemes to the 'heathen abroad' and the 'sinful at home'. Women's chief 'mission', however, as laid out in the Bible, is to be the helpmeet of man.[94]

James' elevated view of Christian women's position in Britain in comparison with women in 'pagan' lands is then deployed to come down firmly in favour of female subordination and 'separate spheres'. It is up to the husband to support the household financially, and to wives to focus on family life, in contrast to the situation among 'uncivilized' heathen tribes and even among some British industrial workers, where 'the woman is the drudge of the family, while the husband lives in lordly sloth', to the detriment of domestic life. Women's proper sphere is the home: their contribution to the 'strength and stability of the nation' and to the 'empire's prosperity' lies in their role in cementing 'the domestic constitution and in well-trained families'. Contra Wollstonecraft, this domestic confinement of women does not, he claims, imply that British men will act 'with the jealousy and authority of an oriental despot'. Rather, in her roles as 'companion, counsellor, and comforter of man', the Bible gives women supremacy in the heart of the family. Woman's subordination is a law of nature and of God, but it is not a condition of slavery, and endeavouring to 'throw off the yoke' will simply cause family strife. Those 'wild visionaries' who claim women's right to fill male roles ignore the fact that it is forbidden by Christianity for women to speak at public assembly or in church, or claim the right of suffrage or authority over men.[95]

The 'woman question' in Elizabeth Hamilton's *Translations of the Letters of a Hindoo Rajah*

A comparison between the writings of Mary Wollstonecraft and Hannah More in the 1790s or those of Harriet Taylor and John Angell James in the 1850s is revealing of the polarisation of positions on the woman question between feminist radicals and evangelicals. Eliza Hamilton's *Translation of the Letters of a Hindoo Rajah* (1796) can be interpreted as an attempt to open up a space between these oppositional positions through adopting the voice of a cultural outsider. The adoption of an 'eastern' persona to offer a fresh perspective on controversial issues and to critique facets of contemporary European society was a feature of Englightenment writing that can be traced back to French Enlightenment philosopher Montesquieu's *Lettres Persanes* (1721).[96] The epistolary format common to such texts, Anne Mellor has suggested, 'opens up a space for a critical or ironic response to any given speaker's opinion', facilitating a 'subtle and nuanced' analysis from 'multiple narrative viewpoints'.[97]

The main body of Hamilton's text takes the form of the fictional correspondence of a 'Hindoo rajah' prior to and during a period of residence in England in the late 1770s. Presented as a translation, it is in fact an imaginative crossing of the boundaries of gender and racial difference, potentially exposing Hamilton to the criticism that she is indulging in a form of miscegenation, as a white woman transgressing the sexual and racial order of imperial Britain. Indeed, Hamilton privately referred to her developing text, her first novel, as 'my black baby': not a child of her womb, but 'a child of my brain, towards whom I am so unnatural a parent, that I have hitherto seen them smothered without remorse'.[98]

Hamilton was the sister of Charles Hamilton, an employee of the East India Company. Her brother had invited her to join him in India, and possibly find a husband there, but she decided instead to try to carve out an independent career as a professional writer in Britain. Elizabeth was strongly influenced by her brother's sympathy for the Orientalist scholarship of Sir William Jones, whose positive evaluation of ancient Hindu civilisation contrasted to the deeply negative view of Hinduism propogated by evangelical missionaries. Her text is dedicated to Warren Hastings, late Governor General of India, promoter of Orientalist scholarship and her late brother's patron, whom the Hamiltons had supported during his long and spectacular public trial before Parliament for corruption and abuse of power.[99]

Hamilton's text is not simply a discussion of the woman question. It incorporates a broader critique of British society and also includes an introductory section in which Hamilton exerts her authority as an expert on India, conveying colonial knowledge of India to a British public, and articulates her own position on British imperialism. Her 'preliminary dissertation of the history, religion, and manners, of the Hindoos' presents British imperial conquest of India in pursuit of commercial gain as having opened up new sources of knowledge. Unable to participate actively in the colonial project of rule and the associated creation of Orientalist knowledge of India, enterprises in which her late brother had been heavily involved, she instead adopts the role of an educationalist, conveying some of the fruits of this scholarship to her British readers, particularly those of her own sex. Taking a pro-Hindu, anti-Muslim, and pro-British position, she stresses 'the amiable and benevolent character of the hindoos' and lays most of the blame for problems on the Muslim invaders of India, expressing the hope that life is improving in areas which have now come under British imperial control. While this introductory section does not focus on the position of women, its relatively positive view of Hindus (contrasting sharply with contemporary evangelical accounts) opens the way for readers to take seriously a 'Hindoo' comparative perspective on the education and position of women in Britain and in India, conveyed through a fictional body of correspondence that forms the body of the text. It also presents British rule in a positive light, a stance that is later reinforced through the words of the Rajah himself.[100]

Volume 1 of Hamilton's text is set in India. In the first letter from Zaarmilla to his friend Maandaara, the Rajah conveys his very positive view of the position of English women, gleaned from an English friend in India. In typical evangelical style, this is ascribed largely to Christianity, which considers women as rational beings, frees them from men's despotic authority and admits them to heaven, in contrast to Muslim law, which excludes women from 'happiness in a future state', and the Hindu Shaster only offers a place in paradise to a woman who burns herself on her husband's funeral pyre. His English friend has also informed him of the importance attached to female education in England, and painted a rosy picture of marriage in a country where women can choose their husbands, a man cannot have more than one wife and 'the wife is the friend of her husband'.[101]

In the second letter, the Rajah's friend Maandaara, who has now married the Rajah's sister, is presented as a traditionalist Hindu supporter of the subordination of women in contrast to his critical and reformist friend.

Maandaara forwards a series of letters he has received from a Brahmin, whose observations on his time in England suggest a much more negative view of the nation than the one the Rajah has gleaned from his English friend, highlighting its involvement in the slave trade. The Brahmin also questions the superiority of European women, suggesting that their education is limited to so-called accomplishments, and leads from vanity to vice. He suggests that allowing such ill-equipped women to be left as widows in charge of estates and the upbringing of children is less wise than the Hindu custom of widow burning (*sati*), and argues that English women are as 'equally ignorant, and equally helpless, as the females of Hindostan' and that the situation of those whose families are reduced to poverty is 'far more destitute and pitiable'. The Brahmin also points to the hypocrisy of Christian Englishmen who pretend to be horrified at *sati* in India yet show no compassion for the far greater number of women who perish on the streets of London every year, 'victims of the licentious passions of unprincipled men'. At first dismissive of the Brahmin's statements, the Rajah begins to question his positive image of English women when he encounters a group of colonial wives in Calcutta who seem like 'superannuated dancing girls', bold and gaudily dressed. However, he desperately attempts to interpret their behaviour in a positive light.[102]

Volume 2 opens with two letters from the Rajah to his Indian friend recording the Rajah's voyage to England, letters that signal the major preoccupation of Hamilton's text: to explore the appropriate education and appropriate roles of English women through the use of the eyes of an outsider. The Rajah compares the manners of three English women he meets on board: the virtuous widow, who, rather than commit *sati* like a Hindu widow, is devoting herself to the education and care of her children; the frivolous and bored colonial wife, who is uneducated and so cannot be a true companion to her husband; and the young woman unhealthily obsessed with romantic novels.[103]

In these early letters, then, comparison between the position of Indian and English women is a central feature, with the practice of *sati* acting as a key reference point in discussion as to whether or not the position of English women is better than that of Hindu women. The following letters record the Rajah's experiences in London and the country, focusing on his observations of the female members of the family of Sir Caprice and Lady Ardent. Comparison between the position of Indian and English women is now largely dropped, as the Rajah's letters home to India become a vehicle for Hamilton's comparison between different forms of female education in Britain, and a comparative evaluation of the characters which these cultivate in women, and their resulting impact on women's behaviour. Here, it becomes clear that Hamilton's central preoccupation is with reforming the education of British women rather than examining the lives of Indian women.

Through the observations of the Rajah, Hamilton articulates her condemnation of a boarding-school education overfocused on female accomplishments for creating women of weak character, and her equal objections to those who educate women in the same way as men for creating overforceful women who violate social propriety, meddle inappropriately in the masculine political sphere, and come to a sticky end. The ideal female education is presented as a good maternal upbringing enabling girls to take advantage of formal education, so that they can combine understanding with accomplishment, vivacity with modesty, and feeling for others with decorum.

Given her apparent alignment with the educational agenda and feminine ideal of Hannah More, the reason why Hamilton decided to use the voice of an outsider to articulate her views is, at first sight, unclear. However, sections of the text indicate that Hamilton's position was more complex than this and that an outsider voice provided her with the opportunity to articulate a position which showed some sympathy for the discredited views of Wollstonecraft. This is evident in the account that the Rajah gives of witnessing the differing responses of the Ardents' three daughters to an accident. Julia, the product of a boarding-school education, flees home, faints and has an hysteric fit; Caroline, the product of maternal education, tends the injured man; Olivia, the product of a masculine education, rushes off and rounds up male help 'with a tone of authority'.[104] While the selfish sensibility of Julia is uneqivocally condemned, the combined actions of the two other (twin) sisters are shown as saving the man's life, suggesting that there may be a role in the world for women in both the More and the Wollstonecraft mould, or perhaps for a woman who combines the qualities of both their ideal types.

Ambivalence about the tendency of Hannah More's approach to female education to cultivate timidity and passivity in women is also suggested in the rather negative portrayal in the text of Charlotte Percy, the sister of the Rajah's diseased English friend. The Rajah has travelled to England in order to deliver a packet to Charlotte. She is portrayed as devoted to her brother, as highly religious and as a writer.[105] As such, she seems to be modelled on Hamilton herself, who had recently lost a beloved brother who had also worked in colonial India. However, the Rajah is shocked that she has sunk into a depressed and purposeless existence in England, feeling that her life has no purpose without any family to care for, and making no attempt to publish her writing because she feels publishers are prejudiced against women's work.[106] This woman, who, like the Hindu widow who commits *sati*, feels that there is nothing to live for after the death of her male relatives, is set up in contrast to Hamilton, for whom the text represented her first venture into publication, and an honouring her brother not through private mourning but through conveying his knowledge of Indian culture to a wider British audience.

While using the Rajah's voice to express shock at women of Wollstonecraft's type who offer forceful opinions on imperial politics, Hamilton also uses his voice to offer her own take on the most publicly debated recent issue in imperial politics: the impeachment of Warren Hastings. Here, the Rajah becomes an apologist for Hastings: encountering a gentleman in a coffee house ranting against Britain's terrible treatment of India, he publicly contradicts the rumour that he has come to Britain 'on behalf of the Hindoo inhabitants of Bengal' to complain of the maladministration of the British governor and expresses his high respect for the British government of India.[107] As Rendall has pointed out with reference to her *Memoirs of Agrippina* (1804), Hamilton believed that imperialism could be a benevolent force in the world if it were promoted by enlightened Christians.[108]

Feminist Utopianism in James Henry Lawrence's *The Empire of the Nairs*

While Hamilton sought to articulate a respectable and practical reformist position on the woman question at a time of political polarisation, James Henry Lawrence's *The Empire of the Nairs; or, the Rights of Women. A Utopian Romance* was, in sharp contrast, a Utopian vision written by an author unconcerned with either practicality or conventional respectability. To describe it, as Gregory Claeys has done, as 'the most important feminist tract' between Mary Wollstonecraft's *Vindication* and William Thompson's *Appeal*, is to accord it a cultural influence that it most probably did not have beyond select sexually libertarian circles.[109] Nevertheless, it is a fascinating text, and interesting in its attempt to set up an indigenous Indian culture as an ideal model for gender relations in the West at the very time that missionaries and liberals were denigrating Indian culture on the basis of its treatment of women and beginning to press for its reform through British imperial intervention. Published in London as a four-volume edition in 1811, it combines Lawrence's own translation of his essay on the Nair system, published in Germany in 1793, with his Utopian novel, originally published in German in 1801.[110]

Like Hamilton, Lawrence uses the medium of cultural outsiders from the Indian subcontinent to throw critical light on British society; like Hamilton, his particular preoccupation is with the position of women, including their education; and like Hamilton, he presents Muslims as despotic oppressors of women. However, whereas Hamilton's Indians are presented as living under benevolent British imperial rule, Lawrence focuses on a non-European 'empire': a community loosely based on the matrilineal society of the Nair of the Malabar Coast in Kerala in south-west India in the period prior to British conquest.[111] Whereas Hamilton provides a critical perspective on Indian and British culture, Lawrence sets up the Nair as the ideal society in contrast to Britain. Whereas Hamilton's fiction presents faithful companionate marriage as the social ideal, Lawrence's launches an out-and-out attack on the institution of marriage, clearly influenced by William Godwin, the bogeyman of Hamilton's book, and presents himself as an unequivocal supporter of Mary Wollstonecraft. His Utopia is presented as existing within a hierarchical Indian feudal society structured along matrilineal lines in which women can take as many male lovers as they please, motherhood is seen as women's highest achievement and women get state support for their children, descent is in the female line, and there is no concept of fatherhood. It would have been scandalous for a woman to publish such a novel in Britain at this period, but Lawrence, as a wealthly, well-travelled and highly educated old Etonian, could get away with it.

Lawrence's introductory essay clarifies the purpose of the work as a whole: 'to shew [*sic*] the possibility of a nation's reaching the highest civilization without marriage'. It positions this as 'the system of nature' which has always existed among the Nair, a very old civilization, and which is also practised by some savage tribes in America. Marriage is condemned as a 'domestic yoke', the Nair system as 'freedom'. Adopting the Nair system would ensure population growth, security of noble inheritance and 'the happiness and liberty of mankind'.[112] The novel itself is a convoluted story of travel, cultural exchange and intimate relationships between Nairs and Britons. Britain, its system of marriage being one of lifelong bondage oppressive to male and female alike, is positioned between the despotic and polygamous Muslims and the matrilinear Nair in its treatment of women. Nair knights, not Christian missionary crusaders, are presented as the true saviours of women from slavery, rescuing women from the harem and tearing off their veils.[113]

The novel is structured partly as a quest for two lost women. The first is Emma, sister of the novel's English hero Walter de Grey, whose loss De Grey describes in language echoing missionary critiques of *sati* in India: 'unhappy victim! Whom my pride sacrificed to the blindest superstition'. The second is Agalva, heir to the Nair Empire's ruler, whose disappearance is a result of her own spirit of adventure and curiosity, and whose own memoirs of her experiences as a visitor to Britain comprise two major sections of the text. Agalva had an excellent education at a mixed college, and with social sanction took lovers and had a child. In contrast, Emma became pregnant after being seduced by a married man unable to divorce his mad wife, and her brother has killed him in a duel to defend her honour, forcing them both to flee the country. Emma lost her baby, then took the veil and was confined in a convent, described as the Abbe's 'seraglio' where the abbess held 'a despotic sway'; she is then taken captive by pirates and taken to Morocco, apparently to the fate of enslavement in a harem.[114]

Volume 2 begins with Firnos, Agalva's son, arriving in England with de Grey. In contrast to Hamilton's Rajah's focus on the question of female education, Firnos focuses on the question of women's sexual freedom. He is shocked at encountering prostitutes for the first time and shocked that a country with a reputation for liberty should treat women as men's private property. A section from Agalva's memoirs follows, providing a female outsider's perspective on the treatment of British women. She recounts her arrival in Britain with her lover, the Baron of Naldor, and her decision to cross-dress in his clothes rather than pass as his wife, an idea 'so shocking to a freeborn woman'. Later she passes as an Italian marchesa and describes her difficulties in donning fashionable European women's apparel, likening it to the binding of women's feet in China and suggesting it could also be attributed to a similar desire to restrict women's movement. She expresses an ethnographic interest in this female clothing, and in an amusing satire on British imperial men's mania for collection, asserts: 'When I return home, I shall present a pair of high-heeled shoes, a pair of stays, and a hoop, or perhaps a doll dressed in the English fashion for the Christian year 1775, to the Imperial Society in Calicut'. At a time when evangelical discourse was presenting infanticide as characteristic of superstitious 'Hindoostan' and alien to Christian Britain and positioning missionaries as the saviours of Indian infants and widows, Agalva describes rescuing an illegitimate baby thrown from a bridge into the Thames by its mother, who has been cast out by her family. She then helps the woman, who later states that 'she not only saved me from an ignominious death, but freed my mind from prejudice and superstition'. In the final volume of the novel, thanks to the efforts of the Nair knights, Agalva, De Grey and Emma are all rescued from imprisonment in Muslim harems and the members of both Nair and English families are happily reunited in the Empire of the Nair. The final words of the novel are 'Success to the rights of women!'.[115]

Despite aligning himself with Wollstonecraft's feminism, however, Lawrence's wider political beliefs are clearly at variance with her political radicalism. His ideal society is a feudal rather than an egalitarian one, his vision apparently fuelled by aristocratic nostalgia rather than revolutionary fervour. Coming from a wealthy family who had settled in Jamaica,[116] he expresses his hostility to the anti-slavery agenda that Wollstonecraft supported. Elevating the freedom to have sex as the most important freedom, he criticises those who think black men are worse off as slaves to enlightened Europeans than as castrated eunuchs in an Eastern harem, and grotesquely argues that English wives are less free than female colonial slaves because their sexual relationships are far more regulated. He also calls for British reformers to rescue their sisters and free their wives before focusing on the wrongs of African slaves.[117]

The 'woman question' in imperial Britain

Lawrence's and Hamilton's texts are suggestive of the richness of approaches to the 'woman question' in the late eighteenth and early nineteenth centuries, and of the variety of ways in which debate on the position of British women drew on cross-cultural comparison and referenced contemporary debates on imperial issues, particularly colonial slavery. Far from being parochial or inward looking, much discussion of the nature, condition and roles of women in the nation situated British women within a broad global framework of historical development that drew on Enlightenment stadial theory developed during the 1770s but which increasingly made use of new cross-cultural comparisons based on knowledge of non-Christian cultural others developed with the expansion of missionary activity in Britain's overseas Empire from the 1790s onwards.

In the feminist texts discussed in the first part of this chapter, critical engagements with Enlightenment stadial theory, the drawing of analogies between the treatment of white Western women and the oppression of black colonial slaves, and the deployment of cross-cultural comparisons between European women and women in extra-European societies are not incidental or marginal features of the texts. Rather, they are central to the construction of feminist arguments. They help position feminism within the European cultural mainstream, enabling feminists to claim that the oppression of women is alien and anachronistic within a civilised nation and to present the emancipation of women not as an outlandish demand but, rather, as the fulfilment of Britain's destiny as a progressive nation, an achievement that will mark the final step along the road to the creation of a fully enlightened society. Women's rights discourse thus becomes securely tied to discourses of Western progress, and in the process, here, a self-consciously modern Western feminist identity is consolidated.

While the central purpose of these feminist texts was not, of course, to contribute to colonial discourse or to debates on Empire, much feminist writing, in stressing the bad treatment of women outside the West, reinforced stereotypical views of non-Europeans as cultural inferiors, views that buttressed the justification and implementation of imperial rule. At the same time, assertions of anti-slavery sentiment positioned feminists as supporters of the reform of the most oppressive aspects of imperialism and combated racist ideas about black peoples' natural inferiority to whites. Complacency over the extent of European progress was also called into question, as were the progressive credentials of leading male thinkers, such as Jean Jacques Rousseau and James Mill, as regards both women and non-European cultures. A minority of feminist writers also made use of cross-cultural comparison to suggest that some contemporary non-European societies offered women more rights than supposedly 'civilised' nations.

In these texts, the oppression or liberation of women in extra-European lands is not the focus of concern; rather, the use of cross-cultural comparison makes it clear that the 'woman' who is the subject of British feminists' concern is the European woman, and often more specifically the upper or middle-class British or English woman. Just how this woman is positioned in relation to others is, however, variable. Among 1790s radicals and 1820 Utopian socialists there is a universalising tendency, notably in Robertson's formulation of the ideal of the woman of the world. In Aikin's cautiously feminist work of 1810, there is a narrower, patriotic and Anglocentric positioning of the woman writer and reader, while in Taylor's 1851 essay there is a more culturally arrogant and imperialist tone in relation to non-European cultures, participating in the 'turn to empire' among liberal thinkers which Jennifer Pitts has identified as characteristic of the mid-nineteenth century, in contrast to the more critical perspectives on Empire adopted by some late-eighteenth-century writers. There is a direct route from Taylor to J.S. Mill and the 'imperial feminist' campaigners for women's suffrage of the 1865–1914 period.

Evangelical texts on women drew on many of the same cultural resources as feminist texts. However, they reworked Enlightenment stadial theory to link progress with the spread of Christianity. In their cross-cultural comparisons they highlighted the role of religion rather than the socio-economic or political stage of development as the key factor in either degrading or elevating women, focusing on men's attitudes to women rather than on women's material social position. This enabled them to draw British women's attention to their privileges, and to argue that they should focus on helping to extend these to others through missionary work rather than be seduced by 'wild visionaries' who sought to disrupt the social order by calling for women's rights. Evangelicals also drew on that strand in Enlightenment thought that stressed the natural differences between male and female minds and positioned companionate marriage and female domesticity as the ideal condition of women, buttressing this with biblical authority to assert the necessity of female subordination in marriage.

In Hannah More's writing, however, there is a more positive assertion of women's power to influence the state of the nation. In order to emphasise the vital importance of her reformist agenda for female education she stresses the danger of allowing cross-cultural comparison to lead to complacency about British women's position. She also expresses ambivalence about supposedly innate differences between men's and women's minds through drawing on an analogy with the present differences in mind between 'uncultured' Africans and 'civilised' Europeans. Christian education is the key to the elevation of both European women and African 'savages'; but, for More, spiritual equality is perfectly compatible with social hierarchy between rich and poor, male and female, and white and black. While her views were in direct conflict with advocates of the rights of woman, they did provide openings of women's assertion of moral power and influence not only from within the family, but also through organised philanthropy and movements for social and moral reform. The important imperial dimensions of such voluntary work, notably the anti-slavery, anti-*sati* and foreign missionary movements, as we will see in the following chapters, provided an important grounding for middle-class women in self-organisation, in the use of pressure from without, and in assertions of agency and power, experiences that helped to lay the ground for the emergence of an organised feminist movement in the second half of the century.

2   Sweetness and power

The domestic woman and anti-slavery politics

As Chapter 1 has shown, debates on the position of women in imperial Britain were interlinked with critiques of colonial slavery. Feminists' use of analogies between the position of British women and of African colonial slaves reflected British women's close involvement in all phases of the anti-slavery movement, from the campaign for the abolition of the British slave trade, which achieved success in 1807, through the campaign for the emancipation of slaves in Britain's colonies, an objective achieved in 1833–8, to the 'universal abolition' movement, which continued into the 1860s.

In my earlier work on the anti-slavery movement I have explored the relationship between British women's anti-slavery campaigning and feminism from a number of angles. One area I have examined is the extent to which female abolitionists moved from calling for the emancipation of slaves to calling for their own emancipation and for equal rights within the anti-slavery movement. My conclusion was that the link between abolitionism and equal-rights feminism was less direct than in the United States: it occurred mainly after the abolition of colonial slavery, when British women turned their attention to 'universal abolition' and forged ties with American abolitionists. Following the dispute over the refusal of the British and Foreign Anti-Slavery Society to allow women from the radical wing of the American movement to take their place as official delegates at the World Anti-Slavery in 1840, some British campaigners forged strong friendships with American abolitionist-feminists, though British women supportive of feminism differed as to whether or not women's rights should be promoted within the anti-slavery movement or kept as a separate issue.[1]

More recently, I have explored the implications of analysing female anti-slavery as a feminist movement itself, rather than simply as stimulating the development of feminism. In the case of African-American women it is clear that resistance to enslavement provided the basis for the emergence of a black feminism in which anti-slavery, anti-racist and women's liberation agendas were inseparable, an agenda articulated to British audiences in the mid-nineteenth century through the public lectures of the radical black abolitionist Sarah Parker Remond. White British women anti-slavery activists, whatever their position on the British 'woman question', focused their concern on the sufferings of enslaved women from the outset, developing an analysis of black women's sexual oppression and exploitation at the hands of men, and focusing their campaigning energies of female emancipation from slavery. They also adopted the rhetoric of sisterhood that emphasised empathetic identification between women across racial divides. However, this woman-centred approach also involved a 'maternalist' stance characterised by assertions of white women's power to speak on behalf of powerless black women, who were represented as the passive victims of slavery. White British women also developed a vision of black freedom that stressed female domesticity without reference to black women's own visions of freedom. In addition, they unselfconsciously measured black women's worth by their own standards of respectability, showing little awareness or respect for enslaved women's African cultural heritages. Concerned to avoid offending sheltered middle-class British women's notions of female propriety, they also censored information on the full range of women's everyday forms of resistance to slavery, including elements of the story of Mary Prince, whose 1831 account of her experiences of slavery is the only surviving slave narrative by a woman from Britain's Caribbean colonies.[2]

In this chapter I approach the question of the relationship between anti-slavery and feminism in Britain from a new and rather different angle. Focusing on women's leading role in the boycott of slave-grown sugar, I draw out the ways in which female anti-slavery activists harnessed women's domestic power both as consumers of colonial produce and as designated guardians of morality to a radical anti-slavery politics that challenged the authority of the male leadership of the movement and called into question male domination of the public and political sphere.

As noted in Chapter 1, Mary Wollstonecraft, writing in 1792 at the height of the first phase of the 'anti-saccharite' campaign, as the slave sugar boycott was popularly known, placed sugar at the heart of a rather complex analogy between the treatment of women and colonial slaves in her *Vindication of the Rights of Woman*. Her emotive talk of 'vital blood' and her call for principle rather than self-interest to guide behaviour towards both women and slaves is suggestive of the radical and feminist potential of the boycott. Both British women and African slaves, Wollstonecraft suggests, are oppressed in order to 'sweeten the cup of man'. The title I have chosen for this chapter is intended to evoke both Wollstonecraft's association between women, sugar and slavery and anthropologist Sidney Mintz's pioneering study of the place of sugar in modern history.[3] It also signals my central aims: to explore the association of sugar with the ideal of the domestic woman and then to discuss how the slave-grown sugar boycott involved women not only abstaining from a sweet substance, but also in moving beyond their metaphorical sweetness as domestic women.

Over the past decade, scholarship has established both the powerful influence of the prescriptive evangelical ideology of 'separate spheres' and the ingenuity of middle-class women in finding practical ways of working around such prescriptions in their everyday lives, notably through developing an intermediate 'social sphere' in which they actively engaged in community-based philanthropy and social reform, often through taking on the role of social mothers of the poor.[4] Women's anti-slavery organisations formed an important part of this social sphere. However, anti-slavery was uniquely important in connecting the two arenas of life that were placed furthest apart in the 'separate spheres' model of gender roles: at one pole, the woman-centred world of domestic life within the nation's homes; at the other, the male-dominated world of imperial commerce and the exclusively masculine world of parliamentary politics and imperial policy making. Through the consumer boycott of slave-grown sugar, this chapter argues, women not only politicised domesticity, harnessing their domestic duties to the end of imperial reform, but also mobilised women's role as consumers as the base for a radical anti-slavery politics that sought to erode the economic basis of slavery and challenge the cautious policies of the male leadership of the movement.

Leading radical abolitionist Thomas Clarkson signalled the importance of the abstention campaign in his *History of the Rise, Progress and Abolition of the Slave Trade*, claiming that by the winter of 1791–2 around 300,000 men, women and children were refusing to consume West Indian sugar and rum.[5] Nevertheless, subsequent historians have often dismissed it as a minor and unsuccessful aspect of the popular campaign against slavery, perhaps failing to take it seriously because of its association with women in the home rather than men in public.[6] Recent trends in historical scholarship, however, provide resources for a re-evaluation of the significance of slave sugar abstention, and women's leading role in the boycott campaigns. Scholars have highlighted the rise in eighteenth-century Britain of a consumer society heavily dependent on 'exotic' colonial produce, and studies of Enlightenment debates on luxury have revealed participants' twin preoccupations with the female consumer and with the consumption of colonial produce.[7] In addition, literary critics have drawn out the repeated textual associations made between women and sugar in the seventeenth and eighteenth centuries, and highlighted the contributions of women writers to debates on the politics of sugar and slavery in the 1790s.[8]

In order to appreciate the significance of women's role in the abstention campaigns fully, it is necessary to appreciate the immense practical and symbolic importance of sugar in eighteenth-century British society and culture, and to be aware of sugar's long-standing association with women. Thus, this chapter begins by examining the growth of sugar consumption in Britain, and its centrality to new rituals of sociability among the middling sort. It then explores the cultural politics of the tea table among a 'polite and commercial people',[9] looking at the development of a highly gendered debate over the merits and dangers of new fashions for exotic consumption and their associated social rituals. Moving on to the launching of anti-slavery campaigns from the 1780s, the chapter then discusses how abolitionists, drawing on these existing social and cultural associations of women with sugar, redirected gendered anxieties and moral panics about the consumption of exotic produce onto the hitherto largely unproblematised link between sugar and slavery. In so doing, it is suggested, abolitionists were able to harness the established link between women's consumer power and their cultural power. The chapter then proceeds to show how the moralising of domestic consumption became linked in the 1820s to a radical female challenge to the cautious approach to slave emancipation among the male leadership of the British anti-slavery movement. A section then considers the positioning of white anti-slavery women as saviours of the nation's virtue, and their promotion of 'legitimate' commerce as a way to reform rather than to undermine the British Empire. In conclusion, the significance of women's participation in the slave-sugar boycott is evaluated in terms of this book's focus on the relationship between emergent feminism and Empire.

'Patronesses of the fair SUGAR': sugar, slavery and domesticity

From the establishment of Britain's first sugar plantations on the Caribbean island of Barbados in the 1640s, Africans, forcibly transported across the Atlantic from the West African coastline to work as slave labour for British plantation owners, provided the ruthlessly exploited workforce that enabled white colonists to feed the growing demand for sugar from domestic consumers in Britain, where the protective duties characteristic of the era of mercantile European imperialism ensured that sugar from Britain's colonies had a virtual monopoly of the nation's domestic sugar market.[10,11] By the early eighteenth century Britain had become Europe's leading slave-trading nation, and the 'polite and commercial' society of eighteenth-century Britain was shaped not only by the political and economic power of the 'West India interest', but also by new patterns of consumption and new rituals of sociability centred around the use of slave-grown sugar.

During the seventeenth century, sugar was an exotic luxury and rarity used mainly by the aristocracy as medicine, spice, decorative material or preservative. However, from the beginning of the eighteenth century it began to have a much broader impact on patterns of consumption in Britain. Sugar as a sweetener came to the fore in connection with three other tropical products: tea, coffee and chocolate.[12] All began as luxury items of consumption, but tea prices fell rapidly during the eighteenth century, enabling the drinking of sugared tea to become central to middle-class sociability. By the early nineteenth century, sugar formed an essential weekly item in the budgets of all British families, rural and urban, rich and poor.[13] Britain's current image as a nation of sweet-toothed tea drinkers is thus rooted in its imperial legacy – and its legacy as a leading slave-holding power.[14]

Merchants with trading interests in the West Indies and returned or absentee planters were important promoters of the fashion for colonial produce in Britain. From the mid-eighteenth century, a fashion for male socialising around the consumption of rum punch, produced from sugar cane, spread out from port cities such as Glasgow and Liverpool, whose business wealth rested largely on the slave trade.[15] In 1767, George Dickinson, a wealthy Liverpool merchant, specially commissioned the production of an enormous decorated ceramic punch bowl bearing images of British ships and the motto 'Success to the African trade', suggesting the unself-conscious celebration of wealth derived from slavery.[16] Attempts were made to reconcile slavery with the eighteenth-century Enlightenment view of commerce as bringing progress, culture and civilisation through disguising the brutality of the slave system. James Grainger, who married the daughter of a West Indian planter and went on to take charge of a plantation himself, wrote a poem entitled *The Sugar-Cane* in 1764 in which he portrayed the cane-fields as an idyllic rural landscape populated by contented black workers. Women were also complicit in producing such images: a similarly prettified view of the sugar cane field is presented in Janet Schaw's journal of her 1774–5 visit to the West Indies.[17]

Britons with links to the slave system also initiated a fashion in Britain for keeping black slave-servants as marks of wealth, status, and refinement and visual foils highlighting the fashionably white skin of the aristocratic lady of leisure. Many were young boys, attired in exotic costumes often of vaguely eastern 'Moorish' style, their presence interchangeable with that of the lap-dog, their youth enabling them to be 'domesticated' as harmless pets, rather than feared as potentially dangerous rebels or rapacious threats to white women's bodies, as were adult African men in the Caribbean.[18] Slavery (and the African slave) was thus domesticated in aristocratic circles within Britain itself, and its violence and exploitative nature rendered invisible.[19] China coffee sets produced in 1760–5 in Liverpool, decorated with a scene showing a black servant waiting on a well-dressed white couple who are drinking sugared coffee in the grounds of a country house, further suggest a cosy absorption of the exotic into English genteel domesticity.[20] As late as 1782 a picture of *A Lady and her Children Relieving a Cottager* incorporated the figure of a black servant in livery, carrying a parasol to protect an elaborately dressed white women with her daughters who are offering alms to a poor countrywoman and her baby; here, the horrors of slavery that lay behind the presence of the black boy are obscured in a decorative scene of fashionable feminine charity.[21] It was the acts of rebellion by such black slave-servants in running away from their masters and mistresses that led to the first stage of the anti-slavery campaign in Britain, with efforts by the lawyer Granville Sharpe culminating in Lord Mansfield's judgment in the case of James Somerset in 1772, widely interpreted at the time as outlawing slavery within the British Isles.[22]

In eighteenth-century Britain, women of all classes played a central role in increasing the consumption of slave-grown sugar in the home, whether as leaders of entertaining in elite or middling households, as domestic servants emulating employers' eating habits, or as impoverished housewives seeking to provide family meals. The association of women with sugar consumption can be traced back to the seventeenth century, when aristocratic Englishwomen's standing was linked to elaborate rituals involving the creation of banquets of decorative sugar moulds and sweet-meats.[23] As Mintz has noted, male observers tended to believe that sweet things 'in both literal and figurative senses' were 'more the domain of women than of men'. In 1715, when physician Frederick Slare wrote a book promoting the value of sugar, his dedication expressed the hope that women would become 'Patronesses of the fair SUGAR', since their palates were more refined than men's. He recommended the use of sugar for infants as a substitute for the 'Sweetness of Breast-Milk', thus connecting the substance with the most intimate bodily functions of domestic femininity.[24] Charlotte Sussman has suggested that this association helped to naturalize sugar consumption within the nation as sugar shifted from luxury to necessity.[25]

Slave-grown sugar also formed the material basis for the rise of new rituals of sociability in the eighteenth century. Tea parties formed a central component of a new culture of civility among the middling ranks that was linked to the rise of consumer society. They were the domestic-based, woman-centred counterparts to the rise of masculine coffeehouse culture and of male sociability around the drinking of rum punch. The custom of afternoon entertaining was centred on the drinking of sugared tea, often accompanied by sugar-sweetened pastries and puddings made to recipes taken from Hannah Glasse's immensely popular special confectionary cookery book, first published in 1760.[26] The ritual stimulated the purchase by women of increasingly expensive and elaborate items for the drawing room: mahogany tables and chairs, china tea-services and silver tea-trays, sugar caddies, tea-spoons, tea-tongs and tea-pots. Such items were frequently singled out for individual description in their wills, suggesting that they attached especial significance to them. The tea table was an arena for the display of refined goods, refined codes of behaviour and the art of polite conversation, attributes of domesticity that became associated with national refinement and good taste. The delicate rituals of polite tea-drinking included a stress on avoiding contaminating the sugar; for example, sugar tongs were used rather than the bodily contact of hands – niceties in which other nations, such as the French, were seen as lagging behind.[27] While middle and upper rank ladies supplied their domestic servants with regular allowances of sugar, together with tea and coffee, a Lancashire lady recorded her horror at catching a female servant using white sugar in her coffee. This reaction suggests that attempts were made to maintain social distinctions by reserving highly refined sugars for use in 'refined' rituals of consumption – the whiteness of the sugar, like the whiteness of an English gentlewoman's skin, was associated with refinement, in contrast to the association of brown sugar with the brown skin, which was a marker of the outdoor labour of the poor Briton or the slave status and supposed racial inferiority of the African.

In the eighteenth century, women's drinking of sugared tea in the home became increasingly linked with morality and respectability and with a highly gendered culture of sensibility which, as Barker-Benfield argues, 'became a culture of reform, aiming to discipline women's consumer appetites in tasteful domesticity, but thence reforming male behaviour', directing it away from tavern to tea table.[28] Refinement, taste and luxury could be presented as female virtues when linked to enlightened conversation, charity and patronage of the arts in venues such as Elizabeth Montagu's bluestocking salon.[29] However, the woman-dominated tea table also became a focus for critics of consumption concerned about the moral implications of the new consumer culture of the middling classes. While some saw the expansion of global trade and the influx of exotic goods like sugar as a mark of the progress of civilisation, others saw it as a corrupting force in the body politic of the nation.[30] In this debate, as Beth Kowaleski-Wallace points out, 'woman herself is defined as a force having the ability to advance or destroy civilization', her appetite for the exotic linked with their appetite for scandalous gossip as potential threats to the family and national economy.[31]

What was strikingly absent from these debates about women, morality and the consumption of exotic goods was the question of the morality of slavery, on which the supply of sugar, and thus the rituals of the tea table, depended. In the pre-abolition period, David Dabydeen has suggested that the leading eighteenth-century artist William Hogarth mostly closely approached a critique of slavery in his use of figures of black slave-servants as crucial components of his satirical images in attacking the moral decay that could result from commercialism.[32] In his satirical series of prints *A Harlot's Progress* (1732), the figure of the merchant's mistress symbolises this decay: her excessive sexuality is linked to the overturning of the domestic order of the tea table and associated with the exotically clad figure of the black boy with teakettle.[33] However, Hogarth's critique seems to promote moderation in, rather than abstention from, the consumption of the bodies of white woman and black slave, and of the exotic produce associated with the tea table.

'A Subject for Conversation at the Tea-Table': creating anti-slavery culture

By the time the abolition campaign was launched in the late 1780s, slave-grown sugar had thus become a staple part of the British diet, central to male and female hospitality rituals in well-to-do households, and symbolic of the power and social integration of the West India interest within imperial Britain. Could the morality of slavery and the ethics of consuming slave-grown produce ever be made into suitable subjects for conversation at the tea table? Could polite etiquette ever open a space for the voice of the suffering, exploited slave? In Jane Austen's domestic novel *Mansfield Park* (1814), the English country estate is sustained by wealth derived from its owner Sir Thomas Bertram's slave sugar plantation in Antigua; but, when the novel's heroine Fanny Price asks Sir Thomas about the slave trade, 'There was such a dead silence'. Edward Said has argued that Austen suggests here 'that one world could not be connected with the other since there simply is no common language for both'.[34] While this may have been the case in households with a direct involvement in slavery, however, the ground had been laid for consideration of the question of slavery by polite society with the emergence from the 1760s of sentimental poems, tales and novels that encouraged sympathy for the sufferings of enslaved Africans as part of the cult of sensibility and which were aimed particularly at a female readership.[35] However, it was not until 1783 that sympathy for the slave began to be translated from fashion into action: the consumption of slave-grown sugar at the tea table now finally began to sit uncomfortably with the reading of sentimental verse.

In drawing public attention to the way in which everyday domestic life in Britain was dependent on the produce of colonial slaves, and in moving debates about sugar consumption away from its potential ill effects on the British body politic to its demonstrably devastating impact on Africans in the colonies, campaigners challenged the cosy relationship between slave-based colonial production and metropolitan sugar consumption on which the economic and political power of the West India interest rested.

British women were ideally placed to take the lead in the sugar boycott campaign launched by abolitionists in 1791. In their role as housewives and household managers who purchased groceries for the family, they were the ones with the responsibility for, and direct opportunity to shape, patterns of domestic consumption. Colonial women had very recently played a leading role in the tea boycott that formed part of the American Revolution, a successful assertion of independence from British imperial rule that was widely admired in British radical circles.[36] Excluded from any voice in Parliament and actively discouraged from signing anti-slavery petitions before 1830, abstention empowered British women to take action against slavery: it was acknowledged that their full participation was not only appropriate, but also essential to success. As a newspaper article of 1791 recognised, 'City meetings might make resolutions upon resolutions in such a business to little purpose indeed, unless we first gain over our wives and daughters', or, as a leading female promoter of abstention put it in during the new wave of abstention campaigning in the 1820s, 'in the domestic department they are the chief controllers; they, for the most part, provide the articles of family consumption'.[37]

Women's ability to make a major contribution to the anti-slavery campaigns through the abstention movement was rooted not only in their practical roles as purchasers of sugar, but also in middle-class women's central role in rituals of polite sociability focused around the tea table, and upper-class women's role as arbiters of fashionable taste. The campaign against the slave trade saw the marketing to women of new forms of ethical consumer produce, cultivating a fashion for the consumption of items of personal ornament, tableware and imaginative literature with an anti-slavery message alongside abstention from slave-grown sugar.[38] The Wedgwoods, who in the 1760s had targeted the politicised consumer in goods for the supporters of John Wilkes, servicing a radical popular culture centred on the male venues of the club, tavern and coffeehouse, now turned their hand to the production of anti-slavery goods aimed at the female abolitionist consumer concerned to create a home-based anti-slavery culture. While aristocratic ladies had kept black children as fashionable markers of their status and wealth, anti-slavery women purchased brooches, hairpins, bracelets and pin boxes produced by Josiah Wedgwood which bore a cameo image of a kneeling and enchained male slave, making a fashion out of abolitionism and signalling their sympathetic identification with the slave.[39] Leading abolitionist Thomas Clarkson recalled in 1806 that 'the taste for wearing them became general; and thus fashion which usually confined itself to worthless things, was seen for one in the honourable office of promoting the cause of justice, humanity and freedom'.[40]

Thus adorned, the female body, as Charlotte Sussman has put it, became 'an exemplary model of compassion imagined as an ethics of consumption'.[41] Black bodies moved from commodity to victim; but, at the same time, the image of the victimised African slave was itself commodified as an item of commercial exchange between white male entrepreneurs and white women consumers. Marcus Wood has argued powerfully that such images present 'the black as a blank page for white guilt to inscribe', erasing the complex cultural contexts in Africa from which slaves were seized.[42] I would also suggest that, when worn round a white woman's neck, taking the place often occupied by a cross, the kneeling black man becomes a Christ-like figure: removed from his African cultural context through slavery, he was not a dangerous rebel man like the contemporary 'black Jacobins' of San Dominigue, but a potential convert to Christianity. His image becomes a signal not only of the Christian woman's anti-slavery credentials, but also of her support for the closely allied foreign mission movement, which, as will be discussed in the following chapters, was developing at this period.

Members of the West India interest had pioneered a fashion for domestic entertaining that revolved around the consumption of West India rum and sugared coffee and tea; to counteract this, anti-slavery campaigners attempted to spread a fashion among women for debating abolition at tea parties from which slave-grown sugar was banned. As Lynne Walker and Vron Ware have discussed, an 'abolitionist interior' was created as women brought the issue of slavery 'into the fabric of their homes and their everyday lives'.[43] The Society for the Abolition of the Slave Trade had William Cowper's poem *Pity the Poor Africans* reprinted on fine quality paper and distributed to thousands with the superscription, 'A Subject for Conversation at the Tea-Table'.[44] In 1792, a public appeal was made to the Duchess of York to set a fashion for sugar abstention that would be emulated first by the nobility and gentry and then by the middling orders; the success of such appeals is suggested by Gillray and Cruikshank's satires of the 'anti-saccharites' in cartoons showing Queen Charlotte discouraging sugar use at the royal family's tea table.[45] In what might be labelled 'negative emulation', some domestic servants are recorded as voluntarily following their master's example and leaving off the use of slave-grown sugar.[46] This new world of ethical consumption, where slavery had become a subject of concerned discussion at the tea table, is suggestively pictured in Kathryn Gleadle's analysis of the diaries of the late-eighteenth-century Shropshire gentlewomen Catherine Plymley, whose brother was an active abolitionist and friend of Thomas Clarkson.[47]

In the 1820s, the domestic consumer culture of anti-slavery developed in new directions. With the emergence of ladies anti-slavery associations, the drawing-room became the hub of female abolitionist organising: meetings were held, propaganda produced, read and discussed, and sewing circles were held, producing anti-slavery images on workbags that were filled with abolitionist propaganda; Walker and Ware have even identified a seat cover embroidered with the image of a kneeling enchained slave.[48] Anti-slavery ladies began holding tea parties using special abolitionist china, bearing images that contrasted strikingly with eighteenth-century coffee sets showing a black slave serving a white couple. Such china was an integral part of abolitionist propaganda, recirculating images and lines of verse from pamphlets and broadsheets. An engraving by Richard Westall produced to illustrate a publication of William Cowper's famous poem *The Negro's Complaint* was reproduced on a milk jug together with a quote from the poem and the motto 'Am I not a Man and a Brother'.[49] A series of engravings showings women's sufferings under slavery commissioned from Samuel Lines by the Birmingham-based Ladies' Society for the Relief of Negro Slaves was used to decorate a china dinner service.[50] A scene by George Cruikshank of a woman being flogged by a white overseer, which appeared on an election leaflet of 1832, was also used to decorate a cup.[51] Like the earlier cameos, the production of such items involved commercial entrepreneurs serving the female humanitarian consumer. Most directly linked to the abstention campaign were the sugar bowls in various styles that were produced bearing the motto 'East India sugar not made by slaves'.[52] Such sugar basins were advertised for sale to 'the Friends of Africa' by a B. Henderson, a businesswoman who owned a china warehouse in Peckham, near London, suggesting that female entrepreneurs were also beginning to exploit the business opportunities opened up by women's anti-slavery activism: her warehouse was located in an area with a strong local ladies anti-slavery association that promoted the slave-grown sugar boycott.[53]

Abstention thus lay at the heart of a feminised anti-slavery culture rooted in a politicised domestic sphere. The concern felt by supporters of slavery by the 1820s was that this culture meant that the tide of public opinion had turned against them, as suggested in this letter to *The Times* by a pro-slavery sympathizer:

> In this neighbourhood we have antislavery clubs, and antislavery needle parties, and antislavery tea parties and antislavery in so many shapes and ways that even if your enemies do not in the end destroy you by assault, those that side with you must give you up for the weariness of the subject and resentment of your supineness.[54]

'No more the blood-stain'd lux'ry choose': purifying the body of the nation

This feminised anti-slavery culture combined fashionable sentiment with a deeply serious moral outlook rooted in both Quakerism and Evangelicalism, and in the particular roles they assigned to women. Quakers' stress on the spiritual equality of women encompassed a female ministry and a stress on following the inner voice of God – the individual conscience – rather than the dictates of established worldly authority; Evangelical Anglicans positioned women as guardians of morality from a domestic base and idealised the domestic arena as a haven from a heartless world.[55]

In its earliest manifestation, abstention was more a matter of individual moral choice than a concerted attempt to use consumer power to bring down the slave system. It began in the 1760s and 1770s as an individual decision by British and American Quakers who were concerned to purify their sect from involvement in the sin of slavery. Quakers, as pacifists, condemned the seizure of slaves as an act of war: for John Woolman, an instigator of the abstention movement, just as refusal to purchase slaves would diminish the seizure of Africans by slave traders, so refusal of slave produce would diminish slave owning. Abstention probably also appealed to a sect who were accustomed to emphasising their distinctiveness by a self-denying lifestyle characterised by 'plain' dress and the renouncing of 'frivolous' entertainments and to following the dictates of their own conscience rather than custom or fashion.[56] In addition, as Quakers became very wealthy through involvement in industry, commerce and banking, and some abandoned 'plain' for 'gay' dress as they moved into new mixed social circles, involvement in philanthropy and slave-produce abstention could be ways of dealing with ambivalent feelings about worldly success.[57]

Abstention seems to have particularly appealed to Quaker women. The first anti-slavery appeal by a woman directed at her own sex, Quaker poet Mary Birkett's 1792 *A Poem on the African Slave Trade*, calls on women to moralise consumption. It castigated the thoughtless indulgence of the 'the giddy and the gay' who sip 'the sweets of charming tea' with little thought for '*The extreme of human mis'ry*' which it is the slave's lot to taste. The poem then urges women to take moral responsibility for the impact of their consumer habits:

> Yes, sisters, to us the task belongs,
> 'Tis we increase or mitigate their wrongs.
> If we the produce of their toils refuse:
> If we no more the blood-stain'd lux'ry choose;
> ....
> And in our brethrens sufferings hold no share,
> In no small part their long-borne pangs will cease,
> And we to souls unborn may whisper peace.[58]

Josephine Teakle's fascinating unpublished study of Mary Birkett's life and works throws new light on the appeal of slave sugar abstention to a young Quaker woman, who published this poem when she was only 17 years old. Birkett spent her childhood in Liverpool and then in Dublin. Both ports were heavily involved in the Atlantic trade, and both were centres for refining slave-grown sugar from Britain's Caribbean colonies, a world of commerce and manufacturing in which both her father and future husband were involved. For Birkett, abstaining from slave-grown sugar must have seemed a perfect performance of self-denying Quaker femininity in the face of the temptations of 'polite and commercial' society in a bustling imperial port.[59]

In Birkett's poem, however, there is already a move from a stress on individual to collective responsibility and morality, from purifying the self to achieving change in the wider world. It was written after the emergence of a non-sectarian but strongly Quaker-influenced abolition movement, in which Birkett's uncle George Harrison played a leading role alongside William Wilberforce and members of the Evangelical Anglican Clapham Sect. Promotion of abstention as a popular movement in the 1790s had resonances with other moral crusades that the Evangelical Clapham Sect were leading at the period against such 'vices' as the excessive consumption of alcohol. For members of the sect, slave-sugar abstention could be seen as forwarding their twin preoccupations: with the abolition of the slave trade, and with the reform of the manners and morals of the nation – a campaign in which home and family were seen as the primary arenas of struggle against sin.[60] Evangelical reformers emphasised women's role as self-sacrificing domestic guardians of morality and stressed that the roots of female power lay in the haven of the private sphere, away from the contamination of the outside world of commerce and of politics. The earliest anti-slavery appeal to British women, published in Manchester in 1787, drew on this sense of middle-class women's lack of contamination with the world of imperial commerce:

> If the Young Men, if the husbands of Manchester are so much involved in the Cares of the World, in the Bustle of Trade, that the still small voice of pity cannot be listened to, it is the duty, and I trust it will be the earnest Inclination of the Fair Sex, in this town at least, to remind them, that some Attention is due to the Humanity of our Commerce as well as to the Gains of it.[61]

However, with the launch of the 'anti-saccharite' campaign, attention was drawn to the fact that the domestic world was not in fact a haven from the heartless world of imperial commerce. The myth of rigidly separated spheres was exposed: only through women's refusal to purchase and consume slave-grown sugar could a true domestic haven be created, for, in bringing in slave-grown sugar from the outside world, women were letting the world of imperial commerce contaminate the home. Colonial sugar, apparently white and refined like the women who consumed it, was graphically presented by abolitionists as polluted by the blood of black slaves, its consumption contaminating the white bodies and staining the virtue of its British female consumers. William Fox, whose pamphlet launched the abstention campaign in 1791, described slave-grown sugar as a 'loathsome potion' that was 'steeped in the blood of our fellow creatures' and suggested that its consumption amounted to cannibalism, a horror normally associated with the indigenous peoples of the Caribbean and of Africa: 'in every pound of sugar used … we may be considered as consuming two ounces of human flesh'.[62] In James Gillray's 1791 cartoon *Barbarities in the West Indies* the European colonist is shown boiling the body of a slave in a huge vat of sugar juice, suggesting that white sugar itself was made up of the boiled-down bodies of black slaves. Deidre Coleman has suggested that 'such a radical internalization of black within white' within a cauldron might signal not only condemnation of the violence and inhumanity of slavery, but also fears of 'the melting pot of miscegenation' and in particular over sexual relations between white women and black men – foreign bodies contaminating the English home.[63] In the work of Romantic poet Robert Southey, the consumption of sugar is also linked with the incitement of slave revolt, itself evoking fears of black men's violation of the bodies of white women. Writing in 1797, Southey argued that, in the absence of progress in Parliament, the slave trade would be ended in one of two ways: either by people abstaining from slave-grown sugar or by bloody slave revolt.[64]

Women took up these associations of slavery with the contamination of their bodies. Mary Birkett in 1792 urged women to 'no more the blood-stain'd lux'ry choose'.[65] A newspaper appeal to women in Sheffield in 1791 urged them to replace West India produce with 'food unstain'd with unoffending blood'.[66] By the 1820s, the sense of slave-grown sugar as contaminating the white female body was so well established in anti-slavery literature that the writer of an 1829 poem entitled *An Answer to the Question 'Do you take Sugar in your Tea?'* did not feel it necessary to make it explicit. The question is answered with the refrain:

> No dear lady, none for me!
> Though squeamish some may think it,
> West Indian sugar spoils my tea:
> I can not, dare not drink it.[67]

Abstention transformed middle-class women from self-indulgent weepers over poems on the sufferings of the poor slave, the kind of women who were crit-icised by both Mary Wollstonecraft and Hannah More for their false sensibility and vapid idleness, into women willing to taking action to right wrongs. This harnessing of sensibility, sentiment and sympathy to positive political ends involved white women in the imperial metropole distancing and distinguish-ing them from white women in the colonies.[68] Indeed, as Deirdre Coleman has discussed, female abolitionists of the 1790s condemned white colonial women for manifesting sentimentality without humanity. In *A Vindication of the Rights of Men*, Wollstonecraft criticised women who, 'after the sight of a flagellation, compose their ruffled spirits and exercise their tender feelings by the perusal of the last imported novel'. Unitarian writer and educationalist Anna Laetitia Barbauld in her *Epistle to William Wilberforce* attacked 'pale Beauty' reclining on 'sofas of voluptuous ease' who 'With languid tones imperious mandates urge;/With arm recumbent wield the household scourge;/And with unruffled mien, and placid sounds,/Contriving torture, and inflicting wounds'.[69]

From 1825, the abstention campaign moved out into the wider community, promoted by the newly formed network of ladies' anti-slavery associations. A concerted attempt was made to involve working-class women by promoting abstention using the established philanthropic approach of district visiting.[70] Systematic house-to-house canvasses were conducted, with women visiting every house in Birmingham over a period of several years, for example. Women also produced special forms of propaganda to bring home their message. The Sheffield Female Anti-Slavery Society handed out cards bearing the information that 'by six families using East India sugar instead of West India sugar one slave less is required'.[71] The Ladies' Society in the Birmingham area sold or lent out thousands of copies of pamphlets variously targeted at the poor, at children and at the 'higher classes', reinforcing class distinctions while seeking to create a cross-class campaign.[72] One such tract addressed at children from better-off families was Amelia Opie's 1826 poem *The Black Man's Lament; or, How to Make Sugar*. Couched in educational format, with a series of colour illustrations of sugar production linked to a set of poems, this sought to paint a very different portrait of slave labour to the idyllic picture presented in pro-slavery productions, such as the poem by James Grainger discussed in the previous section:

> There is a beauteous plant, that grows
> In Western India's sultry clime,
> Which makes, alas! the black man's woes,
> And also makes the White man's crime.

The beauty of the plant and its sweet contents are seen to disguise the horrors of white men's violence and black men's sufferings which go into the making of sugar for consumption in the British home:

> For know, its tall gold stems contain
> A sweet rich juice, which white men prize;
> And that they may this sugar gain,
> The Negro toils, and bleeds and dies.[73]

From 1825, abstention also became linked to the particular role articulated by ladies' anti-slavery associations for women in the movement: to highlight and help relieve the sufferings of women under slavery. The female consumer of tea sweetened with slave-grown sugar, it was suggested, was directly implicated in the sufferings of enslaved women. A copy of a compilation of poems entitled *The Negro's Forget Me Not* (1829) had on the back cover a poem *The Sugar Cane* and on the front an engraving accompanying a poem entitled *The Negro Mother's Appeal*. In the 'Appeal' an enchained black woman whose child is being dragged away by a slave trader is shown appealing to a 'white lady, happy, proud, and free', who has a baby on her lap and is seated in a domestic setting next to a table carrying the slave-grown coffee and sugar she is unthinkingly consuming.[74] The image of the black woman echoes that of the emblem that ladies' anti-slavery associations used with their slogan 'Am I not a Woman and a Sister', and here this sisterly bond is seen as taking the form of a mother's love for her child, a love shared by women regardless of their race. The white woman's happy domestic life and familial role in Britain is shown as being unthinkingly pursued at the expense of the destruction of a black woman's happiness through slavery severing her ties with her child.

There are striking similarities between this image and a 1988 photograph of a South African home interior showing a white mother and daughter with a kneeling black maid, which forms the frontispiece to Rosemary Marangoly George's collection of essays, *Burning Down the Home*. George analyses the image thus: 'What Rosalind Solomon has caught so unflinchingly is the necessity of the servant's presence to complete the mistress's proud display of herself as an established, prosperous, fulfilled woman'.[75] Both anti-slavery and anti-apartheid images also expose the difficulty of producing visual images with an unequivocally radical political message: in each case, the representation of the black woman reproduces her subservient position and that of the white woman her domestic power.

'We, the people ... will emancipate him': Elizabeth Heyrick and the radical politics of abstention

Abstention, then, rooted anti-slavery in the domestic culture of the nation, bringing home the sufferings of the victimised slave to British households. However, it also had more politically radical connotations. It was promoted as a way of bringing about the downfall of the slave system as rapidly as possible, without awaiting the result of parliamentary deliberations. It was tied in to early calls for immediate emancipation, which involved female criticism of the policy of amelioration and gradual emancipation adopted by the male leadership of the national Anti-Slavery Society on its foundation in 1823. A Quaker woman from Leicester, Elizabeth Heyrick, led this radical challenge, gaining the backing of the national network of ladies' anti-slavery associations. Female abstention was thus associated with political radicalism as well as with philanthropic humanitarianism, linked to a collective grassroots challenge to the London-based male leadership of the movement as well as being a matter of individual moral choice.

From its earliest stages the anti-slavery movement had two interdependent strands: the campaign within Parliament and the popular extra-parliamentary campaign. It is interesting to compare abstention with the other main form of popular action against slavery, namely petitioning. A conventional way of distinguishing the two would be to describe abstention as a cosy private, domestic-base campaign dominated by women, and petitioning as an outspoken public and political campaign dominated by men. As we have seen, however, this characterisation fails to acknowledge the ways in which abstention broke down sharp distinctions between the private and the public, the domestic and the political, between satisfying the individual conscience and endeavouring to change the world. What it also fails to consider is the evidence that female abstention could be linked to a more radical anti-slavery politics than male petitioning.

Abstention encouraged universal participation. While the collectors of signatures to petitions were concerned to maintain credibility by collecting the names only of the right kind of people – not children, not the illiterate, and, until 1830, not women – abstention campaigners recognised that their effectiveness depended on gaining the widest possible public participation and, thus, actively solicited the support of children, of the poor and, most notably, of women. While individual or family acts of abstention did not threaten, and perhaps even bolstered, the divide between public and private spheres, the concerted pamphleteering, public debating and canvassing in favour of abstention in the 1790s and 1820s threatened to break down this divide by bringing the politics of imperial commerce into the domestic arena. As domestic consumption was politicised, so private abstention became an expression of public anti-slavery opinion. In so doing, the movement politicised women, subverting the Evangelical programme of completely separating women in the home from the masculine worlds of commerce and politics.

Abstention, as a form of direct action, also carried connotations of political radicalism and popular protest. Members of the ladies' anti-slavery association at Worcester, it was reported, 'withhold their countenance from grocers who sell, and from confectioners who use, West India sugar', an act echoing labouring women's traditional use of exclusive dealing to enforce the 'moral economy' and keep down the price of bread.[76] Individual decisions made by women concerning domestic consumption were brought into the public arena as local and national registers of abstainers were established.[77] Abstention also subverted the class- and gender-based divide between the leaders and the led within the anti-slavery movement. As an expression of public opinion, petitioning involved appeals by those without formal political power to those men with political power; in contrast, abstention involved direct action by the masses. Slavery, Quaker pamphleteer Elizabeth Heyrick asserted, 'is not an abstract question, to be settled between the government and the Planters – it is a question in which we are *all* implicated' through the purchase of slave produce. There was no neutral ground: 'the whole nation must now divide itself into the *active supporters*, and the active *opposers of slavery*'.[78] The moral language of abstention was utilised to appeal to those removed from the allegedly immoral or amoral world of parliamentary politics: as members of the Sheffield Female Anti-Slavery Society stated, slavery was 'not exclusively a political, but pre-eminently a moral question; one, therefore, on which the humble-minded reader of the Bible, which enriches his cottage shelf, is immeasurably a better politician than the statesman versed in the intrigues of Cabinets ....'[79] Here, the idea of a corrupt and unrepresentative Parliament echoed that of political radicals of the period.

Abstention was thus linked to an unwillingness to rely on governmental action. In both 1791 and 1824–5, abstention campaigns were initiated in response to disillusionment with the effectiveness of attempting to influence Parliament by petitioning – the argument was that deeds must replace words. In response to defeat of an abolition bill in the Commons in 1791, William Fox's *An Address to the People of Great Britain*, widely distributed around Britain thanks to its energetic promotion by the leading radical abolitionist Thomas Clarkson, argued that if the government would not take action then people must bring about the end of the slave trade themselves by putting economic pressure on planters and slave traders to change over to a system of free labour and to trade in free-grown produce.[80] In the 1820s, Heyrick's pamphlet *Immediate, not Gradual Abolition* adopted a similar line, arguing that endless petitioning of Parliament for gradual abolition would achieve nothing: 'Too much time has been lost in declamation and argument – in petitions and remonstrances against *British* slavery. The cause of emancipation calls for something more decisive, more efficient than words'. It was by mass abstention from slave-grown produce that slavery would be '*most safely and speedily abolished*'. Government could be bypassed and, through abstention, 'We, the people, the common people of England – we ourselves will emancipate him'.[81]

Abstention campaigns were thus about the people taking things into their own hands rather than relying on the authorities. Their radical nature had been clearly recognised in the 1790s, when the radical Thomas Clarkson's enthusiasm for the abstention campaign was not shared by the anti-Jacobin William Wilberforce, and the campaign only received official endorsement from the committee of the Society for the Abolition of the Slave Trade for a brief period in the summer of 1793. The committee then decided to suspend both petitioning and abstention campaigns, concerned that both would be viewed as subversive activities in the context of the government's clampdowns on public meetings and extra-parliamentary protest in the context of the outbreak of war with revolutionary France. In this context too, radical abolitionists' support for the slave rebellion in France's richest sugar colony of San Domingue on the grounds of the 'rights of man' became seen as unpatriotic in the face of the British government's decisions to conquer the colony from the French and restore slavery. When the anti-slavery movement was relaunched in 1823, the year of a massive slave revolt in Britain's Caribbean sugar colony of Demerera, a conflict between conservative and radical approaches again became apparent.[82] In *Immediate not Gradual Abolition* (1824), Elizabeth Heyrick followed Thomas Clarkson's earlier analysis in justifying slave insurrection as 'self-defence from the most degrading, intolerable oppression', arguing that it was the result not of black men's innate propensity for violence, but of their frustration at their inability to protect their families from attack by white men. To prevent massacres of the white population in the colonies and enable a peaceful transition to freedom, she argued, abolitionists should shift from their current approach of promoting the amelioration and gradual abolition of colonial slavery to campaigning for immediate emancipation.[83]

If the abstention campaign of the 1790s was an expression of despair at the inaction of the government, then under Heyrick's inspiring lead the abstention campaign of the 1820s became associated with a questioning of the authority of the male leadership of the anti-slavery movement itself. When, in 1824, Heyrick called on ordinary people to abstain from slave-grown sugar, she linked her call to an attack on the anti-slavery leadership for being too compromising, and too concerned not to offend the West Indian interest in Parliament. Convinced that 'truth and justice are stubborn and inflexible; – they yield neither to numbers or authority', she attacked the male abolitionist leadership as 'worldly politicians' who had 'converted the great business of emancipation into an object of political calculation'.[84] This challenge to the leadership was echoed by members of the Sheffield Female Anti-Slavery Society, who distributed Heyrick's pamphlet, promoted a systematic boycott of slave sugar and criticised MPs who proposed anything short of immediate emancipation for their 'vain attempts to make humanity and interest meet'.[85] The criticisms could take an explicitly gendered form, with female moral authority being asserted over male worldly authority. Thus, the Sheffield society argued: 'we ought to obey God rather than man. Confidence here is not at variance with humility. On principles like these, the simple need not fear to confront the sage; not a *female* society to take their stand against the united wisdom of this world'.[86]

Promotion of abstention was thus tied to radical shifts in anti-slavery policy. In the 1790s, whereas petitioning focused on ending the slave trade, abstention attacked the system of plantation slavery itself, thus paving the way for the emancipation campaign of the 1820s. In the 1820s, whereas petitioning was for the amelioration of slavery and its gradual emancipation, abstention was linked to calls for rapid transition to waged labour, paving the way for petitions calling for immediate emancipation in the 1830s. Elizabeth Heyrick's pamphlet *Immediate, not Gradual Abolition* is crucial in this regard. It was the first clear call by a white Briton for the immediate emancipation of slaves, and it urged people to boycott slave produce as a means of achieving this objective. Heyrick became a member of the national network of ladies' anti-slavery associations that systematically promoted the boycott movement and which gained the reputation of favouring immediate rather than gradual abolition. While Kenneth Corfield has concluded that she and other women 'had little influence in persuading men to shift their ground and press for immediate emancipation', my own research suggests that this is to underestimate the vital place that ladies' anti-slavery associations were acknowledged to occupy within the anti-slavery movement.[87] By 1828, the Anti-Slavery Society, lamenting the lack of progress achieved by its own approach of male petitioning for amelioration and gradual abolition, was appealing to ladies' anti-slavery associations to promote abstention as one of the main remaining channels for achieving progress towards emancipation.[88] It was a call reiterated in Heyrick's 'Apology for ladies' anti-slavery associations', though in her text this call was again tied to an attack on gradualism as a 'delusive phantom'.[89] The year 1828, then, marked the beginnings of a rethinking of national anti-slavery policy that by 1830–1 resulted in petitions for immediate emancipation from both men and women.[90] Indeed, it is possible that the lack of female petitions prior to 1830 may partly be attributed to the lack of enthusiasm among women activists for the bills for mitigation and gradual abolition presented by parliamentary supporters of abolition prior to that date.

Heyrick advocated immediate emancipation and the sugar boycott in a radical language of rights rather than as an expression of philanthropic concern for the victimised other. While she did not directly address the questions of women's rights in the set of radical pamphlets she wrote on a wide range of issues, she was clearly strongly influenced by 1790s radicalism and was not afraid to link the question of rights at home with that of rights in Britain's overseas colonies. In her *Exposition of One of the Principal Causes of the National Distress* (1817), written at a time of renewed working-class radical activism during the economic crisis that followed the end of the wars with France, she exclaimed (incidentally implying approval of women's rights) that: 'The Rights of Man – the Rights of Woman – the Rights of Brutes – have been boldly advanced; but the *Rights of the Poor* still remain unadvocated'. In this pamphlet she made use of analogies with slavery throughout, complaining that despite 'our invectives against colonial slavery' the labouring classes in Britain had been reduced to a 'state of wretchedness and despair' by 'the *spirit* of the *slave-trade*' – 'the lust of wealth'. Labourers were only nominally free, and the condition of both slave and labourer is '*directly contrary to the Divine will*'. Breaking with the established philanthropic framework within which middle-class women engaged with the poor at this period, she argued that charity was not enough: we should 'investigate the claims of the poor' to more than 'humanity and benevolence', then 'we may discover, that, so far from having obeyed the requisitions of *charity*, we have not yet discharged the demands of *justice*'. Anticipating the immediatist rhetoric of her later anti-slavery pamphlet, she asserted that present distress would most speedily, radically and easily be relived by an immediate wage rise to, say, a guinea a week: 'in the present emergency, no timid, reluctant half-measures, must be resorted to: – no gradual emancipation'.[91] Heyrick made similar points in a pamphlet published in 1819, the year of the Peterloo massacre, addressed to the leading Parliamentary advocate of anti-slavery, Thomas Fowell Buxton. In this she criticised those who said one should not incite the poor but preach submission to them as making a similar argument to West India planters and slave-holders who wish to perpetuate slavery, and urged the British Parliament to take up the cause of justice for the poor 'that England may be as conspicuous and exemplary in breaking the galling yoke of oppression from off the necks of her own sons, as from those of Africa'.[92]

In consistently pointing to the similarities between slave and waged labour, Heyrick challenged hegemonic middle-class anti-slavery ideology. David Brion Davis has convincingly argued that 'the growing power of antislavery in early industrial Britain was at least partly a function of the fit between antislavery ideology and the interests of an emergent capitalist class', suggesting that attacks on slave labour helped legitimise industrialists' consolidation of a system based on a low waged and highly disciplined workforce by presenting wages as a symbol of freedom.[93] Heyrick, in contrast, attacked political economy in the name of Christian economy and presented waged labour as little better than slavery for British workers who suffered from starvation wages.

Given her family background, Heyrick's identification with the sufferings of the labouring poor is, at first sight, surprising. Her father, John Coltman, was a worsted manufacturer in Leicester, and in the riots of 1785, when Elizabeth was a young woman, the family home was plundered by a machine-breaking mob. Despite this family economic interest and related traumatic personal experience, in 1825 she wrote a pamphlet urging the pressure of public opinion on the injust and inhumane hosiers of Leicester who had lowered wages, driving industrious framework-knitters to strike. Widowed at a young age, Heyrick seems to have channelled her rebellious spirit into religious conversion to Quakerism, which gave her space to find a voice and to follow the dictates of conscience and affirmation to her desire to challenge convention and the more conservative political opinions of male relatives.[94] Certainly Heyrick's advocacy of British labourers' rights at the same time as her advocacy of the rights of slaves, and her willingness to draw analogies between the sufferings of the two, represent a radical positioning for a middle-class woman, one that provided a potential political bridge with working-class activists hostile to slavery but suspicious of what they saw as the hypocrisy of middle-class abolitionists who wished to extend rights to slaves but not to workers. That she was able to carry leading ladies' anti-slavery associations along with her in her challenge to gradualism is testament to the power of her voice, but also suggestive of a broader radicalism lurking just below the surface of the respectable humanitarianism of organised female anti-slavery. The crossover from charitable philanthropy to political radicalism, and from the exertion of female influence to the assertion of female power, was always a possibility, particularly when middle-class women began to identify with the lack of rights of the slave or the labourer. Within British abolitionism, Elizabeth Pease Nichol and Anne Knight, supporters of women's rights, Chartism and anti-slavery, provide later examples of such radical middle-class womanhood.[95]

'Thy vessels crown'd with olive branches send': promoting 'legitimate' imperial commerce

Such a radical abolitionist stance, however, did not entail an anti-imperial position: the British anti-slavery movement promoted the reform of Empire rather than its dissolution. Heyrick did not challenge this, and some of her female anti-slavery co-workers positively endorsed this project, promoting 'free' grown sugar and praising 'legitimate' imperial commerce.

In 1791–2, British sugar refiners and the East India Company had begun to challenge the West Indian sugar monopoly, 'free sugar' was first advertised in the English provincial press and the Wedgwood family switched to East India sugar.[96] However, very little Bengali sugar was being produced at this period and there was uncertainty about the possibility of producing quantities of cheap sugar without resort to slave labour.[97] Consequently, pamphleteers advocated abstention rather than substitution. In contrast, by the 1820s, when East India sugar production was better developed, abolitionists such as James Cropper felt able to assert that West India sugar was only cheaper because of protective duties, echoing Adam Smith's view that the slave system was archaic and economically inefficient and that the removal of commercial restrictions could only benefit humanity.[98] Women abolitionists were influenced by such propaganda: in a pamphlet of 1829, Charlotte Townsend, daughter of Lucy Townsend, the founder of the Birmingham Ladies Negroes Friend Society, pointed out that 'when my mother was a little girl, she went without any sugar at all, rather than partake of the sin of slavery' but that now one could use East India sugar instead, since this was cultivated by free men who are paid for their work.[99]

Mention of James Cropper leads to the question of the relationship between the anti-slavery abstention campaign and the 'East India interest'.[100] James Cropper himself was a leading East India sugar merchant in Liverpool and a member of the Liverpool East India Association, as well as a founder of the Liverpool Society for the Amelioration and Gradual Abolition of Slavery and a leading member of the London committee of the national Anti-Slavery Society. He promoted the equalisation of sugar duties – a campaign that was taken up by local men's auxiliary societies – and the substitution of East Indian 'free labour' sugar for West Indian sugar – a campaign on which local ladies' associations focused and in which the female members of his own family were involved.[101]

There has been a major debate among historians concerning the relationship between capitalism and abolitionism, between economic change and humanitarianism.[102] Eric Williams, concerned to stress the predominance of economic interest over disinterested humanitarian motives for British abolition, presents Cropper as a key example of a leading anti-slavery activist motivated primarily by economic self-interest.[103] David Brion Davis, in contrast, presents Cropper as a man in whose mind 'the intensity of Quaker Quietism had fused with the economic optimism of Adam Smith' and whose anti-slavery position was based on a conviction of the 'unity of moral and material progress'.[104] This certainly seems to be the position adopted by his fellow Quaker, the Liverpool-born Mary Birkett. Birkett's poem, which, as discussed earlier in this chapter, was directed primarily at women, suggests that abolishing the slave trade does not entail abandoning the use of Africa's wealth. She discusses the Janus-faced nature of commerce, and in particular British imperial commerce, as a bringer of luxury and of vice, of wealth and of woe. She argues that, after abolition, Britain should 'let the mild rays of commerce there expand' by sending 'thy vessels crown'd with olive branches', so that Britain could benefit from legitimate commerce, by 'tides of wealth by peace and justice got'.[105] Birkett then went further to advocate the colonisation of Africa in order to spread Christianity and civilisation: having restored the rights of man to Africans, Britain should save their souls:

> Plant there our colonies, and to their soul,
> Declare the God who form'd this boundless whole;
> Improve their manners – teach them how to live,
> To them the useful lore of science give.[106]

There is a similar message in Hannah More's *The Slave Trade*. The poem, as Kate Davies has pointed out, presents abolition as transforming British commerce into 'a moralised and ameliorative philanthropy' spreading Christianity and civilization throughout the globe.[107] Britain will then emerge as a supremely virtuous nation, or, as Birkett put it:

> When Albion shall supreme delight bestow
> And with supreme delight, feel her own bosom glow;
> Thus mutual good, conferring and conferr'd,
> Will prove that 'virtue is it own reward'.[108]

Here, Albion, the Roman name for Britain, derived from the Latin for 'white', is personified as a woman, who can stand for the virtuous white woman consumer to whom the poem is addressed: her abstention from slave-grown sugar, it is implied, will help bring about this moralisation of Empire.

More broadly, in female abolitionist literature and visual imagery, representations of Britain as a virtuous woman granting freedom to the slave contrasted with the image of the violent woman-beating colonial planter, who, as one female anti-slavery poet put it, did not deserve to bear a man's or a Christian's name.[109] Such images anticipate the process of the distancing of Britain (and British women) from the nation's 200-year slave-holding history and the construction of its new national image as saintly abolisher of slavery, setting a moral example to the rest of the world. In the words of the Victorian historian W.E.H. Lecky, 'the unwearied, unostentatious, and inglorious crusade of England against slavery' was 'among the three or four perfectly virtuous acts recorded in the history of nations'.[110] Sussman points to the way in which, in abolition pamphlets, 'the compassion of British women symbolizes a specific national identity, a quality which distinguishes England from the rest of the world'.[111] William Allen's abstentionist pamphlet, for example, asked: 'Is it possible ... that the LADIES OF ENGLAND, possessing a sense of *Virtue*, of *Honour*, and of *Sympathy* beyond those of any other nation, is it possible for THEM to encourage the SLAVE TRADE?!'.[112] The abolition of slavery, promoted through domestic abstention as well as parliamentary petitioning, like the abolition of *sati* discussed in Chapter 3, laid the ground for the promotion of a new moral imperialism in which women were seen as having a crucial role to play. It was a role that women's suffrage campaigners of Lecky's era were to take on with gusto as a way of promoting a more directly political role for women in the imperial nation.[113]

Evaluating women's role in the slave-sugar boycott

In both the 1790s and the 1820s the abstention campaign in which women played such a leading role gained widespread public support. Thomas Clarkson, recalling his extensive anti-slavery tour of England and Wales in 1791–2, estimated that 300,000 people had abandoned the use of slave-produced sugar.[114] While no comparable estimates of total numbers of abstainers survive from the 1820s, the painstaking canvassing by ladies' associations almost certainly produced an even higher figure: Elizabeth Heyrick claimed that nine out of ten families visited agreed to abstain.[115]

Abstention campaigners did not achieve direct success: at neither period did they succeed in destroying the market of slave-grown sugar. This does not, however, mean that abstention campaigns lacked significance. In transforming Britain from a nation of households that accepted slavery as a necessary adjunct to sugar consumption and fashionable sociability into a nation of anti-slavery households, local interventions by women in the sphere of 'private' domestic culture were as crucial as national interventions in the sphere of 'public' political culture. In playing a leading role in abstention campaigns, women thus played a vital role in creating a national anti-slavery culture in Britain, setting up a distinction in people's minds between the West India interest and the national interest, widening the anti-slavery public to include women, children and the poor, and creating a chain linking individual, family, community and national action to imperial reform.

In the 1820s, women also linked abstention to a challenge to the authority of the male leadership of the anti-slavery movement, calling on them to switch policy from gradual to immediate emancipation, and urging ordinary people to take direct action to bring about the end of slavery. In the process, the slave-sugar consumer boycott moved from moralising consumption to politicising the domestic sphere, from unthreatening example of feminine moral influence from a domestic base, compatible with evangelical 'separate spheres' ideology, to a radical dissenting female challenge to the male establishment. Slave-grown sugar, the abolitionist women were determined, was no longer to 'sweeten the cups of man', and the domestic woman would not be sweetly obedient to male authority. The roles of this domestic woman – as purchaser of household groceries, as organiser of family life and sociability and as guardian of morality – were thus politicised by abstention campaigners in order to purify the nation of the stain of slavery. The compassionate white Englishwoman, they asserted, had the power to make the nation virtuous through moralising the Empire and thus transforming it into a legitimate source of prosperity and civilisation. The link between anti-slavery and the development of imperial feminism, then, lay not only in the tentative move by some women from championing black slaves' rights to advocating white women's rights or in the ways in which white women positioned themselves as the representatives of enslaved black women, but also in British women collectively harnessing their feminine domestic power to imperial political ends.

3 White women saving brown women?

British women and the campaign against *sati*

Imperial concerns featured prominently in the evangelical reform agenda between the 1790s and the 1830s. If the eradication of British involvement in the slave trade and colonial slavery was among their key campaigning priorities, then a second preoccupation, viewed as of equal or even greater importance, was to bring Christianity to the peoples of Britain's expanding empire and, in particular, to transform the society and culture of the immense population of the nation's growing empire in the Indian subcontinent. Women's active involvement in anti-slavery campaigns is now well established; much less well known is their participation in one of the first evangelical reform initiatives directed at colonial India: the campaign to abolish *sati*, or widow burning, a practice generally referred to as *suttee* in British texts of the period. While female anti-slavery activists highlighted the oppression of black women by white men under the system of colonial slavery, the female anti-*sati* campaigners who form the focus of this chapter highlighted 'Hindu' women's oppression by 'Hindu' men. Both groups of women stressed the importance of combining legislative intervention with direct social action; however, while the former stressed the need to reform the coloniser, the latter stressed the need to reform the colonised.

Between 13 February 1829 and 29 March 1830 a total of 15 separate groups of women from around England sent petitions to Parliament calling on it to abolish *sati*, or rather what they described as 'the practice in India of burning widows on the funeral piles of their husbands'.[1] Women's participation in the anti-*sati* petitioning campaign directly preceded their much more extensive petitioning for the abolition of colonial slavery between 1830 and 1833. This step into direct engagement with parliamentary politics was taken not by women who identified as political radicals or supporters of the 'rights of women', but rather by women associated with the evangelical missionary movement. The petitions formed part of a broader campaign against *sati* that was linked to garnering female support for the foreign missionary enterprise and also led to English women being drawn into organising the dispatch of the first single women to India to provide Christian education for Indian girls and women.

The abolition of *sati* is highly significant in the history of British imperialism because it became used as a major moral justification for imperial rule over India through positioning British men not as violent conquerors and coercive rulers, but rather as rescuers and protectors of non-Western women. As Gayatri Spivak has so pithily put it, in this colonial discourse, 'White men are saving brown women from brown men'.[2] In assigning to British men the credit for the abolition of widow burning, British evangelical missionary and official government discourses presented Indian women as passive victims and Indian men as their violent abusers. They also obscured the part played by British women in the campaign against *sati*. This chapter examines the extent to which white women, too, were able to position themselves as the saviours of brown women and, thus, actively contribute to the moral justification of Empire and simultaneously to justifying their active engagement in missionary work overseas and in the petitioning of Parliament.

Lata Mani's detailed study of the debates about *sati* that took place within colonial India has effectively challenged the way in which 'the abolition of *sati* has been canonized both by colonialist and nationalist texts as a founding moment in the history of women's emancipation in modern India'.[3] Mani argues very convincingly that the colonial debate on *sati* focused on the proper interpretation of Hindu scriptures rather than on the sufferings of women or questions of women's rights: 'women are neither subjects nor objects, but rather the grounds of the discourse on sati'. The debate on *sati* that took place within colonial India was a contest between colonial and indigenous patriarchies rather than between Eastern patriarchy and Western feminism.[4] However, as she herself acknowledges, evangelical arguments against *sati* circulating within Britain were cast not in relation to brahmanic scriptures – the approach adopted within colonial India – but in terms of the degradation of contemporary indigenous society, the oppression of women, and the horror of burning a woman alive.[5] British representation of the abolition of *sati* as the emancipation of women thus first took place in the imperial metropole rather than in the colony, and, in exploring British women's involvement in this process, this chapter throws new light on the roots of imperial feminism in Britain.

This chapter begins by examining the complex and variable ways in which *sati* featured in British women's travel writing and imaginative literature between the 1770s and the 1810s, prior to the launch of a public campaign in Britain against widow burning. It moves on to highlight the ways in which stress on the horror of *sati* was deployed to drum up female support for the foreign mission movement from 1813, and to encourage British women to sponsor the sending of the first single woman into the foreign mission field in 1820. The significance of female petitioning of Parliament against *sati* in 1829–30 is then explored within the broader contexts of the history of public petitioning, women's entry into petitioning on imperial issues, and British women's involvement in transatlantic networks of female reform. Finally, the chapter highlights how, despite the dominant celebration of British men as abolishers of *sati*, British women began to position themselves as the saviours, educators and imperial representatives of Indian women and, thus, in varied ways, laid the grounds for the later emergence of imperial feminism.

'A barbarous exertion of virtue?' British women's early representations of *sati*

Sati attracted the attention of European observers from the earliest stages of the establishment of trading enterprises in India in the seventeenth century. Indeed, Kate Teltscher has described the *sati* as 'a troubling and ambiguous figure who becomes a central topos in the European literature of India'. She sees 'the highly ambivalent masculine responses to the act' as linked to 'the patriarchal appeal of sati as the ultimate demonstration of wifely submission and chastity'.[6] Tensions between admiration and revulsion led to representations of the *sati* ranging from tragic heroine to coerced victim. Many accounts positioned the European male viewer not only as witness, but also as potential heroic and chivalrous rescuer of the widow. The trope of *sati* also provided a useful way for eighteenth-century Enlightenment writers to engage in coded critiques of the Roman Catholic Church: the Brahmin (Hindu priest) who presides over the *sati* ceremony stands in these texts for the religious fanaticism, authoritarianism and corruption of the Catholic clergy.[7]

Accounts of *sati* by British women begin to appear in the late eighteenth century as more British women began to accompany husbands employed in administrative, legal and military positions by the East India Company, at the period when the company was using military force to shift from a commercial enterprise into the territorial ruler of large swathes of the subcontinent on behalf of the British government. From this date onwards, women became important shapers of views of India among the British reading public. Excluded from power within the emerging structures of imperial rule, British women do not imagine themselves as the potential rescuers of Indian women in the memoirs and imaginative literature on India that they produced at this period. Rather, writing prior to the consolidation of a hegemonic colonial discourse on *sati* in the 1820s, they articulate a range of perspectives on the practice, and compare their own social position in a variety of different ways with that of Indian women.[8]

Probably the first recorded impressions of an Englishwoman concerning the lives of women in India are contained in Jemima Kindersley's *Letters from the Island of Teneriffe, Brazil, The Cape of Good Hope, and the East Indies*, published in 1777 and drawing on her stay there as wife of a lieutenant colonel in the Bengal Artillery between 1765 and 1769. Kindersley's description of *sati* as 'a barbarous exertion of virtue' suggests that it was a voluntary act by a woman acting within inferior codes of femininity to those of civilised Europeans. This representation, however, is rather contradicted in her record of the two reasons for the practice that had been proposed to her (reasons that had already been advanced in earlier male-authored European texts). First, that it had been common for women to poison their husbands, and the threat of *sati* was necessary to prevent this; second, that Brahmins encouraged the practice so that they could get their hands on the dead women's jewels. In her text, then, Hindus are not only barbarous, but their women murderous and their religious leaders calculating thieves. Her hope 'that the English will in future prevent those Nabobs we are in alliance with, from giving any such permission' constitutes an early suggestion that Britain should exert its growing imperial authority to eradicate the practice.[9]

Eliza Fay's *Original Letters from India* (1817), a published version of letters written in the 1780s and 1790s, offers a rather different take on *sati*, drawing out similarities between the positions of Indian women and of European women. Her letter of 28 August 1781 begins with the dramatic news that she has been abandoned by her lawyer husband in Calcutta, and obtained an official separation from him. She then proceeds, for the first time in her correspondence, to describe aspects of 'East Indian customs and ceremonies', beginning with *sati*. Coming directly after her story of her own marital woes, this encourages the reader to link her lot as abandoned wife to that of Hindu widow. Rather than stressing that *sati* is an exceptional practice unique to India, as Kindersley does, Fay links it to the widespread oppression of women by men throughout the world: husbands 'have not failed in most countries to invent a sufficient number of rules to render the weaker sex totally subservient to their authority'. She goes on to mock Englishmen who represent *sati* as evidence of Hindu women's superior character 'since I am well aware that so much are we the slaves of habit *every where*' that, were it necessary for a woman's reputation to burn herself in England, many wives who had little regard for their husbands 'would yet mount the funeral pile with all imaginable decency and die with heroic fortitude'. This is not to say, however, that she views Indian and English women to be cultural equals: she goes on to argue that greater sacrifices are made by a woman who tries to be a devoted wife to a difficult husband than by 'the slave of begotry [*sic*] and superstition' who commits *sati*. Here, wifely self-sacrifice in the form of dogged persistence by the Englishwoman is presented as superior to the dramatic act of unthinking adherence to custom by the Indian woman, and is linked to Fay's overall view that Indian culture is inferior to British.[10]

Fictional accounts, too, offered a range of female perspectives on *sati* to a British audience at this period. Phebe Gibbes' *Hartly House, Calcutta* (1789) is a novel in the form of a letter-journal by 'Sophia Goldsborne', an Englishwoman moving in official circles in Calcutta, written to her friend Arabella in England. Sophia forms a close attachment to a Brahmin and becomes enamoured of Hindu religion. In keeping with her positive views of Indian culture, she describes the practice of *sati* as generally voluntary, as motivated by wifely affection, and as heroic if misguided: 'And of this number are those wives, who, with a degree of heroism, that, if properly directed, would do honour to the female world, make an affectionate and voluntary sacrifice of themselves upon the funeral pile of their departed husbands'. Sophia also stresses the posthumous religious reward that women gained from this sacrifice.[11]

While some English men imagined themselves in the role of romantic heroes saving Indian women from *sati*, in Gibbes' novel an English woman explores the appeal of becoming a romantic heroine by adopting the position of the *sati*. However, rather than commit *sati* herself on the death of her beloved Brahmin, Sophia instead opts for a very English cultural response: she cut off a lock of his hair as a private keepsake, and pledges to build a public monument in his memory on her return to England. After flirting with marriage to a wealthy nabob (the term used of corrupt East India company officials who returned to Britain having grown immensely wealthy off the spoils of India), she opts instead for the familiarity of a match with a rather impoverished Englishman selected by her father. Such conventional feminine self-sacrifice within the safe confines of English domesticity is presented as preferable to the dramatic sacrifice of the Hindu widow or the easternised life of luxury of the nabob's wife. The sensible English woman thus comes home, abandoning her dangerous youthful flirtation with the role of the romantic heroine and her cross-cultural love affair. [12]

Gibbes' heroine's flirtation with a Brahmin, with Hinduism and with *sati* contrasts sharply with the Christian critique of Hindu fanaticism in a near-contemporary play by another female author, Mariana Starke's *The Widow of Malabar* (1791). Starke had spent her childhood in India, where her father was a leading official in the East India Company, acting as governor of Fort St George (Madras). However, her play did not draw directly on this experience, but was an adaptation of a popular drama by the French playwright Antoin Marin Lemierre, first performed in 1770. Lemierre's play is about an Indian widow who is saved from committing *sati* by a European military leader who has fallen in love with her. Starke, modifying the play to make it more suitable in style for an English audience, changed the nationality of the commander and his troops besieging an Indian city from French to English. These British Christians are credited with conquering in order 'To save and humanize Mankind'. Indian endorsement of this project is signalled by the widow's brother asking his sister's British rescuer to teach them both the precepts of Christianity. Starke's play was given an explicit role as imperial propaganda by the addition of a prologue by T.W. Fitzgerald, which contrasted the 'unhappy race' of India, confined by chains of body and mind, with the natives of Britain, 'home of freedom' and urged 'Europe's sons' to use reason to bring in laws to improve the situation in India.[13]

Other fictional accounts of *sati* by British women from this period are less convinced of the good treatment of women in Britain or of the merits of British imperial rule. Elizabeth Hamilton's *Translation of the Letters of a Hindoo Rajah* (1797), as discussed in Chapter 1, uses the voice of a Hindu priest to criticize British men for ignoring the sufferings of women at home while crying over widows who commit *sati* overseas. Sydney Owenson's (Lady Morgan's) historical novel *The Missionary* (1811), which deploys *sati* as a central plot device, is critical of religious fanaticism among both Hindus and Christians. A tragic love affair between Hindu priestess Luxima and the Spanish Catholic missionary Hilarion results in both being punished by intolerant religious authorities, and a parallel between the European Inquisition's burning of heretics and the Hindu Brahmin custom of burning widows is suggested when Luxima tries to commit *sati* on the pyre made by the Inquisitors to burn Hilarion. In addition, Morgan links the act of voluntary *sati* by a woman to male political rebellion against imperial rule: Luxima's leap onto the funeral pyre is the signal for an armed Indian rebellion against Spanish colonial authority. In her earlier and more famous novel, *The Wild Irish Girl* (1806), Morgan had attacked English prejudices against the Irish and religious strife between Irish Protestants and Catholics; in *The Missionary* she uses the trope of *sati* to suggest her broader opposition to religious bigotry and colonial arrogance.[14]

'Family, fireside evils': the foreign missionary movement and *sati*

The varied and ambivalent representations of *sati* circulating in Britain at the turn of the century contrasted with the unequivocally negative representation of widow burning in evangelical discourse that emerged with the beginnings of missionary activity in India by the new foreign missionary societies set up by British evangelical Protestants in the 1790s.[15] This 'foreign mission' movement was concerned with the conversion of the heathen abroad, particularly within the British Empire, but it had close links with the 'home mission' movement, which focused on the propagation of 'active' Christianity to the working class within Britain.[16] The missionary movement as a whole was informed by the evangelical conviction that the key to the eradication of vice and sin lay in combating both religious infidelity at home and 'heathen' idolatry in the Empire.[17]

One of the first battles that evangelicals fought was to get the Charter of the East India Company modified so that India would be opened up to missionary activity. The missionary campaign was spearheaded in Parliament by Evangelical Anglicans, members of the influential Clapham Sect who were as concerned to save souls through missionary work in the Empire as to emancipate the bodies of colonial slaves. In their propaganda, the position of women, and in particular the practice of *sati*, played a crucial role in arguments that Britain had a duty to bring Christianity and civilisation to its Indian subjects. A practice that was confined to a minority of Hindus came to stand for the depravity of the culture of the Indian subcontinent as a whole. Charles Grant, who had spent over 20 years in India and was elected to the Board of the East India Company in 1794, sought to combat positive views about ancient Hindu civilisation promoted by eighteenth-century British Orientalist scholars such as William Jones by claiming that 'the cruelty of the hindoo people appears in no way more evident than in the whole of the treatment to which *their women* are subjected in society' and stressing the suffering of women 'doomed to joyless confinement through life, and a violent premature death'.[18]

William Wilberforce, who led the successful parliamentary campaign to open India to missions in 1813, gave a powerful speech in the House of Commons in which he paid particular attention to the ill treatment of women, as evidenced by polygamy and *sati*, contrasting this with the equality to which women were entitled in all Christian countries.[19] In the published edition of his speech he added evidence of the inhumanity caused by 'accursed super-stition' in the form of an eye-witness account of a widow burning by Joshua Marshman, one of the pioneering trio of Baptist missionaries who had estab-lished themselves at the Danish enclave of Serampore near Calcutta in the 1790s. In his gruesome account, Marshman stressed the violation of normal familial and community relations involved: relatives and neighbours partici-pated 'with bursts of brutal laughter' and the children were 'stripped of both their parents in one day'. As Lata Mani has emphasised, in such accounts 'sati circulates as emblematic of indigenous degradation and the oppression of women'.[20]

Wilberforce described 'the evils of Hindostan' as 'family, fireside evils' that both 'pervade the whole mass of the population' and 'embitter the domestic cup of almost every family', language which echoed that of the 'anti-saccharite' campaigners discussed in Chapter 2. Wilberforce's rhetoric of 'fireside evils' would have had a powerful resonance for evangelicals. It set up a contrast between the fireside as the scene of the horrible spectacle of the Hindu widow burning on the funeral pyre, and evangelicals' idealised view of 'fireside enjoy-ments, homeborn happiness' as the hub of the Christian family.[21] Indeed, interlinking the domestic and the political in a way that was also characteris-tic of the campaign against the slave trade, Wilberforce would read out at the dinner table a list of women who had recently committed *sati*.[22] Evangelical women were expected to exert an important influence over moral and religious matters from a domestic base and, while women did not themselves sign the 900 petitions from across the nation in 1813 urging Parliament to open up India to Christian missionary, the leading female member of the Clapham Sect, Hannah More, worked energetically behind the scenes to encourage signatories.[23]

As well as achieving its immediate objective, the evangelical campaign gave wide exposure to missionary propaganda. As missionary activity in India expanded in the period after 1813, and missionary societies became increas-ingly reliant for fund-raising on networks of local ladies' associations, *sati* became the focus of appeals designed to draw women into the missionary movement.[24] In June 1813, for example, the *Missionary Register*, a widely read interdenominational journal promoting missionary work, based its appeal to British women on an item 'On the burning of women in India' that they had selected from the influential four-volume *Account of the Writings, Religion, and Manners of the Hindoos* by the Rev. William Ward, one of the early group of British Baptist missionaries at the Danish enclave of Seramapore.[25] The appeal, in contrasting the lot of women living in a Christian land with that of Indian women living in a land of superstition, set a pattern for future calls for British women's help:

> Let every Christian woman, who reads the following statement, pity the wretched thousands of her sex who are sacrificed every year in India to a cruel superstition, and thank God for her own light and privileges, and pray and labour earnestly for the salvation of these her miserable fellow subjects.

Soon, members of the new ladies' associations began themselves to contribute to discourse on *sati,* presenting missionary accounts in ways which they felt would most gain women's interest. An early example is the 1814 address of the Southwark Ladies' Association, one of the first female auxiliaries of the Church Missionary Society, which had as its patroness Mrs Henry Thornton, wife of one of the Clapham Sect leaders of the society. The women's address described *sati* as 'one picture of misery ... which appeals to their own sex'. Breaking with the usual pattern of a lurid account accompanied by general expressions of horror at the barbarous practice, the appeal instead set out to draw women into sympathy for, and empathy with, Indian women. Defining a characteristic of the female sex as being 'to commiserate with suffering humanity', it opened with an attempt to get women to identify as mothers with the sufferings of Indian widows, taking it for granted that Indian and British women shared the same loving feelings for their children:

> Let the anxiously fond mother, who trembles lest her tender offspring should, by a wise but inscrutable Providence, be deprived of either of the guardians of their early years, for a moment endeavour to realize the poignant anguish which must rend the breast of that other, who in the decease of her children's best support, hears the summons for her to forsake them, at a time, too, when they most need her fostering care; and to immolate herself on her husband's funeral pile! – The affecting representation excites our sympathy: let it stimulate our exertions.[26]

Female supporters of missions thus couched their opposition to *sati* in terms of an Indian widow's duty as a mother. This accorded with evangelical idealisation of motherhood; it also linked their support for missions in the Empire to their preoccupations in the domestic philanthropic arena with work among working-class women and children.[27] Here, we see 'women's mission to women' taking on an imperial dimension at a very early stage.[28] Here, too, we see the evangelical ideology of domesticity being deployed to promote a pro-imperial message. Readers were encouraged to evoke the following scene of family prayer along the ideal evangelical model:

> [E]nter the dwelling where your messenger has proclaimed the glad tidings of salvation. Behold a father, a mother, a family, forming an assembly of humble, grateful worshippers, who, while they adore the Fountain of their mercies, are fervently craving Heaven's richest blessings on the British Isles, the medium through which those blessings flowed.

The building block of this ambitious missionary project for the conversion and moral reform of India is represented not as the individual convert but rather as the Christianised family, in accordance with the centrality of the household to the Evangelical project.[29] The reward for women's exertions will be the gratitude of Indian families towards both Christian missionaries and the British nation. In such ways were evangelical British women encouraged to imagine that they had the power, under the auspices of the British Empire, to extend their own 'privileges' to other women, and so to mitigate what Wilberforce had labelled the 'family, fireside evils' of 'Hindostan', epitomised in the horror of *sati*.

To 'rescue from ignorance, and by that means from these funeral piles': *sati* and female education

From the outset, a central element of missionary activity in India was the spread of education. The setting up of mission schools was motivated by the belief that intellectual enlightenment would lead to rejection of Hindu idolatry, conversion to Christianity, and the moral reform of society.[30] Since missionaries identified many of the evils of Hindu society as involving the ill treatment of women, promoting Indian female education was potentially crucial to their success. Given the refusal of Indian parents to have their daughters educated by men, women teachers were essential if progress was to be made. However, the wives of the early missionaries often did not necessarily have the interest, qualifications or time to get involved in female education.[31] The obvious solution to such limited progress was to recruit qualified English women as teachers, but there was considerable resistance in Britain to the idea of employing single women. In 1815, for example, the Church Missionary Society, after discussing an offer by three women from Bristol to act as missionaries in India, concluded 'not to send unmarried women abroad, except sisters accompanying or joining their brothers'.[32] As a result of such reluctance, missionary provision for girls' education lagged well behind that of boys during the first two decades of the nineteenth century.[33]

Tensions between missionaries in the field and the leadership of missionary societies in London were not uncommon, and they are evident over the question of female education. In a tone rather similar to that adopted by Elizabeth Heyrick in her criticism of the male leadership of the anti-slavery movement in the 1820s (see Chapter 2), Baptist missionary William Ward argued that if the male leadership of missionary societies in Britain were reluctant to act, then women should take the initiative, impelled by their concern over the persistence of *sati*. This willingness to bypass central male authority in the imperial metropole was probably linked to Ward's radical political background: the son of a cabinet maker, he had been an editor of a radical newspaper in the 1790s, before experiencing religious conversion in 1796 and deciding to become a missionary. His recognition of women's potential contribution to the mission field was also doubtless inspired by the example of Hannah Marshman, wife of another member of the Serampore missionary trio, who worked efficiently with him in running the practical affairs of the mission and its out-stations and who was also a pioneer of girls' schooling.[34]

In a series of appeals made to English women between 1817 and 1821, Ward gave a picture of the female missionary role, placing it firmly within an imperial framework.[35] The treatment of women, he argued, was a marker of the terrible cruelty of superstitious and idolatrous 'Hindoo' society. *Sati* exemplified this ill treatment: 'the awful state of female society in this miserable country appears in nothing so much as in dooming the female, the widow, to be burned alive with the putrid carcass of her husband'.[36] British imperial rule had come about so that 'one of the smallest portions of the civilized world' would have the opportunity to 'accomplish some very important moral change' in the 'long-degraded state' of India.[37] British women were themselves privileged – 'raised by gracious Providence to the enjoyment of so many comforts' and British society was 'much improved by their virtues'.[38] It was thus their duty to help the 75 million less fortunate Indian women. As Stanley has concluded in his study of the relationship between missions and Empire, the 'Christian belief in divine providence led by logical steps to the concept of Britain's imperial role as a sacred trust to be used in the interests of the gospel'.[39] Here, we see articulated British women's duty to help fulfil this sacred trust.

To fulfil this duty, Ward advocated organised support for female education in India. British women should organise themselves into societies to 'rescue from ignorance, and by that means from these funeral piles'.[40] Just as anti-slavery campaigners argued that petitioning must be backed by abstention from slave produce, so Ward argued that government action against *sati* would fail without educational initiatives to back it up: 'government may do much to put an end to these immolations; but without the communication of knowledge, the fires can never to be wholly quenched'.[41] Appealing to both British and American women, he suggested that they could bring about the permanent end of *sati:* 'Let the females of both countries give the means of affording the education of their sex in India – and these infants must be saved; these fires must be put out; these graves must be closed for ever'.[42] Indian women's rescue from ignorance was thus presented as the means of rescuing them from *sati*.

This project, Ward argued, was capable of success. His optimism was grounded in evangelicals' belief in the potential of all, regardless of cultural background or 'race', to become 'civilised'. He had a greater faith than many missionaries in the potential of Indian men's and women's own agency to bring about positive social change, and a greater sense of their potential equality with Europeans. Described by Daniel Potts as 'a strong advocate of an active role for converts' who was keen to create an Indian-based church, he believed that Indian women had as much intellectual potential as Indian men: 'a few individuals have been found, by their knowledge of letters and of letters and of philosophy, putting the other sex to the blush'.[43] They also had the potential to emulate British women: with education they would be 'behind none of the sex in the charms which adorn the female character; in no mental elevation to which the highest rank of British females have attained';[44] they could become the Hannah Moores and Elizabeth Frys of India – the moral reformers of their own society.[45]

Ward's high evaluation of Indian women's potential was accompanied by expressions of confidence in the power of British women to bring about social improvements: 'There can hardly be a misery, connected with human existence, which the pity and the zeal of British females, under the blessing of Providence, is not able to remove'.[46] This was truly a women's cause, one only they could successfully carry out: 'Other triumphs of humanity may have been gained by our Howards, our Clarksons, our Wilberforces; but this emancipation of the females and widows of British India must be the work of the British fair';[47] this was 'the cause of woman – but especially of every christian widow – of every christian mother – of every christian female'.[48]

Ward's appeals to women were translated into a specific plan of action in 1820 by the British and Foreign School Society. The society, whose promotion of female education in metropole and colony will be discussed further in Chapter 4, issued an 'Appeal in behalf of Native Females', based on information furnished by Ward. This evoked the horror of *sati* to overcome doubts about the propriety of employing single women missionaries. Pointing to the lack of girls' schools in India, the appeal argued that Indian female education was vital to dissolving the superstition of Hindu women, which led to female infanticide and widow burning, and essential to improving society as a whole. It urged British women to contribute to a special fund set up to raise the money to send out of one of their countrywomen to train Indian women as teachers, given that 'The state of Indian Manners forbids females to be placed under the tuition of men'. The appeal continued:

> [I]s it not manifest that the Ladies in Britain are the natural guardians of these unhappy Widows and Orphans in British India? Is it possible that our fair countrywomen ... can ... continue unmoved by the cries issuing from these fires, and from the thousands of orphans which surround them .... This appeal cannot be made in vain: such a tale of woe was never before addressed to the hearts of British Mothers. Let every Lady of rank and influence in the United Empire do her duty, and these fires cannot burn another twenty years.[49]

British women were now being urged to take on an active, guiding, 'maternalistic' role as tutors and guardians of suffering Indian women under the aegis of Empire.

The *Missionary Register* urged support for this initiative, pointing out that the issue of *sati* was currently being raised in Parliament and suggesting that: 'If the Females of the United Empire will act on the appeal now made to them, the Voice of the Country will be so decisive in behalf of just and efficient measures on this subject, that the wishes of humane Senators will be fully accomplished'.[50] In other words, widespread female support for the educational initiatives would, in itself, act as strong public pressure on Parliament to take action against *sati*.

By May 1821, a total of £521.9s had been collected by the Ladies' Committee of the British and Foreign School Society to fund sending a woman teacher to Calcutta.[51] Mary Anne Cooke (1795–1861) was selected: she had worked as a governess in England, and 'to a sincere love of her sex and fervent piety towards her Saviour, united long acquaintance with the work of education'.[52] Cooke, who went on to marry Church Missionary Society missionary the Rev. Isaac Wilson but was soon widowed, was highly successful in setting up a network of schools in the Calcutta district that taught over 800 pupils over a 3-year period to 1825.[53] As will be discussed in Chapter 4, Wilson (*née* Cooke) was to act as an inspiring example to later missionary women.

In developing girls' education, Cooke did not simply rely for direction and funding from Britain; rather, she sought support from a range of sources. First, there were prominent local Hindu reformers in Bengal who were supportive of girls' education despite their suspicion of missionaries' religious agenda, and who lent private support to her work though they stopped short of publicly promoting it. Second, there were British women resident in Calcutta, who in 1824 set up the Ladies' Society for Native-Female Education and brought Cooke's schools under female management.[54] Third, there were women in Britain itself: voluntary financial support from Britain was particularly important given that it was against imperial policy to give official financial support to schools in India that had an explicitly Christian curriculum.[55] An 'Indian Female Education Fund' in aid of the Ladies' Society was opened in England in 1825, under the auspices of the Church Missionary Society, and it issued an 'Appeal to the Ladies of the United Kingdom'.[56] In 1829 the fund-raising passed into the hands of the Ladies' East India Female Education Society, set up in London by Amelia Heber, widow of the former Bishop of Calcutta. Drawing support from a number of aristocratic ladies and Evangelicals associated with the Clapham Sect, it was the first society in Britain to focus specifically on Indian female education.[57]

Conversations between Cooke and the Indian girls and their mothers in her schools were reported in the *Missionary Register* with the comment that 'This is the beginning of an intercourse between the Christian Females of India with the Heathen Women of that land, which will, we trust, rapidly increase, and be imitated in all quarters'.[58] From reports of Cooke's own words we can get some sense of the ways in which she conceptualised her mission to Indian women. She saw the aim of her educational work as being to raise Indian girls from ignorance so that they would be able to gain the respect and affection of their husbands, to 'properly discharge the important duties of their sex', and to exercise good influence from a familial base.[59] An image of such an ideal type of young Indian woman pupil appeared in the *Missionary Papers*: bearing book and sewing workbag, symbols of education and domesticity, her demeanour is poised and serious, she is foregrounded against the open sky and a neat landscape with schoolhouse. The sense of Mary Ann Cooke as bringing order into Indian women's lives through education is also emphasised by an image in the *Missionary Register* that shows the scene inside one of her schools: the neat rows of Indian girls, supervised by two English women, with three Indian women looking on, all set in a peaceful rural scene complete with bathing children. These images are in stark contrast to the violent images of *sati* that appeared in British missionary publications of the period.[60]

Throughout the 1820s, support for female education was presented as a vital complement to the evangelical campaign to get the British government to ban *sati*. The Church Missionary Society quarterly *Missionary Papers*, distributed free to supporters, juxtaposed engravings and accounts of the horror of *sati* with appeals for support of Mary Anne Cooke's schools.[61] Urging children to raise funds for schools for girls in Orissa in Bengal, an article in *The General Baptist Repository and Missionary Observer* evoked the image 'of a girl of twelve or fourteen years old, burnt alive with the body of her dear husband'.[62] Anglican vicar Thomas Shuttleworth Grimshawe's 1825 pamphlet, *An Earnest Appeal to British Humanity in Behalf of Hindoo Widows*, which called on the British government to abolish *sati*, concluded by urging support for Mrs Wilson's schools in an appeal that contrasted the 'high and manifold privileges' of British women with 'the situation of the ignorant, the abject, and deluded Hindoo female, offering her tender infant as a propriatory sacrifice to the Ganges, and finally expiring amidst the flames of the funeral pile'.[63] In this way he included women in the project of bringing freedom from 'heathen' superstition, which, he claimed, could, by emancipating India (and, he implied, emancipating Indian women), atone for the violence of imperial conquest:

> It is thus that India, emancipated, through our Instrumentality, from the yoke of a cruel Superstition, and admitted to a fellowship in the peace and hope of the Gospel, will recognise in Britain no longer a Conqueror to whom she is bound by the terror of our arms, but a Benefactor indissolubly endeared by the triumphs of our mercy.

Sati continued to be evoked in calls for British women to support missionary work in India even after 1829–30, when it was officially banned in areas of India under direct British control. Mrs General M. Mainwaring's 1830 novel about an Indian brother and sister who convert to Christianity and become missionaries in the East was entitled *The Suttee; or, the Hindu Converts* and included a dedication to the Duchess of Gloucester expressing the hope that 'it may, in some degree, contribute to that impulse of sympathy, now excited in behalf of a people less known by their virtues than their sufferings'.[64] Jemima Thompson's *Memoirs of British Female Missionaries* (1841) – a text discussed in more detail in Chapter 4 – had as its frontispiece a picture of the 'burning of the wives and slaves of Runjeet Sing. June 1839'. The tract, designed to encourage British women to become missionaries to heathen women, used India as an example of the way the 'heathen' treated women, focusing particularly on *sati*, with information on the British campaign for its abolition and on the continuance of the practice in regions outside Britain's immediate control.[65] The plight of the poor children left orphaned by *sati* was also evoked in female missionary propaganda targeted at children, particularly girls. Ann Taylor Gilbert's 'Hymn', sung by some 6000 children at the children's missionary meeting held in Exeter Hall, London, lamented the 'little heathens' who 'stand and see, with bitter cries,/Their mothers burnt before their eyes' and thanked the Lord for the 'mercies we possess' in a 'Christian land'.[66]

'Impelled by the convictions of conscience and the claims of benevolence': female petitioners against *sati*

Alongside attempts to undermine Hindu support for *sati* through Christian education and conversion, missionaries and their supporters put increasing pressure on the British authorities to take legal steps to eradicate the practice. This pressure was stepped up when official statistics suggested that the regulation of *sati* introduced from 1813 onwards had actually led to an increase, rather than a decline, in widow immolation. Campaigning for British government action intensified in 1816, with the publication of William Johns' pamphlet *A Collection of Facts and Opinions Relative to the Burning of Widows with the Dead Bodies of their Husbands.* Johns had been a Baptist missionary doctor at Seramapore in India between 1812 and 1813, working with Ann Chaffin, described by Potts the first missionary nurse. He included (without acknowledgement) among his evidence a revised version of Chaffin's eye-witness account of a *sati*, the only detailed account of its kind by a British woman. While, as Mani points out, Chaffin's original account was distinguished from most British men's accounts by the way in which *sati* is situated 'firmly in the domain of every day practice, undermining the tendency to idealisation found in many other accounts', her conclusion was in accord with that of her male missionary colleagues, namely that the spread of Christianity was the only way to eradicate a horrific practice. In the preface to the book, Johns acknowledged that this introduction of Christian religion would 'necessarily be very slow in its progress and greatly limited in its effect' in India and expressed the hope that his pamphlet would encourage the British government to take action to stop the practice. [67]

The British campaign against *sati* also drew on the writings of the influential Bengali Hindu reformer Rammohum Roy (*c*.1772–1833), best known as the founder of the Brahmo Somaj movement. Set up in 1828 as Brahmo Sabha, this advocated worship of one god alone on the basis of the divine authority of Hindu scriptures (the Veda). An English edition of Roy's first tract on *sati* was published in 1818 as a *Conference between an Advocate for, and an Opponent of, the Practice of Burning Widows Alive*. This was followed by an English edition of his *Second Conference* in 1820, which was dedicated to Lady Hastings, wife of the Governor-General, and which championed the cause of Indian women's education. Within colonial India his evidence that Hindu scriptures did not sanction *sati* became a major resource for British officials and missionaries arguing with indigenous religious authorities over the issue; in Britain, extracts from his tracts, printed in British missionary magazines such as the *Missionary Register*, helped arouse metropolitan campaigners.[68]

Within the British Parliament, missionaries gained vital support from Thomas Fowell Buxton, Wilberforce's successor as leader of the Evangelical Anglican group of reformers. In 1820, the first Blue Book on *sati* was published, and the following year Buxton initiated the first Parliamentary debate on the issue.[69] Public pressure on Parliament began to be exerted at just the same time as the Anti-Slavery Society was launching its campaign for the end of colonial slavery: in 1823, the first anti-*sati* petition was presented to Parliament.[70]

The campaign gained renewed momentum in 1827, following the publication of the first edition of what became the most widely circulated and extensively reviewed anti-*sati* tract, the Reverend James Peggs' *The Suttees' Cry to Britain*.[71] Peggs (1793–1850) had been one of the first missionaries sent out by the General Baptist Missionary Society to India and had worked at Cuttack, Orissa, between 1821 and 1825. On his return to Britain he promoted female support for missionary work and girls' education in India and, at the same time, urged that petitions be sent to Parliament against *sati*. Peggs raised funds for the distribution of his pamphlet by tours around England, preaching and addressing local missionary meetings. On 1 January 1828, for example, after he preached at Mr Mackenzie's Particular Baptist Chapel in St Ives, Cornwall, the Miss Barneses gave a sovereign to enable copies of *The Suttees' Cry* to be sent to British officials in India.[72]

In Coventry, in November 1828, Peggs set up the Society for the Abolition of Human Sacrifices in India.[73] Its remit was broader than *sati* alone: it aimed to campaign for the passage of British laws to abolish a range of 'heathen' practices, including infanticide. By the beginning of 1830 the society had circulated thousands of pamphlets, arranged a public meeting in Coventry to petition Parliament against *sati*, and stimulated the formation of similar committees in both London and Birmingham.[74] Altogether, between 1823 and 1830, a total of 107 petitions against *sati* were presented to the House of Commons, the majority from 1827 onwards, with petitioning reaching a peak in the first months of 1830.[75]

Despite this substantial expression of public opinion, historians have largely ignored the extra-parliamentary campaign against *sati* that took place in Britain, probably because it was completely overshadowed in scale by the contemporary anti-slavery campaign.[76] What, then, was the extent of women's involvement? All three human sacrifice abolition committees were led by men, as was customary at the period, and there is no evidence for the formation of related ladies' associations, in contrast to the anti-slavery movement. While Peggs and other activists were keen to draw women into active support of the campaign, they were cautious about urging women to petition.

In the first edition of *The Suttees' Cry* (1827), Peggs included a tentative call for public action by women, closing his text with a quote from the *Asiatic Observer* of 1824 that included the suggestion that the ladies of Calcutta should petition, to 'impress on their husbands the importance of rescuing a degraded part of the female sex'.[77] Here, female petitioning is safely removed to a distant colonial setting and is presented as nothing more than a way of exerting private wifely moral influence on husbands. Peggs, however, made a bolder suggestion in March 1828, when he produced a second updated edition of *The Suttees' Cry*. In this he suggested 'petitions to the British Parliament, signed by females from the principal Cities and Towns in Britain and Ireland'. He justified his call in these terms: 'should it be objected – this is an unprecedented method of expressing public opinion: it may be replied, "Is not the destruction of so many hundred unhappy widows annually in British India, a sufficient justification of it?"'[78] Peggs' suggestion, cautiously confined to a footnote, was followed by a poem by a woman, *A voice from India; or, the horrors of a suttee* by Ellen of Matlock Bath, which foregrounded women in its call for pressure to be put on Parliament:

> Ye British matrons, husbands, sires,
> Your souls with soft compassion glowing,
> O! haste to quench the horrid fires
> Whence human blood is daily flowing!
> With your lov'd king and country plead,
> Implore the Senate of your nation,
> That British India may be freed
> From scenes of such abomination.[79]

Women began to petition Parliament against *sati* from March 1829, but the male leadership of the campaign continued to be torn between the desire to involve women actively in the campaign and wariness of promoting female petitions. 'An Appeal to the Pious and Humane', issued by the anti-*sati* committee formed in London in June 1829 after a speech by Peggs, suggested that, should English men refuse to take action:

> the sisters of these Eastern victims, living in a land of science and charity, will surely unite to quench this murder and fire! Were each British female to shed one honest tear on these flames, they would go out for ever;

for such an influence would then be employed, as would secure the glorious object.

The appeal went on to call for petitions from all over the nation, and reproduced verses from Ellen of Matlock's poem but did not explicitly endorse female petitioning.[80] It was not until January 1830 that the London committee finally openly urged women to join the petitioning campaign, though recommending separate female petitions because 'by those who are well informed on such subjects, it is deemed by far the better way'.[81]

Despite the cautious approach by the male leadership, between February 1829 and April 1830 a total of 15 separate groups of women from around England sent anti-*sati* petitions to Parliament, comprising around one-fifth of the petitions on the topic presented over this particular period, and around one-eighth of total anti-*sati* petitions. Petitions were presented to the House of Commons from the female inhabitants of the towns of Castle Donnington and Loughborough in Leicestershire, from Melbourne, Heanor and Ilkestone in Derbyshire, from Stroud in Gloucestershire, from Worcester, from Alcester in Warwickshire, and from Blackburn in Lancashire. They were also presented from the female members of the following congregations: Protestant Dissenters of the Independent denomination meeting at Bassingbourn in Cambridgeshire; Protestant Dissenters of Old Gravel Pit Meeting in Hackney in Middlesex; Protestant Dissenters' meeting in Eagle-Street, London; Protestant Dissenters of the Calvinistic Meeting House in Kettering, Northamptonshire; and Baptists of Cockspur Street Chapel in Liverpool, Lancashire. In addition, a mixed petition was sent from the male and female inhabitants of Falmouth in Cornwall. Five of the groups also presented petitions to the House of Lords.[82] The number of signatories to each petition is uncertain, except in the case of the petition from Melbourne, which its presenter stated was signed by 300 or 400 ladies.[83]

Female petitions thus came from a wide range of English counties, from both dissenting religious congregations and town inhabitants, and from communities ranging from small rural towns to large industrial cities. Many were probably stimulated by Peggs' tours of the country to address missionary meetings: several of the towns (Castle Donnington, Melbourne, Loughborough and Ilkestone) had earlier sent considerable sums of money to support the General Baptist Missionary Society.[84] Many came from the same towns at men's petitions.

Interestingly, there is no evidence that female petitions against *sati* excited the disapproval or ribald dismissal that greeted women petitioners against Roman Catholic emancipation at this period.[85] Anti-Catholic petitions flooded Parliament between 1828 and April 1829 as the government attempted to secure the passage of the Relief Act, with Anglican clergy and activists of the Religious Tract Society stirring up religious bigotry with stories of Protestants being burned alive on fires by Catholics – at just the time that dissenters and Clapham Sect Evangelicals, both generally sympathetic to

Catholic emancipation, were purveying rather similar images of the burning alive of Hindu widows. There was confusion over whether women should
be allowed to sign these anti-Catholic petitions, leading to an interesting
debate about women's relationship to Parliamentary politics. Hart Davis, presenting one of the largest – a petition from Bristol signed by 38,894 – to
the House of Commons on 26 February 1829, stated that the signatures had
been examined and, to his regret, the names of all females had been struck
out. He wanted to know 'on what principle this was done' and argued: 'Had
not the female housekeeper as great a right to express the interest she felt
in a question of such vital importance ...? Did not the laws of this country permit a female to sit upon the throne, and had not a charter of one
of our kings given to the females of Bristol who were daughters of freemen
the right to make their husbands free?' He expressed the hope that his 'lady
constituents' would be treated better in future.[86] The ultra-Protestant peer
Lord Eldon, presenting a petition 'signed by a great many ladies' against
Catholic emancipation to the House of Lords on 19 February 1829 – a few
days after the first female anti-*sati* petition as presented to the Commons –
stated that he was 'not aware that there was any precedent to exclude the ladies'
from 'forwarding their remonstrances' to the House of Lords 'against measures
which they considered injurious to the constitution' and defended the petitioners on the grounds that 'there were many women who possessed more
knowledge of the constitution, and more common sense, than the descendants
of chancellors'.[87]

Supporters of Catholic emancipation attempted to take away the anti's
advantage in terms of numbers of signatures by questioning their validity
as genuine expressions of respectable public opinion through alleging that
women as well as small boys, prisoners, vagrants and illiterates had signed
them – thus lumping all women with the ignorant, the unrespectable and the
underage. On 19 March 1829, Alderman Waithman questioned the validity a
petition against Catholic emancipation presented to the House of Commons,
which its presenter claimed was signed by 113,000 householders of London,
by attacking the 'new and extraordinary doctrine' that allowed signatures by
women and children, arguing that:

> women were very well in their proper place; but he did not think they
> were in their proper place, when they came forward to petition parlia-
> ment. If, however, they insisted upon their right to petition, let them
> come forward in their proper character, and avow themselves, as in all
> probability they were, ladies of a certain description. The question came
> to this – were hon. members to be influenced and governed by the
> discussion and determinations of that house, or were they to yield up
> their judgments to the representations contained in parchments, signed
> by women and children, and the most ignorant part of the commu-
> nity? This petition was prepared at a meeting held at the Crown and
> Anchor Tavern.[88]

Such attacks resembled those that had been made in an attempt to discredit petitions against the slave trade in the 1790s.[89] Given that anti-*sati* campaigners came from sectors of the population – Evangelical Anglicans and Protestant Dissenters – who supported Catholic emancipation and were thus keen to discredit anti-Catholic petitions by any means possible, it was obviously problematic for these groups to simultaneously urge women to sign anti-*sati* petitions. It is thus not surprising that when Mr B. Lamb presented the anti-*sati* petition from the ladies of Melbourne to the House of Commons on 2 April 1829 he explained that 'he had withheld for some time' because of the objections that had recently been raised to ladies petitioning on Catholic emancipation.[90] Practical considerations based on their experience of the use of the presence of female signatories to discredit petitions against the slave trade and against Catholic emancipation, as much as ideological objections based on 'separate spheres', were clearly at play in the decisions of the male leadership of both anti-*sati* and anti-slavery campaigns not to encourage female signatures to general petitions, but instead cautiously to condone separate female petitions.

In this context, female petitioners against *sati*, and the female petitioners against colonial slavery who followed in their wake, were concerned to present their petitioning as a respectable activity that lay within their appropriate sphere. This was easier to do in the case of both anti-*sati* and anti-slavery campaigns than in the case of opposition to Roman Catholic emancipation because a specifically feminine take on the issues could be articulated, focused around deep concern for the sufferings of 'other' women, namely colonized black and brown women in the Empire. This feminine approach was first articulated in anti-*sati* petitions and then replicated in the very similar wording of anti-slavery petitions, whose content I have discussed in my earlier work.[91]

In classic evangelical style, women petitioners against *sati* stressed their awareness of 'the benefits that they themselves have derived from Christianity', emphasising their own privileges and signalling contentment with their own position in society. They also claimed a particular feminine empathy with the sufferings of their own sex: *sati* was 'a subject in which, as females, they are deeply interested' and which demanded their 'peculiar sympathy'. Female petitioners also represented their public action as an extension of their private familial roles, stating that 'as Wives, as Mothers, as Daughters, or as Sisters' they could not contemplate practices such as *sati* and infanticide 'but with emotions of the most painful Nature'. They stressed that the issue as one of humanity – and thus within their sphere as philanthropists and guardians of morality – rather than one of politics. Acknowledging that they were 'aware that it is unusual for persons of their sex to express opinions on matters of legislation' they attempted to disarm criticism by stating that this was a matter of humanity rather than politics.[92]

Finally, women petitioners diffused the potential interpretation of their action as usurping men's role by couching their petitions as pleas to powerful men to extend their paternal protection to colonized women. The London anti-*sati* committee's June 1829 Appeal, discussed above, had suggested in the language of sentimental humanitarianism that 'were each British female to shed one honest tear on these flames, they would go out for ever; for such an influence would then be employed, as would secure the glorious object'.[93] One group of female petitioners from Loughborough appended the following lines of verse to their appeal, suggesting that these accumulated female tears, expressed in the form of pleas to Parliament, could be transubstantiated into a single word from men, a decree that would have the power to end *sati*:

> Say but a single word and save
> Ten thousand mothers from a flaming grave,
> And tens of thousands from that source of woe,
> That ever must to orphan'd children flow.[94]

The humble feminine tone of female petitions against *sati* seems to have successfully disarmed those concerned about female interference in politics. The *Baptist Magazine* of March 1830, recording the presentation of the petition against *sati* from the women of Worcester, stated that:

> Among the petitions now presenting to parliament for this purpose, we are happy to find some from that sex whose sympathies must be supposed to be peculiarly alive to this subject, and who, touched by the urgency of the case, are coming forth from their accustomed retirement, clad in the veil of modesty, and in a tone of amiable commiseration to express their feelings, and to solicit on behalf of these daughters of oppression the protecting shield of a British and a Christian government.

The article proceeded to give the full text of the petition for the congregation at Eagle Street, London, implicitly offering this as a model for other female petitioners.[95]

Women campaigners' success in gaining acceptance of their petitions through the use of the language of feminine plea should not, however, be allowed to submerge the potentially radical implications of female petitioning. As Susan Zaeske has pointed out, 'petitioning's ability to place demands on rulers or representatives, even while it obscured the signers' motive of demand' gave petitioning 'a deeply subversive potential'.[96] Female petitions against *sati* asserted a public role for British women in moralising the imperial nation and reforming the Empire, based on their particular ability as women to represent the interests of colonised women to the imperial Parliament. Emphasising the special national character of British women and their own sense of themselves as full members of the imperial nation, the female inhabitants of Alcester stated that *sati* was 'degrading to the character, and disgusting to the moral feelings, of every *British* female'. In describing colonized women as having 'an equal right to the paternal protection of the British Government' they combined the rights-based language of political radicalism and feminism with the conservative and anti-feminist language of paternalism and protection. In stating that they had only moved out of their usual sphere because they were 'impelled by the convictions of conscience and the claims of benevolence' the female members of the congregation of Protestant Dissenters of the Calvinistic Baptist Meeting House in Kettering associated the ameliorative language of charitable concern, which could be accommodated within the existing social order, with the uncompromising language of conscience, which was drawn on by religious dissenters resisting Church establishment authority. This language, as discussed in Chapter 2, had earlier been used by Elizabeth Heyrick and her female supporters to challenge male authority in the anti-slavery movement.[97]

In engaging in collective petitioning, women were participating in a way of expressing public opinion to government that had radical political roots and associations in Britain. Collective petitioning had emerged with the Levellers during the English Civil War, some of whose petitions were signed by women. It resurfaced in the 1760s with the use of petitions by North American colonists to bring their grievances against British rule to king and Parliament in the build up to the American Revolution, and was in turn taken up by Wilkite agitators for radical parliamentary reform in the 1770s, though neither group encouraged female signatories. Petitioning then became an important part of the campaign against the slave trade, but was then abandoned because it became tainted with associations with political radicalism during the period of reaction against the French Revolution.

Middle-class reformers' desire to avoid opening their movements to charges of political radicalism was probably one of the reasons why leaders of the campaign against the slave trade discouraged female petitioners at a time when women's active engagement in politics was associated with French revolutionary fervour. In the 1820s, however, mass petitioning was revived as an effective and acceptable way for reformers within Parliament to force repeated debates on the issues they wished to press. By 1829, when women joined the petitioning campaign against *sati*, a huge proportion of parliamentary time was being taken up with debate on public petitions. Nevertheless, the presence of female signatories was still used to discredit petitioning campaigns: witness the reactions to anti-Catholic petitions. It was only by presenting the issues of *sati* and slavery as moral rather than political in nature, and by separating out female from male petitioners, that female petitioning was able to gain respectability and acceptance.

Cross-currents of influence between religiously motivated reform movement in Britain and the United States were also important in stimulating the almost simultaneous entry of women into petitioning in the two nations in the 1820s and early 1830s. In the United States, women began local temperance petitioning in 1818, national petitioning to halt the removal of the Cherokee from their native land in 1829, and petitioning against slavery in 1831;[98] in Britain, women began anti-*sati* petitioning in 1829 and mass petitioning against slavery in 1830. British women anti-slavery campaigners strongly influenced the emergence of organised female abolitionism in the 1830s in the United States,[99] while transatlantic links between female anti-*sati* campaigners can be dated back to 1817–21, when, as discussed earlier in this chapter, William Ward promoted the anti-*sati* campaign among women on both sides of the Atlantic. Interestingly, Julie Roy Jeffrey points out that the founding constitutions of a number of American female anti-slavery societies condemned Americans for expressing sympathy for the plight of widows burnt on their husbands' funeral pyres in India while ignoring the evil of slavery in their midst.[100] Further research is clearly needed into anti-*sati* campaigning in the United States, and into the links between anti-*sati*, foreign missionary and anti-slavery campaigns both within and between the two nations.[101]

In her examination of American women's anti-slavery petitioning, Zaeske has noted how women moved from a 'rhetoric of humility and disavowal' and stress on Christian duty in the 1831–6 period to an assertion of their constitutional rights as citizens.[102] In the context of US anti-slavery then, the subversive radical potential of female petitioning seems to have been realised. In Britain, however, this potential, though suggested by the radical historical associations of collective petitioning in Britain, and hinted at in aspects of the language of female anti-*sati* petitioning discussed above, was not fulfilled: the rhetoric never completely shifted from humility to self-assertion. This can partly be attributed to the facts that, in Britain, both campaigns achieved success very soon after women entered into petitioning – in 1829–30 *sati* was outlawed, and in 1833 the Emancipation Act was passed – and that at the same time women were explicitly excluded from direct participation in parliamentary politics as voters under the terms of the 1832 Reform Act.

Abolition and beyond: evangelicals, Unitarians and the roots of imperial feminism

By 1830 the British campaign against *sati* had achieved its objective. The recently appointed Governor-General of India, Lord William Bentinck, was an Evangelical Anglican who supported missionary activity and was determined to tackle the question of *sati*.[103] After canvassing opinion in India, on 4 December 1829 he issued his regulation on *sati* that forbade widow burning in the Bengal Presidency; the Governors of Madras and Bombay followed suit in February and April 1830.[104] News of these developments filtered back to Britain, and petitioning came to a halt in the middle of 1830. Indigenous reaction in India was mixed: a group of orthodox Hindus made a petition appeal to the British government against Bentinck's ruling; this, however, was countered by a petition by Hindu reformers in support of Bentinck, brought personally to London in 1831 by Rajah Rammohun Roy.[105]

The successful conclusion of the missionary campaign against *sati* marked the beginnings of a more culturally interventionist imperial policy by the British in India during the 'Age of Reform' associated with Bentinck's governorship (1828–35) as the era of expanding military conquest was succeeded by a period of consolidation of administrative control.[106] In British evangelical circles the abolition of *sati* was represented as the rescue of Hindu widows by feeling Christian men, erasing the earlier impotence of missionaries, the initial sanctioning of 'voluntary' *sati* by the British authorities, and the vital input of Hindu reformers such as Rammohun Roy – as well as British women's active contribution to the campaign.[107] Officially, the sensitive British evangelical male – represented by the two European men turning away and shielding their eyes from the horror of a widow burning in the frontispiece image of the 1830 edition of Peggs' anti-*sati* tract – was given all the credit for ending the practice.[108] In Calcutta, a monument to the British Governor-General William Cavendish Bentinck, erected around 1838, commemorated him as the abolisher of *sati*, epitomizing a new ideal of imperial manliness that combined paternalism and Christian moral authority with worldly power. Liberal reformer and historian Thomas Babington Macaulay's inscription on the monument commemorated his friend as a man 'who infused into oriental despotism the spirit of British freedom' and 'whose constant study it was to elevate the intellectual and moral character of the nations committed to his charge'. Indigenous opposition to British cultural imperialism was erased by Macaulay's testimony that the statue was erected by 'men who, differing in race, in manners, in language, and in religion, cherish, with equal veneration and gratitude, the memory of his wise, upright and paternal administration'. An official imperial history of India was being 'made concrete'.[109]

This official imperial version of events was one that some British women were happy to confirm. Mrs Phelps' poem *The Suttee* (1831) represents the abolition of *sati* as story of the rescue of a young widow from the funeral pyre by Reginald Heber, Bishop of Calcutta. Heber appears before the 'passive victim':

> And dashing from his cheek the manly tears,
> Bids the attendants raise the wretched wife
> And stops the fiery brand, and quells the murderous strife.
> Gives to her arms the helpless babes,
> And from the fire the destined Suttee saves.[110]

In fact, Heber had died prior to the prohibition of *sati* and his description of how he had failed to stop a *sati* whilst Bishop of Calcutta in the 1820s had stressed his feelings of impotence: 'I felt very sick at heart, and regretted I had not been half an hour sooner, though probably my attempts at persuasion would have had no chance of success'.[111] But Phelps, of course, is not concerned with literal truth: her description drew on an eighteenth-century literary tradition of the *sati* as a tragic victim rescued by a chivalrous British man, reshaping it to create in Heber the ideal of evangelical manhood: sensitivity combined with steadfastness and moral authority.[112] The poem is an example of what Rajan has described as the use of the 'trope of chivalry' by the 'colonial imagination' to represent the administrative abolition of *sati* – in other words, to draw on the words of Gayatri Spivak quoted at the opening of this chapter, Heber and Bentinck are represented as white men saving brown women from brown men.[113]

The hegemony of this colonial discourse on *sati* did not, however, go completely unchallenged by British women. Fanny Parks, who lived in India between 1822 and 1845, drew on her own experiences of independent travel in the subcontinent, her knowledge of Hindustani and her friendships with Indian women to question dominant accounts. In *Wanderings of a Pilgrim* (1850), the journal of her life in India, she records witnessing a *sati* and finding out that the burning of widows was not commanded by Hindu scriptures. Parks suggests that there would initially have been little resistance to the British government abolishing the practice before missionaries came on the scene. She also casts doubt on the disinterested humanitarianism of the government, pointing out that it was happy to go along with 'native superstition' when it was profitable to do so: 'witness the tax they levy on pilgrims'. Rather than viewing Indian women as uniquely victimised, Parks links *sati* to the universal subordination of women, locating its roots in patriarchal economic interests as much as religion, and expressing her feminist pleasure at its prohibition as a step towards taking women's interests into account: 'Women in all countries are considered such dust in the balance, when their interests are pitted against those of the men, that I rejoice no more widows are to be grilled, to ensure the whole of the property passing to the sons of the deceased'.[114]

Such universalizing feminism, stressing the common oppression of all women, echoed Utopian socialist William Thompson's use of an analogy with *sati* in the 1820s to highlight the patriarchal oppression of English wives and widow (see Chapter 1). While Thompson's use of the analogy was clearly influenced by the anti-*sati* campaigns of the period, however, it became increasingly unusual to equate the positions of British and Indian women. Rather, two main strands of female discourse on *sati* and the position of Indian women emerged. The first developed within the evangelical missionary movement, the second among Unitarian women with close ties to the Bengali anti-*sati* campaigner and reformer Rammohun Roy. These two strands, I will argue, both fed into imperial feminist approaches to Indian women by British women's suffrage campaigners of the later nineteenth century.

To begin with evangelical women. As this chapter has shown, missionary propaganda targeted specifically at women focused on aspects of 'heathen' societies with which they might be expected to be particularly concerned: the ill treatment of women and, most dramatically, the burning of widows. British women themselves, who had earlier been involved in shaping British perceptions of India through travel writings and imaginative literature that purveyed a complex and varied picture of the lives of Indian women, now began to participate in the creation of a more univocal and unequivocally negative evangelical discourse on the position of Indian women. Whereas prior to the nineteenth century only European men had been able to imagine themselves in the role of rescuers of Indian women from the funeral pyre, British women now began to picture themselves in that role. They might not be in the position to snatch women physically from the clutches of the flames, but they considered that they were better equipped than men to empower Indian women through a Christian education that would impel them to abandon the superstition which had led them to accept *sati* as a widow's fate. They also believed that they were better placed than British men to use the recognized power of their moral influence and the emotional appeal of their empathetic identification with female suffering to mount moving pleas for Indian women's rescue from *sati* in the form of petitions to the imperial Parliament.[115]

Through such actions, so evangelical women were convinced, they could emancipate Indian women. In keeping with the evangelical approach to the woman question outlined in Chapter 1, they defined female emancipation not as the abolition of all forms of patriarchy or the granting of civic rights to women, but rather as the enlightenment of Hindu women by Christian education so that they were freed from superstition and ignorance to become good wives within a Christianised and reformed patriarchal family and enabled to fulfil their duties as mothers rather than leaving their children orphaned by committing *sati*. Female emancipation was also envisioned as part of the broader evangelical project of bringing about the moral reform of society by removing the fetters of heathen superstition and ignorance. Western-educated Indian women, it was hoped, might become the moral reformers of society from a domestic base.

In contrasting their own position with that of Indian women, British women campaigners against *sati*, like the women anti-slavery campaigners whose campaigning overlapped chronologically with theirs, signalled acceptance of their existing social role by stressing their own privileges in a civilised and Christian country.[116] At the same time, their concern for women's suffering propelled evangelical women out of their designated domestic sphere into the political sphere as signatories to collective petitions to Parliament. In petitioning Parliament, women became publicly involved in defining the limits of acceptable male behaviour, asserting the value of a woman's life and the unacceptability of male violence.

The other group of women who took a strong interest in the position of Indian women at this period were Unitarian women. From a dissenting denomination who remained outside the evangelical fold and at one remove from the mainstream foreign missionary movement, Unitarians began being interested in the issue of *sati* through their close connections with Rammohum Roy, the monotheist Bengali reformer whom they attempted to claim as one of their own. Roy travelled to Britain in 1831 bearing a petition signed by Indians supportive of the abolition of *sati*, and he mixed in radical circles in London and developed particularly close connections with leading Unitarians in Bristol. Roy provided British men and women with living proof that Indian men could be supporters of women's rights. He also bolstered English women's own sense of superiority to Indian women and belief in the ability of

4 Can women be missionaries?

Imperial philanthropy, female agency and feminism

If Charlotte Brontë's Jane Eyre rejects the self-annihilation required of an Indian widow, she also shies away from the uncomplaining Christian martyrdom required of a dutiful missionary's wife in India, realising that a loveless marriage to English clergyman John St Rivers would make her 'burn inwardly'. She states that she will only accompany him to India on the condition that she may 'go free', participating in the missionary project not as his wife but as his 'adopted sister'. Rivers, however, rejects her offer: he wants a missionary wife, a 'helpmeet' committed to himself as well as to God.[1]

Gayatri Spivak, in a foundational text of feminist postcolonial criticism, argued that in Charlotte Brontë's 'cult text of feminism' the English heroine's 'feminist individualism', while rooted in contrasts with the *sati* and the mad Creole woman, does not encompass an independent female engagement in imperial social mission. The end of the novel, she suggested, emphasises the importance of the work of 'soul making' among colonised peoples over a life of English domesticity; however, when Jane anticipates Rivers' martyrdom in the Indian mission field, Brontë's use of the '*allegorical* language of Christian psychobiography' genders the missionary as male and 'marks the inaccessibility of the imperialist project as such to the nascent 'feminist' scenario'.[2] Jane marries the man she loves and stays in England; John goes on his own to India as a missionary. This fictional representation of the obstacles to independent female missionary agency in the early nineteenth century tended to be reaffirmed in pioneering scholarship on the history of women and missions. Valentine Cunningham, for example, suggested that when the fictional Jane expresses the desire to go out to India not as 'a wifely supplement or subordinate' but as a 'fellow-missionary', she is 'projecting an impossibility' because at this period '*missionary* was a male noun; it denoted a male actor, male action, male spheres of service'.[3] Neither masculine missionary convention nor feminist literary imagination, in these scholarly readings, offered possibilities for envisioning independent female missionary agency in the early nineteenth-century British Empire.

Noting the refusal of the main missionary societies to employ women as missionaries in their own right until the late nineteenth century, scholars still tend to downplay the significance of British women's early engagements with the foreign mission movement.[4] At first sight, then, early nineteenth-century missionary women might seem an unpromising group to study in a book discussing the relationship between imperialism and the origins of modern Western feminism. However, the active involvement of women in the missionary campaign against *sati*, both as petitioners and as promoters of 'native' female education, which has been delineated in the Chapter 3 calls into question the scenarios presented by Cunningham and Spivak. More broadly, missionary scholarship is beginning to expose both the crucial nature of the contributions made by missionary wives in a range of mission fields and the pioneering educational work undertaken by single women as a close adjunct to the foreign missionary enterprise during this early period.[5] In addition, the gendered domestic base of missionary support in early to mid-nineteenth-century Britain and the links between 'home' and 'foreign' missions are coming under increasing scrutiny.[6] Alongside this historical scholarship, but often with little cross-reference to it, there has developed a veritable industry of literary scholarship on *Jane Eyre* from feminist and postcolonial perspectives, some of which explores the place of missions in the text.[7]

Building on this scholarship, but focusing specifically on the promotion in Britain of female missionary work overseas, this chapter considers whether active independent engagement by women in imperial social mission really was 'inaccessible' to British women in the early nineteenth century. Could women, in fact, be missionaries? And what was the relationship between women's role in the foreign missionary movement and the origins of 'feminist individualism' in Britain?

I begin by exploring the emergence of an imperial dimension to female philanthropy in Britain and examining the development of distinctively gendered forms of missionary organisation and concepts of missionary agency in the early nineteenth century. Then, drawing on a hitherto largely neglected genre of missionary texts, early female missionary memoirs, I examine the ways in which women active in the mission field were represented to the British missionary public at home. I move on to consider both the obstacles facing single women who wished to become missionary agents in the field and the discursive openings for female missionary agency offered by broader evangelical discourses on women and on imperial social mission. The positioning of the missionary woman in a quasi-maternal relation to the 'heathen' woman is then examined in terms of the increasing fixing of missionary hopes in India on the orphan girl. Finally, the boundaries of early female missionary agency are explored through a study of a debate that took place in the pages of a leading English evangelical women's magazine over the distinction between male preaching and female teaching in the foreign mission field.

In going beyond the high-profile publications of the main missionary societies and the classic literary text of *Jane Eyre* to explore early nineteenth-century British missionary texts by, for and about women, this chapter reveals the presence of a more expansive view of female missionary agency at this period than that suggested by Cunningham or Spivak. In the process, new insights are offered into the relationship between British women's engagement in the foreign missionary enterprise and the development of imperial feminism.

Foreign missionary organisations and the gendered division of missionary labour

Local ladies' associations associated with foreign missionary societies were among the most numerous and active of the female voluntary organisations that burgeoned in early nineteenth-century Britain. Indeed, Frank Prochaska has identified the Female Missionary Society in Northampton, founded in 1805 to support the Baptist Missionary Society, as perhaps the first auxiliary established by women in support of any English philanthropic organisation. In Scotland there was an even earlier initiative, when the Northern Missionary Society, based in Inverness, set up an associated women's society soon after its formation in 1800. Foreign missionary societies, together with the British and Foreign Bible Society, pioneered the use of national networks of local ladies' associations as an effective means of fund-raising, distributing information and raising interest in their activities, particularly among women and children. Reporting on the activities of its auxiliary societies in the *Missionary Herald* of 1820, the Baptist Missionary Society stated that 'a very strong testimony is borne to the value and great importance of Female Aid. Associations formed and conducted by our Christian sisters, have always been among the most productive, in proportion to their extent'. Eugene Stock, in his official history of the Church Missionary Society, stressed the vital importance of branch societies as fund raisers during the society's first decade of operation, and stated that 'Ladies' Associations were a great power in those days'.[8]

Women, however, were excluded from the national committees of these foreign missionary societies until the late nineteenth century or even later. These national committees also only formally recruited men as missionaries. It was not until 1858 that the Wesleyan Methodist Missionary Society became the first to recruit women; it was followed by the Baptist Missionary Society in 1866, the London Missionary Society in 1875 and the Church Missionary Society followed in 1887; in Scotland, the United Presbyterian Church began to recruit female missionaries in 1881.[9]

The reasons why foreign missionary societies did not initially recruit women were rooted in women's position within evangelical Protestantism during the early nineteenth century. The work of missionaries was understood to be 'the preaching of the Gospel, the translation and publication of the Holy Scriptures, and the establishment of Schools.'[10] It was acceptable for women to undertake translation and teaching; however, they were excluded, or in the process of being excluded, from preaching by all the main British Protestant sects – Anglican, Baptist, Congregationalist, Wesleyan Methodist – at the time that these denominations were setting up their foreign missionary societies. Public preaching by women became confined to the Society of Friends and to splinter groups such as the Primitive Methodists, neither of which were heavily involved in foreign missionary work, and female preaching was not to re-emerge in the Protestant mainstream until the 1860s.[11] Theological objections to female preaching combined with professional constraints on female training. While denominational patterns varied, most missionaries were recruited from the all-male ranks of the clergy and ministry. They increasingly received formal training of at least a year's duration, this at a time when women where totally excluded from higher education and professional training.[12] These factors, when combined with evangelicals' strong promotion of 'separate spheres' ideology, with its emphasis on the primacy of women's domestic duties, acted as powerful inhibitors to the employment of women as full missionaries.

At first sight, then, women seen to have limited scope for agency within the early foreign missionary movement: only men could sit on the national committees of the foreign missionary societies, only men could gain the formal qualifications of a full missionary, only men could become the salaried employees of foreign missionary societies, and only men could perform that primary component of a missionary's role, namely preaching. However, despite these restrictions, women found ways of carving out a far greater space for female missionary agency than this picture suggests: missionary wives developed their own particular spheres of expertise in the field and forged direct links with female supporters at home, ladies' associations targeted their funds at female education projects, and women-run societies were formed to promote the Christian education of 'native' girls by both missionary wives and single women.

From an early date, missionary societies recognised the benefits of recruiting married men as missionaries; thus, as early as there were foreign missionaries, there were missionaries' wives. Wives were seen as providing an important domestic base for their husbands, and as modelling proper feminine domesticity to indigenous women.[13] Increasingly, however, they were also recognised as playing an important role in the development of girls' education. Given that teaching was a crucial component of the male missionary's work, and indeed often found to be more effective than preaching in bringing the word of God to the 'heathen', the role of male missionary and missionary's wife in practice overlapped considerably. Even though only men were officially employed by the missionary societies, and carried the official title of missionaries, in practice it was missionary couples, rather than single men, who became the building blocks of the missionary enterprise; as a result, as many women as men were active in the early mission field. The extent to which these missionary wives gained unofficial recognition as missionaries in their own right will be explored through an examination of their memoirs in the following section.

Missionary wives played an important role in encouraging British women to promote 'native' female education. Valentine Cunningham notes how Mrs Hill, wife of an early London Missionary Society missionary in India, obtained support for her schools from friends in Newcastle-under-Lyme, who organised sewing circles and sent over articles for sale.[14] From 1820, several ladies' associations of the Baptist Missionary Society began to channel their funds into support for specific schools for 'native girls' set up by Baptist missionary wives in India, rather than simply forwarding it to the general fund of the national society.[15] The public image of centralised male metropolitan control over missionary work in the field thus masked a more complex reality in which British women formed links with specific female missionary educators in the field. Missionary wives also promoted support for female education on return to Britain. W.M. Harvard, one of the first Wesleyan Methodist missionaries in Ceylon, recorded that he and his wife Elizabeth, after they returned to England in the 1820s, travelled around the country to promote missionary work. While he presumably gave sermons and speeches to public meetings, she acted 'in the true spirit of a Missionary agent', giving talks to women about the girls' schools of the Ceylon Mission, and exciting their interest by exhibiting a collection of 'native' needlework.[16] In the 1850s, the cooperative efforts of missionary wives in the field and the wives of the male leaders of the Wesleyan Methodist Missionary Society at home proved crucial in pushing the society to become the first to set up a ladies' committee to recruit single women as missionaries.[17]

Single women also entered into the mission field at an early date as schoolteachers. As discussed in Chapter 3, the ladies' committee of the British and Foreign School Society took the initiative, sponsoring Mary Anne Cooke's work in India. An interdenominational evangelical organisation, the British and Foreign School Society aimed to use the monitorial system of elementary education to instruct the children of the poor. Its domestic agenda sought to buttress existing class and gender hierarchies: concerned at the 'degraded state' of many female servants, which was ascribed to lack of proper instruction in 'moral and religious principles', it wanted to give girls 'such a portion of education in reading, writing, arithmetic, and needlework, as shall enable them to discharge the duties of their stations which, as *women*, they are destined to fill'.[18] The society focused its overseas efforts on Britain's Empire: Cooke's success in Calcutta encouraged the ladies' committee to expand its outreach to girls in newly acquired parts of the British Empire, including Chinese girls in Malaysia and Greek girls in the Ionian Islands and, following the abolition of British colonial slavery, to newly emancipated African girls in both Jamaica and Cape Town.[19]

In 1834 the British and Foreign School Society handed over the main responsibility for recruiting single women from Britain for 'native female education' to the independent, female-run Society for Promoting Female Education in China, India and the East (FES). Unlike the ladies' committee of the British and Foreign School Society, whose main preoccupation was the education of working-class girls at home, this society could devote all its energies to the foreign field. In an initiative indicative of the close links between early British and American missionary enterprise, its foundation was stimulated by an 'Appeal to Christian Ladies' issued by the Rev. David Abeel, an American missionary on leave from China, who urged the need for Christian education to raise Chinese women from degradation and inferiority.[20] Its formation was part of the early stages of what Frank Prochaska has described as 'an explosion of charities managed exclusively by women' in nineteenth-century England, and occurred at the beginning of a decade of renewed popular enthusiasm in Britain for the foreign missionary enterprise.[21] Like the British and Foreign School Society, it was an interdenominational organisation, and adopted its monitorial system of schooling. The Rev. Baptist Wriothesley Noel, 'one of the most influential evangelical clergymen of early Victorian England', was instrumental in its formation, and his wife joined its committee, while the Duchess of Beaufort became its president, lending important establishment respectability.[22] An independent, female-run society, the FES was nevertheless dependent for its success in the field on smooth cooperation with the major missionary societies, and it had particularly close links with the Church Missionary Society.[23]

The society defined its objects as the collecting and diffusing of information on female education, the establishing and superintending of schools in the East (a term that encompassed Africa as well as Asia) and the giving of money and books to schools, and the selection and preparation in Britain of 'pious and intelligent' women to act as the trainers and superintendents of 'native' female teachers. Seeking to select the right sort of women for the work, the FES ladies' committee tested female candidates on their motives, knowledge of the Bible, general education and experience of philanthropy and teaching, and obtained references as to their piety, involvement in good works, interest in the cause, temperament as teachers and 'station in life'. Governesses and ministers' daughters were two of the types of women attracted to and considered suitable recruits for such work. They were required to undertake a period of probation in London in the training institutions either of the British and Foreign School Society in Borough Road or the Home and Colonial Infant School Society in Gray's Inn Road, an Evangelical Anglican foundation. Before embarking, the female agents had to sign an undertaking that, if they voluntarily relinquished their situation or married within five years, they would repay the committee the sum it had expended on their account. In other words, in complete contrast to male missionaries, single status was seen as crucial to successful prosecution of their work. The aim was to pay applicants' outfit and passage but to favour those who could be paid salaries by local fund-raising, following the system initiated by the British and Foreign School Society. The women were sent out under the protection of missionary families and attached to them during their work, a way of combating fears about safety and respectability and providing them with a home in the field.[24]

While the society talked in terms of supported agents based in a familial environment, these single British women, like the women earlier engaged by the British and Foreign School Society, were not voluntary workers but women in salaried employment. Though small in number, they were pioneering a new vocational role for educated single women. This choice, however, was couched in terms of self-sacrifice rather than self-fulfilment: as the *Missionary Register* stated, Mary Anne Cooke had left 'her country, her parents, her friends, and every other advantage' and 'given up great expectations'.[25] Cooke did, of course, risk very real self-sacrifice – many missionaries died of tropical diseases after only a few years in the 'field'. However, she was also moving from a subservient position hidden away as a governess in a private household into a position of public prominence and authority that gave her scope for initiatives, superintendence of others, and the sense of being part of a broader missionary project under the aegis of British imperial rule.[26] Her achievements show that she seized these new opportunities with alacrity.

By 1847, the year *Jane Eyre* was published, the FES had sent out 50 single women 'agents' to the foreign field. In 1854 it launched its own periodical, the *Female Missionary Intelligencer*, which at a price of only 1d was aimed at a wide female readership. By its twenty-fifth anniversary it had raised a total of £43,050 for female education, sent work for sale abroad valued at a further £21,561, trained and sent out 84 qualified teachers to specific posts and assisted 43 others in making their own arrangements to work overseas; and it had been involved in the formation of 128 new schools. In addition to its network of auxiliaries within England, which totalled 57 in the late 1850s, the FES also fostered the formation of associate female education committees in Geneva, Basle and Berlin and stimulated the setting up in Cairo in 1840 of an Egyptian Society for Promoting Female Education in the East, comprising 'leading Turkish and Arab ladies', encouraged by the reformist ruler of Egypt, Mahomet Ali.[27]

The FES also influenced the development of a similar society in Scotland, though here a rather different relationship between male and female missionary organisation developed. The Edinburgh Ladies' Association for the Advancement of Female Education in India (f. 1837) was soon brought under the supervision of a board of seven male presidents, all ministers in the Church of Scotland, the appointment of teachers was taken over by the General Assembly, and women's work in the field was closely supervised by the church's male missionaries. On the one hand, this marked an official endorsement by the Presbyterian church of the employment of single women in the project of 'native' female education'; on the other hand, it meant that female autonomy and interdenominational cooperation was lost within the highly patriarchal and hierarchical structure of Scottish Presbyterianism. Following the Disruption of 1843 – when the Church of Scotland split and its more evangelically oriented members seceded to form the Free Church – many of the members of the Edinburgh-based society split away to form a more effective new group. This Female Society of the Free Church of Scotland for Promoting Christian Education of Females in India in 1844 launched a journal entitled *The Eastern Female's Friend*. Its two successive editors were male, but both were former missionaries whose wives had been active in developing female education in India. In 1857, a highpoint in annual income of £3650 was reached.[28]

'Christian psychobiography' and the early female missionary memoir

Such Christian educational work by missionary wives and single women, while receiving limited coverage in the official publications of the major missionary societies, was regularly reported in the *Missionary Register*, a widely circulated periodical: the Church Missionary Society, for example, purchased thousands of copies a month for free distribution among its subscribers and collectors.[29] The work of the FES was also highlighted by the publication in 1839 of Priscilla Chapman's *Hindoo Female Education*[30] and by a history of the society published in 1847, the same year as *Jane Eyre*. Indeed, Charlotte Brontë showed her awareness in *Jane Eyre* of both married and single women's involvement in female education in India, presenting these as the respective roles in the missionary enterprise envisioned by Rivers for Jane and by Jane for herself.

There also emerged a genre of female missionary memoirs that went beyond a practical focus to celebrate and commemorate the lives of missionary women. When set alongside these now largely forgotten early nineteenth-century memoirs, Charlotte Brontë's presentation in *Jane Eyre* of 'Christian psychobiography' in exclusively masculine terms can be seen in a new light: more as her conscious authorial choice than as a reflection of the limits of the broader cultural imagining of female missionary agency at the period. The memoirs also, as we will see, call into question Cunningham's assertion that missionary remained a 'male noun' until the later nineteenth century.

Early female missionary memoirs, while not as widely read as accounts of the leading male missionaries of the period, frequently ran into several editions of several thousand copies each. Linda H. Peterson, in what appears to be the only previous discussion of the genre, includes them under the rubric of women's autobiography, and develops an insightful contrast between such 'heroic missionary memoirs' and the 'domesticated spiritual autobiography' of *Jane Eyre*.[31] However, it is important to note that, although female missionary memoirs commonly drew extensively on the subjects' own letters and journals, they were posthumous publications. The individual memoirs were generally compiled and edited by the missionary husbands of the deceased and often framed by a substantial introduction by the bereaved husband or by another male supporter of missions, explaining the reasons for publication and suggesting how the memoir should be read as an example to other women, encouraging them to take up the missionary cause. As such, the texts are multilayered, telling us as much about how male missionaries wished to present their wives to the British public as about the views, motivations, activities and self-presentation of missionary women themselves.

One of the earliest memoirs of missionary women to be published in Britain was John Philip's 1824 memoir of Mrs Matilda Smith. Its author and compiler was the Scottish superintendent of the London Missionary Society's recently established mission in southern Africa and an ardent anti-slavery campaigner.

Philip noted in his preface that, while many volumes of female biography had recently been published, in most of these 'we see more of the contemplative than of the active character'. In contrast, Mrs Smith 'was for many years the chief instrument of preserving any degree of vital religion in the colony [Cape Colony], and the grand animating principle of a missionary spirit, and of all the missionary exertions, made by the professed Christian population with which she was surrounded'. Here, British women are presented with a role model who not only undertook missionary work independently of her two successive husbands, but actually played the *leading* role in the promotion of missionary work in southern Africa: a powerful example of independent female agency rather than subordinate wifely assistance.[32] Keen to maximise her role as an example to British women, Philip's presentation of Smith probably deliberately obscured her ethnicity and racial background and her stance on slavery, highlighted in Elizabeth Elbourne's recent study of missions in Cape Colony.[33] Machtelt Smit, whose name Philip Anglicised even while referring to her Dutch extraction, had one grandmother who was a freed African slave and she herself owned a slave. As in most missionary propaganda, the complexities of the relationships between missionaries and colonialism and between coloniser and colonised are smoothed over.[34]

American missionary women were the subjects of a group of four other early memoirs published in Britain. The memoir of Mrs Harriet Newell, which appeared in a British edition in 1815, celebrated this 19-year-old, who had died soon after accompanying her American missionary husband to India, as 'the first Martyr to the missionary cause, from the American world', signalling that from an early date the designation of heroic missionary martyr was not exclusively reserved for men.[35] The memoir of Newell's friend Mrs Ann H. Judson, who helped establish the pioneering American Baptist mission in Burma, was published in a British edition in 1829, at the instigation of the Baptist Missionary Society, and was so popular in this country that it had run into nine editions by 1838. Judson, described as the first American female 'to bear the gospel to the heathen in foreign climes', had visited Britain in 1822 and the interest evinced by her tales of the Burma mission had led her to publish an account of the mission for British audiences.[36] In 1838, memoirs also appeared of Mrs H.W. Winslow of the Ceylon Mission and Louisa A. Lowrie of the Northern India Mission of an American Presbyterian organisation, the Western Foreign Missionary Society. The memoir of Winslow included an introductory essay by James Harrington Evans, a supporter of the Baptist Missionary Society. In this he stated that the memoir showed 'how high and holy may be that station' which missionary wives might occupy as 'fellow laborers [*sic*] in the missionary work', undertaking work that 'though apparently less responsible' than that of their husbands, 'may be equally important'.[37] Lowrie's memoir, published in London at the instigation of Congregationalist minister Andrew Reed, included a prefatory letter by a prominent British Baptist missionary in Calcutta, the Rev. W.H. Pearce. Stressing the importance of supporting the establishment of schools for girls, its author expressed the hope that his account of Lowrie's 'brief but interesting course as a female missionary', together with the other early American women's memoirs of Newell, Judson and Winslow, would act as examples to British women both of the 'mental and spiritual qualifications which render fit for missionary labour' and of how such labour was best conducted.[38] Such exhortations indicate that female participation in the Protestant Christian missionary enterprise was seen as part of a broader transatlantic evangelical enterprise.

Pearce's 1838 description of Lowrie as a 'female missionary' was not the first use of missionary as a 'female noun' in a British publication. The term is also used in a memoir that is probably the earliest missionary memoir of a British-born woman: the memoir of Elizabeth Harvard, written by her husband W.M. Harvard, one of the first Wesleyan Methodist missionaries in Ceylon. Originally published in 1825, this had run into a third edition by 1833. Her husband's presentation of Elizabeth's life focuses less on her wifely role than on her role as a 'female missionary' who 'had the honour to be the first female who *put* her *hand to the plough*' of the Ceylon Mission. Harvard also ascribes to his wife many of the qualities of character that were seen to mark out heroic missionary men in both memoir and fiction. He comments on Elizabeth's 'noble and adventurous spirit' and records the 'zeal and firmness' with which she overcame her father's opposition to her decision to become a missionary's wife. That this strength of character could lead to actions which challenged conventional gender roles is vividly conveyed in his account of their marriage: when her father tries to avoid giving his daughter away, she takes him by the arm in the chapel and she leads him to the alter!

The memoir also records that, after the Harvards arrived in Colombo in 1814, despite coping with four pregnancies, the loss of two children in infancy and bouts of illness and depression, Elizabeth accompanied her husband on his missionary excursions around the island, learned Singhalese and superintended the female departments of Sunday and Day schools catering for over 160 pupils. The memoir stresses that she forged links with her 'missionary sisters', giving a picture of a missionary network bound together not only through family ties, but also through close friendships among women. Her husband also quotes Elizabeth's letters and diary to show 'the admirable blendings [*sic*] of a public and private spirit in her character', her combination of missionary ardour with sensitivity to domestic relationships.[39]

The sense that female missionary work was a public role rather than simply a private wifely duty is also strongly conveyed in the 1829 memoir of Margaret Clough, wife of another early Wesleyan Methodist missionary in Ceylon. Her husband comments in the text that it was rare for such a young women to 'attain the same height in public life … as she did as the wife of a missionary', while extracts from his wife's diary express her alarm at 'entering into such a public sphere of life'. The introduction to the text, by a male family friend, stresses the importance when selecting candidates for foreign missionary work of checking not only their own qualifications, but also whether their wives were qualified to be real helpmeets. This highlights the way in which missionary societies were beginning formally to recognise the role of missionary wives as crucial to the success of their husbands.[40]

The Rev. William Ellis, in his 1835 memoir of his first wife Mary, followed Harvard's 1825 memoir of his wife in presenting Mary as a 'female missionary' and in stressing her close collaboration with her 'sister missionaries' – though, significantly, he reserved the title of Missionary with a capital 'M' for male employees of the London Missionary Society, like himself, signalling an upholding of gender differentiation on the basis of professional status. William presents Mary as an active promoter of domestic values among the indigenous women of Tahiti. This role was, as Anna Johnston has discussed, was particularly crucial in the context of the London Missionary Society's Polynesian mission, where outward signs, such as bonnet wearing by women, were read as crucial evidence of the veracity of islanders' claims of conversion.[41] As secretary of the London Missionary Society, Ellis was a highly influential figure who, in producing this memoir, gave important endorsement to the concept of public recognition of the lives and work of missionary wives, stressing evidence of the salutary influence of the biographies of other missionary wives in promoting 'the interests of missions abroad'.[42]

Ellis refers specifically to the two early memoirs of American missionary wives discussed above, those of Harriet Newell and Anna Judson; and the impact of these early American memoirs in encouraging British women to take up missionary work is further evidenced in the Rev. T. Middleditch's 1839 memoir of his daughter Mary Ann Hutchins, wife of a Baptist missionary at Savanna-la-Mar in Jamaica. Hutchins records 'reading, or rather re-reading Harriet Newell and Mrs Judson' as she decides to become a missionary. Writing to ask her father's permission to marry, she simultaneously confesses her devotion to missionary work and signals her determination to become a missionary wife: 'my dear Parents, duty calls, and great as is the sacrifice, your child must go'. She stresses that she acts not 'from attachment to an earthly object' but from 'desire to promote the glory of that Saviour who died for me'. While acknowledging at the end of her letter that she would, of course, obey her father if he cannot give his consent to her plan, the tone of the rest of the letter is less that of the self-effacing female of much evangelical prescriptive literature than that of the stern male missionary Rivers, who puts religious duty before love in his marriage proposal to Jane Eyre. Despite his initial reluctance to allow her to become a missionary wife, her bereaved father later showed his pride in his determined daughter through compiling her memoir, which, in another example of the use of missionary as a 'female noun,' he entitled *The Youthful Female Missionary*.[43]

A similar stress on female agency is evident in the lengthy memoir of Margaret Wilson by her husband the Rev. John Wilson, employed by the Scottish Missionary Society in Bombay. Published in 1838, the memoir records that in the seven years before her death, as well as fulfilling her wifely duties – providing John with invaluable support by conducting the secular side of the mission, and advising and encouraging him in his work – she had started six schools for 'native females' with a total of 120 scholars, trained teachers, set up a school for destitute girls, and formed close links with the local Indian community through welcoming visitors, visiting homes and learning Marathi to the level where she was able to translate and to write papers for local periodicals.[44] A woman, the text suggested, could be both a supportive missionary wife and make major independent contributions to the development of girls' education; she could foster links to the indigenous community both through acting as hostess in the private sphere and through public engagements with indigenous male cultural institutions.

Such individual memoirs continued through the 1840s and into the second half of the nineteenth century. From 1839 onwards, however, a new development in the genre occurred, with the publication of collective memoirs of missionary women, generally edited by female promoters of missions rather than male missionaries. The earliest of these was *Memoirs of Female Labourers in the Missionary Cause*, by an anonymous female author. It was the first text to celebrate the lives and work of missionaries' wives as a group, and its title conveyed the sense of female collectivity, contrasting with the titles of the individual memoirs discussed above, which identified women through association with their missionary husbands. The text also transcended denominational boundaries, reflecting the sense of pan-evangelical solidarity among missionary women that characterised the operations of the FES. Expressing regret that missionaries' wives were so little known, with the exception of Mrs Newell, Mrs Judson, Mrs Ellis, Mrs Wilson, Mrs Leslie and Mrs Smith (subjects of the individual memoirs discussed above), it profiles seven other women of various denominations who 'hazarded their lives for the sake of Lord Jesus' in India, in the West India, in Sierra Leone and in Greenland, in the hope that their example would 'enkindle a like missionary spirit' in readers, and suggested the purchase of batches of the text for distribution to young women and in Sunday schools. The profile of Mrs Dawson, wife of a missionary in Travancore, echoed earlier memoirs in indicating that women did not simply passively follow husbands into the foreign field, but rather could be instrumental in persuading male relatives to become missionaries, or could deliberately select missionaries as husbands because they themselves wanted to engage in the missionary project:

> Her desire to do good to souls was very great; and, having a cherished wish to make known the gospel to the heathen ... she diligently attended the Central School in York, with the hope that thus qualified, by learning the National System of Education, she would be enabled to labour among the females of India ... if a way in providence was opened for her going thither. These desires were granted about a year afterwards, and with her husband and the brother whose conversion she had been made the honoured means of, she left England for the East Indies, under the patronage of the Church Missionary Society.[45]

This group memoir was followed by the publication in 1841 of Jemima Thompson's *Memoirs of British Female Missionaries*. Adopting a more assertive tone than of the 'authoress' of the earlier work, she prefaced her text with a strong assertion that 'missionary biography ought not ... be limited to ... laborious and apostolic men'. While the earlier memoirs discussed above indicate that this had not, in fact, been entirely the case, official publications of the missionary societies had continued to marginalise women. Thompson's father was a member of the committee of the London Missionary Society, and her text can be read as a riposte to the patriarchal tone of the recently published *The Fathers and Founders of the London Missionary Society*, which, as its title suggests, celebrated the leading men associated with the London Missionary Society while ignoring female contributions to the work of the society.[46]

Thompson's group memoir commemorated the work of 16 women, mainly missionary wives (including Harvard, Ellis and Wilson and two of the wives featured in *Memoirs of Female Labourers*), but also included three single women educationalists. One of these was Hannah Kilham, the Quaker whose educational work among freed slaves in Sierra Leone had already been celebrated in a memoir compiled by her daughter-in-law Sarah Biller in 1837.[47] Another was Miss Bird, who, having joined her widowed (non-missionary) brother in Bengal in 1823, independently set up schools for native girls and visited Hindu women in their own homes, continuing the work after her brother's death and demonstrating the possibility for women to undertake such work regardless of lack of official backing. The third was Miss Smith, one of the early agents of the FES in Bombay, and to her biographical entry Thompson appended some general information on the society, together with a list of the single women it had sent out to India and elsewhere.

Thompson's text, however, was much more than a set of memoirs: it was a kind of manifesto promoting female missionary endeavour. It opened with a long essay on 'the importance of female agency in evangelizing pagan nations', possibly authored by FES founder Baptist W. Noel, and this was followed by Thompson's own extensive 'survey of the condition of women in heathen countries'. The introductory essay lamented that many girls 'spend several years of the most valuable part of their lives in a kind of restless indolence' and argued that 'had they before them some great and benevolent object, such as taking a share in the regeneration of the world they would be much happier, and much more amiable'.[48] Such a religious vocation could offer single women an alternative to what Rivers presents to Jane Eyre as a life in Britain of 'selfish ease' and 'barren obscurity'.[49]

Female missionary memoirs published in Britain from 1815 onwards thus established that 'missionary' could be a 'female' as well as a 'male' noun. They created a feminised form of 'Christian psychobiography' that effectively set up missionary wives as inspiring examples to other women, possessed of many of the same qualities of character for which male missionary heroes were celebrated, occupying a crucial public position within the missionary enterprise, and working with their 'missionary sisters' as well as their husbands as part of a broader Christian family. By 1839, such women began to acquire a collective group identity in addition to their identification with their husbands, and independent female missionary agency also began to be publicly commemorated. When Emma Raymond Pitman published her widely read *Heroines of the Mission Field* in 1880, many of the women she chose to include had been active in the early nineteenth century, indicating how these women were held up as role models to later generations of missionary women.[50]

Jemima Thompson Luke's personal memoir and the obstacles to single women's missionary agency

Thompson's memoir of her own life illustrates both the attraction of missionary work to pious young women and just how difficult it was for single women to overcome familial objections to their working overseas. It is considered in some detail here because it throws interesting light on the family dynamics of gendered power within the missionary movement, on the vocational attraction of missionary work to intensely religious single middle-class women, and on the way in which such a calling led women to push against the boundaries of what was acceptable for women.

Thompson recalls how, as a young woman, she imagined a missionary future for herself in quasi-maternal terms. It would be hard to 'bear the separation from one's native land and loving relatives at home' but she had heard 'missionary women with beaming eyes talk of the loving relations between themselves and their adopted children in India'. If a woman had no children of her own, then it seemed her Christian duty to 'bring up some of the motherless and miserable'; to create a new home in India through gathering together 'a few of these friendless, gentle, guiltless victims of a cruel faith and cruel customs under the happy shelter of a Christian home, to convey to them the knowledge of a Saviour's love'.[51] In conjuring up a cross-cultural family that a single English woman has the power to create for herself, without the need for a husband, Thompson provides a powerful vision of Christian women's agency in the British Empire. Here is a feminised 'Christian psychobiography' that can be counter-posed to the picture of the militant masculinity of St John Rivers, who is described in the closing chapter of *Jane Eyre* as engaging in his missionary work with 'the sternness of the warrior Greatheart' and 'the ambition of the high master-spirit' sharing in 'the last mighty victories of the Lamb'.[52]

Jemima was raised in a well-to-do middle-class family steeped in evangelical missionary zeal. Her father was a supporter of the Bible Society, assisted in founding the Sunday School Union and the Home Missionary Society, supported the work of the early Baptist missionaries in Serampore, became a committee member of the London Missionary Society in 1827 and held missionary parties at home that were attended by leading London Missionary Society missionaries, including John Williams, William Ellis and Robert Moffat.

The Thompsons attended the services and Bible classes of the leading Evangelical preacher the Rev. Baptist William Noel at just the time he was involved in setting up the Female Education Society. Jemima became friends with one of its first committee members, Anna Braithwaite, a Quaker 'to whom having been brought up among "the Friends", the idea of feminine agency was not a new one'. She became a supporter of the society and was involved in interviewing its candidates for missionary work. Influenced by her Quaker friend, she became convinced that 'there was a great field for Christian women to occupy', and that there was plenty in the Bible to support female agency, and she longed to become directly involved in the work herself.[53] Her account of Anna's influence suggests the radicalising potential for women of involvement in interdenominational organisations, which brought them into contact with members of the Society of Friends among which female ministry was fully accepted. Quaker women, including Hannah Kilham and other members of the ladies' committee of the British and Foreign School Society, had been prominent in the earliest initiatives to organise and engage in 'native female education'.[54]

Nevertheless, Jemima remained the dutiful daughter and, following the death of her mother in 1837, she focused on her familial duties as eldest daughter. However, her father's remarriage in 1839 (to Noel's sister) changed her circumstances: she lost a demanding but probably also fulfilling role in the family. Looking back on this point of her life from the vantage point of old age, she stated: 'The force of providential circumstances seemed suddenly to have placed my life before me – and the question what I should do with it'. Interestingly, the idea of finding a husband does not figure in her retrospective account of her deliberations. Instead, it was whether or not she should resign herself to spending her time in comfort and trivial pursuits at home: 'reading interesting books, writing chatty letters to friends, receiving and paying calls, doing Berlin wool-work, and making wax and paper flowers as then in vogue, and knitting babies' socks and antimacassars for bazaars'. She wondered whether this was 'a satisfactory life for an immortal being, or a meet offering for him to whom I owed my all?', given that she was 'in the prime of life, with an excellent constitution, untiring energy, and years spent in mental cultivation'.[55] This sense of herself as physically strong, highly motivated and intellectually self-confident is at odds with the stereotype of middle-class women at this period as frail, dependent and having only an 'ornamental' education. The end result of her deliberations was a resolve to go out to work in female education in India.

According to her memoir, Thompson's father was initially very supportive of her plan. He urged her to become an agent of the London Missionary Society, volunteering to cover the costs of her outfit, passage and allowance – an undertaking that would have overcome any objections the society might have to paying a salary to a woman. He also found a missionary couple willing to act as her surrogate family: she was to travel to India with Mr and Mrs Crisp, missionaries at Bangalore, and work in the schools for girls set up by Mrs Crisp.[56]

While Thompson in her memoir describes this plan to send a single woman out under the auspices of one of the major missionary societies as unprecedented, in fact this was not so: in 1826 the London Missionary Society had appointed Maria Newell to superintend the female department of the Malacca Free School and to promote Chinese female education as part of the society's 'Ultra Ganges Mission' in Britain's newly created Straits Settlements. Newell married the Rev. Karl Gutzlaff, formerly a missionary of the Netherlands Missionary Society, and left the service of the London Missionary Society after two years, although continuing missionary work with her husband; she died in 1831 whilst travelling with her husband through Siam/Thailand.[57]

Jemima recorded that her father's active support was tremendously important, enabling her to withstand opposition from friends and relatives to the idea of a single woman undertaking such work. However, after undertaking training as an infant school teacher she became very ill. Given her stress on her earlier robust health and lack of subsequent mentions of illness in her memoir, the timing of this illness suggests a possible psychological dimension. Her father immediately withdrew his consent to her departure for the missionary field. While this was doubtless based on real concern about her ability to withstand the rigours of travel to and work in India, it is clear from her memoir that he was also having second thoughts about the propriety of the plan. When she told him that she was keen, instead, to take up an invitation to remain in London and become honorary secretary of the Female Education Society her father forbade this, saying she must return to live with him. Looking back in later life on his stance, she speculated that 'perhaps he almost unconsciously sympathised with the prejudice against the Female Education Society. Which in some quarters had been cynically called "The Batchelor's Aid Society"'. This referred to concerns that its agents often got married after a short time in the missionary field, a problem that the society itself acknowledged and tried to solve by instituting a system of financial penalties.

While she does not suggest this in her memoir, it is quite possible that wider events over the 1839–41 period influenced Thompson's father in his diminished enthusiasm for his daughter's involvement in independent philanthropic activities away from her family home. The World Anti-Slavery Convention in London in 1840 brought to Britain the controversy over women's rights that was splitting the American abolitionist movement. The Thompsons were Congregationalists and it was American Congregationalists who were most outspoken in their condemnation of the Quaker Angelina Grimké's public speeches in favour of anti-slavery and women's rights.[58]

Jemima Thompson was thus not able to implement her desire to engage directly in this maternal missionary enterprise, either as a female educator in the mission field in colonial India or as an organiser of single women's missionary enterprise from a base in the imperial metropole. Her memoir demonstrates how family constraints could stop even the most dedicated of single women from translating new visions of independent female agency into practice. The power of a father's control over unmarried daughters here becomes apparent – there is no suggestion in her memoir that she even considered defying his authority.[59]

Thompson's *Memoirs of British Female Missionaries* was published in 1841, which dates it to just after this crisis in her life. In her personal memoir she describes settling at the family home in Poundsford Park and starting to compose hymns, established as an acceptable female occupation by this time.[60] She also describes attending a meeting of a little local society that had been set up in aid of the Female Education Society – the hint of a rebellious gesture given her father's stance towards the organisation. Her *Memoirs of British Female Missionaries* can be read as an indirect, but public, questioning of her father's attitude to the society and to the patriarchal authority of the London Missionary Society leadership as a whole. It includes information of the Female Education Society's activities and a list of its agents. The text also included the following passage that, while probably authored by her new step-uncle, Baptist W. Noel, rather than herself, is so close to the sentiments that she later expressed in the memoir of her own life that it may well reflect her own feelings at this time:

> All human beings, whether they are men or women, require an object for which to live, i.e., not merely the grand object of preparation for the future life, but a subordinate and immediate one for the present. Women, a little removed from the humbler classes of society, commonly labour, in this respect, under a disadvantage not experienced by men. The latter have some profession on which to enter … but women, have none.[61]

With the chance for direct involvement in the female missionary enterprise overseas closed, Thompson was to find this 'object for which to live' through the more conventional and acceptable root of promoting home support for the foreign missionary enterprise, through her advocacy of female missionary agency, through her work with her father in promoting the work of the major male-led missionary societies, and through her publications encouraging children to support the cause: she edited a magazine called *The Missionary Repository for Youth* and wrote widely circulated *Missionary Stories* for children. In 1843, at the age of 30, she married a Congregational minister, the Rev. Samuel Luke, with whom she had three children. She maintained an interest in the plight of Indian women, ending her 1900 memoir with a plea to young single English women to help the still-suffering Hindu widow.[62]

Woman's mission, Christian privilege and imperial duty

How, then, were promoters of single women's missionary work able to create a vision of female missionary agency within an evangelical culture that is best known for prescribing subordinate and domestically focused roles for women?[63] As Frank Prochaska cautioned at the opening of his major study of nineteenth-century English female philanthropy, 'we are perhaps too prone to see limitations where the women of the past saw possibilities'.[64]

In this section, three main resources for this vision of female agency are examined. First, the internally contradictory nature of evangelical prescriptions for women, in particular the combination of expansive vision and constricting prescription contained within the notion of 'woman's mission'. Second, the central place accorded both in prescriptive tracts addressed at women and in missionary tracts promoting the conversion of the 'heathen' overseas to comparisons between the degraded position of 'heathen' women and the elevated position of Christian women. Third, the links made between Christian women's privileges and their duties to their less fortunate sisters in the context of assertions of Britain's imperial responsibilities as a Protestant Christian nation.

The concept of 'woman's mission' was central to nineteenth-century evangelical discourse about women's social roles. In her widely read 1839 tract of that name, Sarah Lewis claimed for Christian women 'no less an office than that of instruments (under God) for the regeneration of the world'. She described mothers as 'prime agents of God in the regeneration of mankind'; maternal love, 'the only purely unselfish feeling that exists on this earth', was a revelation of God's love, showing that he intended women 'for his missionaries upon earth'. She hastened to add, however, that this exalted mission should not entail moving beyond women's proper sphere: women should exert their influence primarily from their domestic base. Lewis herself acknowledged the seemingly 'inconsistent' and 'paradoxical' nature of her prescription for women: 'to recommend at the same time expansion of views and contraction of operation; to awaken the sense of power, and to require that the exercise of it be limited'. Framing her argument both as a riposte to 'the warmest advocates of the political rights of woman' and as an advance on earlier evangelical writers who stressed women's domestic duties, she claimed that women were men's moral and intellectual equals, but that their value and moral influence depended on self-renunciation rather than public usefulness.[65]

In Lewis's text, an exalted notion of woman's mission thus becomes a powerful advocacy of 'separate spheres': while she does not explicitly condemn women's missionary work, she sets herself against the kind of large-scale organised philanthropic and social reforming work by women that was emerging at this period.[66] Jemima Thompson and others, however, found scope for assertions of female public agency within the paradoxes of this concept of woman's mission. The call in Thompson's 1841 tract for British women to take 'a share in the regeneration of the world' perhaps consciously echoed the words of Lewis's tract.[67] However, in urging single women to travel overseas on a vocational educational mission, the text dramatically exceeds the constraints of the spare-time, voluntary and locally based philanthropy that Lewis deemed as marking the acceptable limits of women's activities beyond home and family.

Women's different but complementary qualities to men, which Lewis and others argued were best cultivated and utilised from a domestic base, were presented in Thompson's tract as particularly suiting them to missionary work among the heathen overseas. Indeed, they are seen as offering a valuable complement to those that men brought to the enterprise:

> If less capable of what is bold and hazardous in action, profound in thought, or laborious in investigation, they [women] possess a tenderness of feeling, a depth of compassion, a quickness of perception, and a forgetfulness of self, which are commonly found to less extent elsewhere. They appear also generally to manifest a greater facility for the acquisition of languages, as far as the mere power of conversation is concerned; and they can sooner adapt themselves to the prejudices, and win their way to the hearts, of those on whose welfare they are bent.[68]

In envisioning a 'woman's mission' that encompassed practical engagement in the missionary project overseas, advocates of 'native female education' also drew on another key aspect of evangelical discourse: its stress on the privileges of Christian women and the contrasting degradation of women in non-Christian cultures. This was a key feature of the evangelical prescriptive tracts aimed at British women that have been discussed in Chapter 1, and of the early missionary discourse aimed at gaining support for the expansion of missionary work overseas, discussed in Chapter 3. Indeed, some of the leading promoters of foreign missions were also among the leading writers of religious and prescriptive tracts addressed at British women. They included Francis Augustus Cox, who wrote the first history of the Baptist Missionary Society and who was the author of *Female Scripture Biography*, and Birmingham Congregationalist minister John Angell James, a prominent promoter of foreign missions and the author of *Female Piety*.[69]

When the FES took up the work of promoting single women's missionary agency, they were thus able to draw on an established evangelical discourse contrasting the lot of Christian and 'heathen' women. Developing on the earlier anti-*sati* appeals to women discussed in the previous chapter, they used this as the basis of their assertion of British women's duty towards their less privileged sisters:

> Wives, who are happy in the affectionate esteem of your husbands – mothers, who enjoy your children's reverence and gratitude – children, who have been blest by a mother's example and a mother's care – sisters, who have found in brothers your warmest friends – Christian women, who feel that you can lend to society its charm, and receive from it a loyal courtesy in return – protected, honoured, and loved – impart your blessings to those who are miserable, because they are without them.[70]

Indeed, women were presented as benefiting from Christianity even more than men and, thus, having an even *greater* duty to help the 'heathen'. Thompson's 1841 tract argues: 'if all Christians are bound to exert themselves in this cause, surely the obligation which rests on Christian women is fourfold! They, far more than men, owe to Christianity their present free and happy state – while it is on their sex that, in other lands, the hard bondage of heathenism presses with the heavier weight', and she ends her 'survey of the condition of women in heathen countries' with an appeal to British women, elevated by Christianity to 'their rightful station and dignity' to take action in the face of the 'present degradation of their sex in Pagan and Mohammedan countries'.[71]

Promoters of 'native' female education also articulated women's missionary duty as an imperial duty. Thompson expressed the hope that 'his glory may be promoted among all the tribes of mankind, particularly in our vast colonies, and among all denominations of Christians in the British empire!'[72] The FES presented women's earliest efforts in developing 'heathen' girls' education as their contribution to forwarding a paternalistic imperialist project: 'to aid the beneficent legislation of a paternal government, in the improvement of so large a population committed to our care ... these are the great objects which carried Mrs Wilson to the children of Hindostan, and Miss Wallace to those of China'.[73] The 1840 report of the Glasgow Association for Promoting Female Education in the East placed British women's missionary work as part of providential imperialism:

> Recognising the providence of God, what, we may safely ask, was His grand design in connecting Great Britain, a small island, as a distance of eight or ten thousand miles, with the immense empire of India, with its one hundred and thirty millions of people – an event unparalleled in the history of the world? ... Was it merely to further the interests of trade and of commerce – to supply us with a few more of the luxuries of this perishable life? Was it not rather to place us in the most favourable circumstances for communicating to millions of our fellow immortals the knowledge of the great salvation?[74]

Paradoxically, then, evangelical discourse, generally seen as encouraging women's confinement within the domestic sphere in Britain, could, through the marriage of concepts of woman's mission, Christian female privilege and providential imperialism, be deployed to create an expansive vision of independent British female agency on the global stage, enacting a maternalist Christian-imperial mission to 'heathen' women.

Surrogate mothers and orphan girls

This maternalist mission was particularly powerfully articulated around the surrogate mothering of the orphan 'heathen' girl. Scholarship on the Christian family within Britain's Protestant overseas missionary community in the nineteenth century has focused mainly on the role of the patriarchal family headed by the male missionary in modelling evangelical ideals of gender relations and domesticity to 'heathen' converts. However, within Britain's imperial

Christian community another family model also operated: all-female surrogate families headed by missionary women, providing institutional colonial homes for orphan girls from 'heathen' backgrounds, backed by sponsorship from British women based in both colony and metropole. This section explores the representations of these surrogate families within missionary discourse in early nineteenth-century Britain, and discusses the significance of this quasi-familial model to the envisioning of Britain's imperial Christian community.

Both missionary wives and single women educators were involved in setting up Christian orphanages for 'heathen' girls in India from the 1830s. They were in part humanitarian foundations aiming to take in abandoned, destitute and orphaned children. Mary Anne Cooke, for example, set up an orphanage in response to the floods and famine in Lower Bengal in 1832 and 1833.[75] However, they also marked the beginnings of a new focus for missionary women's energies in India. In keeping with the broader evangelical project of reforming society from the family outwards, female missionary educators had initially pursued a 'top-down' approach, attempting to reach high-caste girls from well-off and influential families who, they believed, could exert the greatest cultural influence both within their own family circles and on the wider society – witness Ward's ambitious hopes in 1820 of creating the future Hannah Mores and Elizabeth Frys of India (discussed in Chapter 3). However, they had little success in persuading parents to send these girls to day schools: lack of social exclusivity, the seclusion of upper-caste and upper-class girls, and objections to the explicitly Christian curriculum, together posed insuperable obstacles. From the mid-1850s, missionaries would attempt to address this problem by developing 'zenana' education within the homes of high-caste women. However, prior to this they continued to focus on schools, but these tended to attract girls from lower-caste, poor, and minority groups. Even these girls attended erratically and often left early to marry. By 1846 the report of the Calcutta Branch of the Scottish Ladies' Association for the Advancement of Female Education in India was describing the aims of day schools in rather despairing terms that did not even mention their evangelising purpose: 'to collect the female children of heathen parents in day schools, and give them the best plain education which their irregular attendance, early marriages, and other untoward circumstances will admit of'.[76]

Promoters of 'native' female education in colonial India thus increasingly pinned their hopes on perhaps the most socially marginal girls of all: destitute girls who were orphans or had been abandoned by their parents. Removed from indigenous society and placed under close supervision in missionary orphanages, these girls would be the easiest to bring under Christian influence. Ignoring the strength of class and caste divides on the Indian subcontinent, and reversing the previous top-down model of social transformation, British evangelicals hoped that orphan girls, brought up 'in the faith and practice of the religion of Christ' as well as ' in habits of domestic and general usefulness' could have a positive impact on wider society.[77] They could either become Christian teachers to 'heathen' children or 'exemplary wives to native Christians or native catechists' who, 'as the future mothers of Christian families', would 'set before the heathen, among whom they will dwell, an attractive example of domestic virtue, intelligence, and affection'.[78]

'True' tales of individual 'heathen' orphan girls were published in Britain to raise funds for these orphanages. Jemima Thompson Luke's set of illustrated *Missionary Stories*, aimed at British children and published between 1842 and 1844, included three stories of orphaned or abandoned 'heathen' girls: 'Hannah Kilpin', 'A Heathen Mother' and 'The History of Mary Gutzlaff'. In these tales the girls are rescued by British missionary women, given Christian first names and in some cases given the surnames of their 'adoptive' missionary family.[79]

A number of longer accounts represented such orphan girls as model Christian converts, fulfilling the hopes placed on them by supporters of missionary orphanages. In the Rev. Alexander Duff's *More Fruits from India; or, the outcast safe in Christ; the life and happy death of Charlotte Green, a poor orphan* (1848), addressed to the Sabbath School children of the Free Church of Scotland, a burial scene illustrates the front cover, and Charlotte's death-bed scene opens and concludes the text, placing it within the genre of evangelical tales of virtuous children who died young. Duff tells the story of this Indian orphan girl, brought up in the Calcutta Institution for Destitute Girls. He states that the child was handed over by an old woman who had probably bought or stolen her but then found her to be sickly. This scenario is presented as typical of heathen lands, which are racked by cruel practices fuelled by superstition, in contrast to Christian lands. Charlotte gains health and learns to read and speak English. She is described as loving reading the Bible and little Christian books such as Luke's *Missionary Stories* – an interesting indication of the way such tales were used in the education of 'heathen' girls themselves.[80]

A girl who lived long enough to fulfil this missionary orphan destiny is the subject of Mrs Weitbrecht, *An Indian blossom which bore fruit. A memoir of Rabee, who died at Burdwan, December, 1848*, published by the Female Education Society for the benefit of the school at Burdwan. This is the tale of a Hindu orphan convert who becomes a schoolteacher and marries a native Christian. One of the orphans created by the floods and famine of 1834, she is taken in to the orphanage run by Mrs Weitbrecht and then allowed to accompany the missionary family when they depart for Europe, acting as a carer for their children and then training at the Home and Colonial Institution in London, where she is financially supported by the FES. She then returns with the Weitbrechts to Burdwan in 1844, where she begins her duties as an infant school teacher.[81]

The text provides a rare transcription of an orphan convert's own words, quoting from a letter she writes to her old school mistress in England, telling her about another girl who converted before her death, and about the violence and punishments in India that show 'how wicked heathenism is'. Clearly, she had internalised the very negative missionary discourse about 'heathen' India.

However, in terms of personal relationships, she shows a keen awareness of the limits of the surrogate mothering provided by British missionary women. Explaining that she is now married to a native Christian who teaches at the English school, she voices her sadness that her own mother was not at the ceremony. While she expresses gratitude that 'my kind benefactor and benefactress stood by me in the place of my parents' – a reference to the Weibrechts – it is two of her Indian relatives by marriage that, as Mrs Weitbrecht herself acknowledges in the text, she regarded as a father and mother because of their kindness to her. It is in this native Christian community, linked with but not identical to the missionary community, that this orphan girl finds a stable home.[82]

In her account, Mrs Weitbrecht praises Rabee's 'earnest concern for the improvement and spiritual welfare of the orphan girls'. This improvement was closely linked to the example of her self-presentation: 'her clean, neat, simple costume' is stressed, and 'the good effect her correct and tidy habits produced upon her young companions, most of whom are not patterns of propriety in these matter'. Weitbrecht suggests that English schoolchildren 'can little imagine the dirty, uncouth appearance of those of their own rank in a heathen country, who are in no degree under Christian influence, or who have but lately come under it'. Here, rather than suggesting parallels between the working-class girl at home and the heathen girl overseas, the suggestion is that, when class distinctions are taken out of the equation, there remains a gulf between the two that can only be bridged by the spread of Christianity. That this gulf was cultural rather than racial, and quite possible to overcome through the creation of a global Christian community, is signalled in the text by Weitbrecht's stress on how impressed British visitors were with her school: 'One of the clergymen said that her infant school was equal in appearance and efficient management to any they had ever seen in Europe: indeed, that they could perceive no other differences than that arising from the tawny colour of the little ones'. Such statements are marked by both an assertion of racial difference and a denial of its significance. Weitbrecht concluded on an optimistic note: 'May the Lord raise up many of Bengal's deeply degraded daughters, to become, like her, ornaments of believers, and a crown of rejoicing to his ministering servants!'[83]

Similar success was trumpeted by the Free Church of Scotland in reference to the orphan refuge run in Calcutta by Miss Laing, catering for around 30 orphaned and destitute girls aged from 3 to 16 from Hindu, Muslim and 'mixed-race' backgrounds, together with three 'Jewesses'. The transformation of these girls, most of whom had been 'rescued from infamy and ruin', is presented as manifested in their behaviour and demeanour. One girl, who had been sold as a slave and branded with the word 'thief', was at first violent, intractable and wild, but is now subdued. Scottish women supporters of the orphanage are informed of the contrast between the girls' backgrounds and their present 'happy, cheerful countenances' that are 'the very emblems of contentment, and expanding intelligence, and prospective moral and social worth'. Drawing on a resonant mid-nineteenth-century image of well-ordered English domestic-ity, the orphanage is likened to 'a well-cultured garden' set in the midst of 'moral waste'.[84]

This sense of order is also conveyed in descriptions of the orphans' lives: they are divided into five classes with a structured day timetabled from daybreak to evening worship. Their work combines the domestic and the academic, encom-passing useful needlework, washing and cooking, reading, English language, knowledge of the Bible and catechism, and geography. The aim is to form mind and character and inculcate 'habits of domestic economy and usefulness' and in so doing to 'to overcome and eradicate the apathy and sluggishness so inherent in the natives of this land'. Such domestic habits are felt to be 'of immense importance by way of example and contrast to Heathen neighbours'. Success stories are provided to illustrate the potential of orphan girls to help transform Indian society. Two girls have married Christian converts: 'In this way the Christian principles inculcated on the mind of the helpless orphan may become the seed plot of superior usefulness in the bosom of a Christian family'. Another girl has become a teacher, at a good salary: 'Let us hail this as an earnest of better days, when India's rescued and enlightened daughters shall become the instructresses of their still benighted countrywomen'.[85]

The actual process of conversion of orphan girls was something to which great importance was attached. It was not enough simply to bring up the girls in the Christian faith. A letter from Alexander Duff published in the magazine *The Home and Foreign Missionary Record for the Free Church of Scotland* in 1847 included the transcript of an account from a Bengali magazine of the baptism of seven orphan children, with the information that the girls had spontaneously applied for admission into the church following a powerful service conducted by Duff. In a following report, Duff commented on the continued work of grace among the inmates of the orphan institution, commenting: 'those lately baptized had for months manifested deep heart-concern for their sins of word and deed – but especially of *heart*-sins'. There is a stress here on genuineness of conversion, and on true religion as being a matter of the heart not just the head, an approach central to evangelical Protestantism.[86] Duff's accounts convey some sense of the pressure exerted on girls to convert in the intensely Christian surrogate home of the orphanage, but also suggest the space for the girls' agency provided by the importance attached to conversions being heartfelt and not superficial. In addition, the simultaneous conversions of several girls hint at a sense of collectivity among the orphans, despite their different ethnic, religious and caste backgrounds. Recent scholarship has stressed the importance of not underestimating Indian women's own agency in converting to Christianity in India, and missionary orphanages clearly offered destitute girls not only the chance of survival, but also rare opportunities for education and a respectable future as either self-supporting teachers or wives of converts.[87]

British women who were home supporters of foreign missions were encouraged to sponsor individual orphan girls. Orphan girls were thus pro-vided with two kinds of temporary surrogate mothers within the imperial

Christian community: missionary women who ran orphanages in colonial India and British women supporters of missions at home.[88] By 1858, concerns were being voiced about the practice of British women wanting to rename the orphans they sponsored. The concern, however, was not about the cultural violence involved in the imposition of completely new identities on the girls, but rather the fear that it might contribute to making them less valuable to carrying forward the missionary project. The Rev. John Pourie warned that: 'there is at present in Calcutta ... a very strong *Anglifying* tendency among native Christians, which, if not carefully watched and kept in check, may very much diminish their influence in favour of Christianity'. He elaborated: 'it is with difficulty sometimes that we can get our Christian girls to acquire and keep up any adequate knowledge of their own native tongue, they are inclined to look on it as *vulgar* to talk in it. ... And thus they unfit themselves for usefulness afterwards among the sunken heathen masses of their native countrywomen'.[89]

Pourie's comments are suggestive of the contradictions within the female missionary educators' global Christian project. As surrogate mothers of orphaned Indian girls, they wished to bring up these girls to share their religion, their language and their cultural values. However, if these girls became too like themselves – Indian in appearance but English in culture, to paraphrase Thomas Babington Macaulay's expression of his aspirations for elite Indian men in the 1830s – then there was a danger that they would not be able to perform their assigned role within the imperial Christian community as mediators between indigenous 'heathen' society and British missionaries, whether as teachers or as model wives and mothers.

The report also suggests that even the most intense forms of missionary cultural imperialism, directed at that most powerless of colonial subject groups, orphan girls, was unable to erase subaltern agency completely. Despite being brought up within the institutional confines of the Christian orphan home, named after and imbued with the beliefs and values of British evangelical women, these surrogate Indian daughters did not always think or act in precisely the ways their missionary mothers prayed for. These difficulties of the female missionary enterprise were, however, only intermittently acknowledged in missionary propaganda. The cover of *The Female Missionary Intelligencer*, in the form of a composite visual image of well-dressed Indian, Chinese and African mothers instructing their children to read and to pray, papered over the immense difficulties involved in the translation of missionary aspiration into reality in the foreign field.[90]

Preaching, teaching and the limits of female evangelism overseas

In the familial imagery of the missionary movement, the missionary woman as surrogate mother of the heathen child complemented that of the male missionary as father of the mission. Similarly, the female missionary teacher complemented the male missionary preacher. If mothering and fathering are, by definition, gender-distinct roles, however, the divide between teaching and preaching was not as clearly demarcated. Men and women shared the designation of 'evangelist': both brought the word of the gospel to the 'heathen'. In addition, it was recognised that women could reach sectors of the 'heathen' population who were inaccessible to men, replacing rather than simply complementing the work of the male evangelist. The *Missionary Register* of 1815 included a 'Call on British females', in the form of a letter addressed to the secretary of the Church Missionary Society, purportedly from an Indian woman of Christian parentage, which urged British women to bring the word of the gospel to women in *purdah* who could not benefit from the preaching of male missionaries.[91]

Female teaching in the foreign mission field could also take a form that was almost indistinguishable from preaching. W.M. Harvard's 1824 memoir of his wife Elizabeth, who worked alongside him in the Wesleyan Methodist mission in Ceylon, records that, when accompanying him on his missionary excursions around the island: 'such was the ardour of her soul for the conversions of those benighted idolators' that she made use of their interpreter to say something to them herself regarding Christianity. Aware that this suggested she was preaching, he hastened to add, 'she never, indeed, conceived that the occupation of the pulpit fell within her line of duty'. Writing at a time when Wesleyans were debating the propriety of female preaching, he clarified: 'Whatever she might have conceded, in that respect, to the peculiar impressions of duty professed by others, her own views of female obligation, led to a different conclusion with respect to herself'. In other words, she did not condemn other women for preaching, but felt it was not her role to do so. Rather, she saw teaching as an appropriate substitute: 'yet, she was apt to *teach*; and with a heart overflowing with the most unaffected love for her race, she generally acted – in a humbler mode – under a sense of duty to impart what little she knew of divine things to any one whom she had reason to suspect had less knowledge of them than herself'. Here, the term 'teach' seems to encompass more than schooling and to refer more broadly to the verbal outpouring of Christian knowledge. In adopting this evangelising role among men and well as women she justified it as appropriate in the particular circumstance of foreign missionary work: 'in a heathen land, she felt perfectly at liberty to act on this principle'. Her husband endorsed her stance: 'she was never more truly amiable, than when thus employed'.[92]

Mary Ann Wilson (*née* Cooke), the first single woman Christian educator in India, shared this belief that female evangelism need not be entirely confined to a woman's mission to women: they might also been instruments for the conversion of men. In a letter dated February 1835, published as an appendix to a sermon by the Rev. Baptist Noel on behalf of the FES, she argues that women are 'as much required as Missionaries, and may be as useful in evangelising these pagan countries'. For 'true, they would come forth in the first instance to teach children, but by no means stop there. They would also endeavour to use every opportunity of giving religious instruction to adults, whether male or female'.[93]

It is interesting to read the quotes above in the context of Keinzle and Walker's recent study of female preaching through two millennia of Christianity. They point out 'how closely religious teaching approximates preaching' and show 'how the boundaries between the two could be purposely blurred to create a space for female voices'. However, they also note that such moves were counteracted by attempts to sharpen boundaries between male and female religious activity by asserting a narrow definition of preaching that confined it to the sermons delivered by authorised clerics in the context of a formal religious service.[94]

Just such a contest over boundaries took place over the role of the FES and the question of female evangelists in a public exchange in 1836–7 in the pages of the *Christian Lady's Magazine*, an influential monthly periodical edited by the popular religious writer Charlotte Elizabeth Phelan (afterwards, Tonna). The exchange provides insights into the tussle over the line between unacceptable and acceptable spheres of female missionary endeavour and shows how the question of single women and missions was part of a broader struggle within British society to define the limits of women's sphere.

Charlotte Elizabeth, an Evangelical Anglican, a Tory, a supporter of anti-slavery and a strong advocate of factory reform to improve the plight of labouring women, was herself the author of the first piece on the FES to appear in the magazine.[95] Publicising the formation of the society to help 'our poor eastern sisters', she argued that this work was becoming an important branch of missionary work among the heathen, and gave the employment of single women as Christian educators important mainstream endorsement as a 'truly Christian, truly feminine undertaking'.[96]

The following year saw the publication in the *Christian Lady's Magazine* of an article by 'Lydia', a supporter of the FES. She began by stressing the powerful influence, for good or ill, of women on the nature of society in all nations. Then, drawing the attention of young Christian women to the terrible situation of 'millions of their sisters in the east', she urged them to go over and help those pioneering women who were already labouring to bring them to Christ. While 'hitherto it has been chiefly the allotment of Christian women to work for their Lord and Master in the quiet and unobtrusive walks of domestic privacy', women were now being called 'to do the work of an evangelist', which she defined as 'proclaiming the glad tidings of salvation'. Here, female evangelism is presented as public speaking rather than simply teaching, though the term preaching is not explicitly used. While presenting this as a break from the past, as a new call from the Lord rather than something justified by Biblical precedent, 'Lydia' also presented it as fulfilling woman's God's allotted role for women to be 'an help meet for man'. This attempt to place her call within the acceptable bounds of an auxiliary and supportive role was, however, contradicted by the tone of much of her appeal. She presented female evangelism in a heroic and glorious light: an opportunity for women 'to distinguish themselves in the eyes of the great Captain of Salvation, and win from him a far more exceeding and eternal weight of glory'. In a final rousing passage, she urged women to 'resolve, that if the hands of woman were foremost to pluck of the tree of knowledge of good and evil those hands also shall be foremost to plant that tree of life which is for the healing of the nations, in every quarter of the globe which "sin unto death" yet reigns in unmitigated bitterness'.

A great sense of the power of women is conveyed in Lydia's text, and a direct challenge to male supremacy – far from simply men's helpers, women have the capacity to be 'foremost' in spreading Christianity. This is female 'Christian psychobiography' presented more in the language used to describe the male missionary hero in *Jane Eyre* than in the more acceptable evangelical language of separate spheres and feminine self-effacement. 'Lydia' seems to be claiming a full missionary role for women, encompassing preaching as well as teaching.[97] That Charlotte Elizabeth was willing to give space to this radical vision of female missionary agency in her magazine is interesting, suggesting she did not consider it completely out of line with mainstream evangelical thinking.

However, immediate criticism of the tone of Lydia's article came in the form of a letter from 'G.H.G'. The author asserted that 'I cannot see any ground for supposing that the work of an 'evangelist' (that is, a professed teacher of the gospel) is in any manner suited to a female'. For a woman to be a missionary's wife was acceptable, but anything more went beyond her sphere as delineated in the Scriptures: 'The whole tenor of Scripture leads me to believe that women's path, with very few exceptions, in intended to be a retiring, unobtrusive one, and that, when unsupported by a husband's countenance, missionary labours are out of her sphere of duty'. Religious philanthropic work by single women was fine if undertaken in a private capacity close to home: 'I am very far from asserting that single as well as married women ought not zealously to do their utmost to win souls to Christ, but then it must be in a *private*, not a *public* capacity, in their own neighbourhood, among the poor and ignorant'. In contrast, if a woman were to 'throw off that "shamefacedness" which ought to adorn her, and sally forth alone to distant lands, as a missionary' then she would not only be acting outside her sphere but also 'shocking the deep-rooted prejudices of those she most wishes to conciliate'. In other words, her work was not only inappropriate, but also unlikely to be effective because it would alienate gender norms in distant lands – an interesting line of criticism, given that missionaries claimed they wished to reform rather than condone indigenous gender relations![98]

This seems a powerful condemnation of single women's work in the missionary field, and the closing passage of the letter, approvingly quoting the opinion of an unnamed public figure that 'women in the present day take too prominent a part in religious societies', can be read in this context as hostility not only to the FES, but also to organised female philanthropy more broadly. Interestingly, though, while drawing attention to those passages in the Bible that stressed wives' duties to husbands as providing guidelines for the role of women in the church, the author also drew on Biblical precedent to suggest the possibility of a wider role for small numbers of exceptional women:

> There have been, and still are, 'Mothers in Israel', who, like Deborah of old, are honoured as instruments of public usefulness in the great Redeemer's hand: but these appear to me *exceptions*, to the general rule; and I cannot but think that an exhortation to women, to cast off the retiring modesty of their sex, and to put themselves forward even in so good a cause as the conversion of the heathen, is likely to prove anything but beneficial to them.[99]

The space is thus left open for individual single women with a true religious calling to become public evangelists overseas – and the author does not even explicitly restrict that role to the teaching of girls and women along the lines promoted by the FES. Indeed, the reference to 'exceptional' women echoes the language of Wesley's early qualified condoning of female preaching. What starts as a reactionary condemnation of a wider role for women thus turns into a willingness to question any all-encompassing prescription of women's sphere.

The FES's own attitude to the designation and role of its women educators was a cautious one. G.H.G.'s letter in the *Christian Lady's Magazine* prompted a response in a letter to the editor from 'J.S.' that probably represents the organisation's official line. Defending the work of the FES and its female educators, it sought to reassure readers of the journal by presenting a narrow interpretation of Lydia's call to women to do 'the work of an evangelist', claiming that she did not mean that women should do 'unfeminine' work by taking on the role of (male) missionaries, who travelled around preaching to large crowds. The author also claimed that the work of the FES's agents took the form of teaching undertaken unobtrusively under the protection of resident missionary families.[100] Already pushing the boundaries of appropriate activity for women, and depending for success in the field on cooperation with the main missionary societies, it clearly did not wish to be seen as directly challenging existing hierarchies within the movement.

Female missionary agency and feminism

Returning, then, to the apparently straightforward question posed in the title to this chapter: could women be missionaries in the early nineteenth century? The evidence of early female missionary memoirs shows that, contra Cunningham, missionary was *not* an exclusively 'male noun' at this period, despite the fact that foreign missionary societies only directly employed men as missionaries. Their authors publicly celebrated missionaries' wives as female missionaries, giving their work public recognition, despite its lack of formal status. What Spivak labels 'Christian psychobiography' was not, as she suggests, an exclusively masculine discourse in early nineteenth-century Britain.

The organised female philanthropy that developed in early nineteenth-century Britain combined the domestic-focused with the foreign, and especially imperially, orientated. Whereas organising support for working-class girls' education within the nation was widely accepted as an appropriate role for middle-class women, the sending of single women overseas to work as Christian educators among the 'heathen' pushed the boundaries of acceptable activity for respectable women. In establishing such work as legitimate, evangelical women were able to exploit the openings offered by contradictions within early evangelical discourse on women, and to bring together concepts of women's mission, Christian women's privilege and providential imperialism to create an expansive vision of female imperial social mission.

The presence of such single women in the mission field from the 1820s onwards suggests that Charlotte Brontë could have ascribed to Jane Eyre independent agency as a 'soul maker' and participant in 'imperial social mission'. She could have created a female version of the 'Christian psychobiography' she narrated for Rivers and presented Jane as a zealous participant in, and brave martyr to, the cause. That she did not opt to do so can be read not as a reflection of the limited possibilities for female missionary agency in early nineteenth-century Britain, but rather as Bronte's conscious authorial choice to prioritise the reform of English domesticity at home over the feminising of imperial mission overseas.

What, then, is the relationship between the representations of female missionary agency discussed in this paper and what Spivak labels a 'nascent feminist scenario' and what was the link with 'imperial social mission'? Susan Thorne has coined the term 'missionary-imperial feminism' to describe the approach of nineteenth-century British women missionaries; however, I think that this term rather obscures the complexities of the triangular relationship between missionaries, imperialism and feminism.[101] Early promoters of female missionary activity were certainly not advocates of liberal feminist individualism. These women did not openly challenge patriarchal male authority or 'separate spheres' ideology, and they did not call for social equality or civic rights either for themselves or for the 'heathen' women and girls towards whom they directed their missionary zeal. However, early nineteenth-century British missionary women did carve out both psychological and institutional spaces for female missionary agency. They did so by articulating a distinctive female imperial mission that implicitly challenged hegemonic understandings of the natures and appropriate roles of white middle-class women, extending the concept of social motherhood onto the imperial stage while promoting the spread of the evangelical ideology of domesticity to 'heathen' women in the empire. Promoters of single women's foreign missionary work held out to pious evangelical women the possibility of a vocation that combined self-sacrifice with self-fulfilment, and which called for both those qualities of character deemed feminine and those more usually associated with men. The circumstances of work in the imperial mission field also opened up opportunities to women to engage in an evangelism that blurred the lines between teaching and preaching, during precisely the period when women were largely excluded from preaching at home.

Empire could, indeed, offer a field of both imagined and actual opportunity for evangelical white British women, and the foreign missionary movement drew women into active engagement in imperial social mission. Women's imperial missionary agency was not identical to 'imperial feminism', but it did play a vital part in laying the ground for its emergence. In the later nineteenth century, when evangelical women such as Josephine Butler began to critique both the Biblical basis of female subordination and misogynist aspects of imperial policy, the marrying of evangelicalism, feminism and imperial social mission began to become a possibility.[102]

5 Feminism, colonial emigration and the new model Englishwoman

In the late 1850s, at around the same time that the Wesleyan Methodist Missionary Society became the first of the major British-based foreign missionary societies formally to begin employing single women as missionaries overseas, women also began to set up new forms of voluntary organisations in Britain, promoting a secular feminist rather than evangelical reform agenda. This chapter explores the relationship between imperialism and the emergence of this organised feminist movement in Britain between the mid-1850s and the mid-1860s.

At first sight, it might appear that the middle-class feminists of what became known as the Langham Place Circle had little interest in Empire. They directed their reforming energies into campaigns designed to improve the position of women within British society through petitioning for married women's property rights and campaigning to improve middle-class women's educational and employment opportunities.[1] They were active prior to the launch of the women's suffrage campaign, when feminists began to highlight British women's potential role as social reformers of Empire as a way of claiming that they had a legitimate place in a national Parliament responsible for policy-making on imperial as well as domestic issues.[2] They also formed a group distinct from women active in the foreign missionary movement: the founding figures of the Circle, Bessie Rayner Parkes and Barbara Leigh Smith Bodichon, both came from Unitarian backgrounds, a denomination outwith the evangelical mainstream, and were strongly influenced by their contacts with the radical unitarians of the 1830s and 1840s who challenged dominant evangelical ideas about women's position in society.[3] In addition, while some were active supporters of the anti-slavery movement, following the abolition of colonial slavery in 1834–8, their focus was not on the British Empire but on slavery in the USA.[4]

The development of Langham Place feminism was, nevertheless, intimately linked to European imperialism. Deborah Cherry has highlighted the significance of the French colony of Algeria to the group, a connection stemming from activist Barbara Leigh Smith's marriage to a French colonial doctor in 1857. Thereafter, she shuttled between a house in a white settler suburb of Algiers and 'home' at the hub of the British Empire in central London, drawing other leading members of the Circle into an imperial circuit within which feminist discourses were shaped. Cherry has concluded that 'at the moment of its emergence as an organised movement, egalitarian feminism's discourses on equal rights were shaped in and by the colonial context of Algeria and founded on the slippery discourses of race' with Algerian women as 'targets for "woman's mission", philanthropy and the imperial project'.[5] In other words, Langham Place feminists, despite their lack of links with the British foreign missionary movement, were caught up in the project of imperial social mission.

This form of imperial feminism was based in a common sense of cultural superiority to the colonised other, a world view that Europeans held in common despite their intense national imperial rivalries. However, as this chapter will demonstrate, there was also a more nationalistic, Anglo-centric dimension to Langham Place feminists' engagement with imperialism, one that was arguably more central to its formation than the association with the white settler community in French colonial Algeria that has been emphasised by Cherry. This grew out of feminist interest in exploiting the opportunities opening up to educated English women in Britain's colonies of white settlement.

The history of British imperial migration has recently been described by James Hammerton as the 'poor relation' of imperial history in general, and the study of gender and Empire in particular.[6] Feminist involvement in female colonial emigration has also occupied a marginal place in general histories of British feminism, despite its consideration in Hammerton's classic study of emigrant gentlewomen and in Marion Diamond's recent biography of the leading early feminist promoter of colonial emigration, Maria Rye.[7] In both Hammerton and Diamond's work, too, Empire and colonial settlement remain taken-for-granted backdrops to accounts that focus on the practicalities of the feminist emigration project rather than its ideological underpinnings and relationship to imperialism. Other studies of single women's emigration from Britain, undertaken as part of the social history of specific white settler colonies, have been neglected by historians of women's lives within Britain, despite the insights they include into the metropolitan scene.[8] Recent attempts to approach the study of Victorian women's emigration from the perspective of postcolonial literary theory have offered some interesting insights into intersecting discourses of femininity and emigration, but have left unclear the precise nature of the discursive relationship between early feminism and emigration.[9] The relationship between British women's promotion of female emigration, their involvement in feminism, and their support for imperialism has been most directly addressed by Julia Bush, who has suggested that there were distinct but overlapping feminist and imperialist women's movements in Edwardian Britain, with their roots in the late Victorian period.[10] The question of the relation between feminism, colonial emigration and imperialism in the mid-Victorian period, however, remains poorly understood.

In this chapter I aim to demonstrate that the issue of colonial emigration was not a marginal side-strand to early feminist debate; rather, it was integral to feminist attempts to construct a 'new model' of middle-class womanhood that linked English femininity to independence rather than to dependent domesticity. *The English Woman's Journal* (1858–64), the mouth-piece of the Langham Place Circle, covered the question of female colonial emigration regularly and fully, devoting far more attention to this than to any other Empire-related issue. In discussing emigration in this periodical, in the mainstream press and at the congresses of the National Association for the Pro-motion of Social Science, feminists, I argue, developed a gendered discourse of Englishness that both drew on and helped shape mid-nineteenth-century British colonial discourse.

It was at this discursive cultural level that feminist engagement with female emigration has its prime historical significance, rather than at the social or demographic level. The number of middle-class women whom feminists actually helped to emigrate to the colonies between 1860 and the winding down of the Female Middle Class Emigration Society in 1886 numbered only a few hundred.[11] Life-changing as emigration was for the individuals con-cerned, as witnessed by the letters from emigrants preserved in the archive of the society in the Women's Library in London, these emigrants were a tiny number in comparison with the around 20,000 that its successor female emi-gration societies helped to emigrate over a similar number of years between 1884 and 1914.[12] They were also a drop in the ocean of the overall outflow of emigrants from Britain over that period, who comprised mainly working- rather than middle-class individuals and families, with men outnumbering women, and totalled around half a million from England and Wales alone over each decade during the second half of the nineteenth century, around a third of these emigrating to the colonies of white settlement and the remainder to the United States.[13]

This chapter, then, focuses on the discursive dimensions of early feminist engagement with colonial emigration. In the first section of this chapter I note the appearance of 'Miss Bull' as the 'new model' Englishwoman in the opening article of the newly launched feminist periodical, *The English Women's Journal*, in March 1858, and discuss how the independent woman was discursively positioned by Langham Place feminists in relation to the dominant Victorian ideology associating Englishness with an ideal of feminine domesticity. I then explore how feminists' preoccupation with finding new employment oppor-tunities for educated single women led them to look to colonial emigration as a possible solution to this aspect of the 'woman question'. Looking first at what feminists claimed that the colonies could offer 'Miss Bull' and then at what 'Miss Bull' was promoted as offering the colonies, I reveal the way in which early feminist campaigners linked improvements in the position of English women with the consolidation of white colonial settlement, reveal-ing the mutual constitution of feminist and colonial discourses through the promotion of female emigration. This project was, however, rendered prob-lematic for feminists not only because of practical difficulties, but also because female emigration was being simultaneously promoted by misogynist writers as a solution to the supposed 'surplus' of single women in the population.

Finally, I place 'Miss Bull' alongside alternative, more racially and ethnically inclusive, models of new womanhood offered by two women of African descent in mid-nineteenth-century England and discuss their relationship to, and impact on, Langham Place feminism.

Miss Bull: feminists and the new model Englishwoman

Interest on aiding English women to emigrate developed out of one of the key campaigning focuses of the organised women's movement in its early years, namely the attempt to increase the employment opportunities of educated single women.[14] *The English Woman's Journal*, the organ of the Langham Place Circle founded by Bessie Rayner Parkes and her friend Barbara Leigh Smith Bodichon in March 1858, signalled its preoccupation with this issue by opening with an article entitled 'The Profession of Teacher'.[15] The anonymously authored article, most probably contributed by either Parkes or Bodichon, is examined in detail here because it is suggestive of the link that feminist campaigners made from the outset between female employment and English identity, a link that was soon to become central to feminist emigration discourse.

The article began by reporting on the work of the Governesses Benevolent Institution, a charitable organisation set up in 1843 to aid the large numbers of governesses left destitute because of overcrowding, low pay and lack of job security in one of the few respectable professions open to middle-class women.[16] Rather than simply concluding with an appeal for funds, however, the author went on to argue that there was a need for a wider range of employment opportunities for the 43% of women in the land who were unmarried or widowed – a reference to the high proportion of single women identified by the census of 1851.

The author poses this problem of female employment in a language of race and ethnicity, asking 'to what ends then must we hope to see the intelligent female labour of this Anglo-Saxon race directed, and how is the current to be turned into new channels?' Rather than focusing on practical remedies, she then launches into a rather convoluted discussion that links racial and ethnic categories to specific character traits. Presenting an ethnographic picture, she claims that 'every race has its *specialité* of function in the great sum total of humanity', continuing: 'while the Hindoo pecks rice, sleeps, bathes, fights, and embroiders coats of many colours, and the Mohammedan Arab sits cross-legged in the sun and play endless games of backgammon, the Anglo-Saxon man digs and ploughs, spins and weaves, buys and sells'. Idle eastern, non-Christian men are thus contrasted with the industrious Anglo-Saxon man, whose physiogamy is linked to his practicality: 'He is a sturdy sensible fellow, has a square forehead and an active body; he can calculate well, and usually knows how to buy in the cheapest and sell in the dearest market'. Drawing on a tradition dating back to the beginning of the eighteenth century of personifying England and the English national character in the figure of John Bull, the author states that this Anglo-Saxon 'Mr Bull', while 'neither literary nor artistic', 'has an unusually fair share of what is termed 'good common sense'.[17]

Just when the thread of the argument concerning female employment seems to be being lost in a cross-cultural comparison of men's relation to work, the author brings the less familiar figure of Mrs Bull into her argument; she claims that Mrs Bull has 'feminine' qualities that are the counterpart to John Bull's 'fine sterling qualities': she is a "motherly body" who 'not only looks after the children, but after the storeroom too'. This domestic Englishwoman in country districts, she claims, 'represents the feminine side of the same active and sterling character which is supposed to mark the Englishman'.[18] This becomes the basis for arguing that the single daughters of tradesmen and small merchants and manufacturers, rather than becoming governesses, could assist in the occupations of their fathers and brothers in business – this should not be seen as losing caste or gentility.

This seems a nostalgic pining for a mythical national past of prosperous farmers and small family-run businesses, before industrialisation led to the separation of home and workplace, at first sight a strange stance to inform the opening article in a new London-based feminist periodical. However, this article is not an aberration; rather, it signals the way in which feminist campaigners, embarking on new and controversial campaigns that challenged Victorian conventions of femininity, attempted to diffuse criticism by presenting their ideas as rooted in English tradition. Mrs John Bull, as Madge Dresser has pointed out, was 'the symbol of the good English housewife, frugal, modest and hospitable' and also 'a nostalgic figure who embodies the domestic virtues of a pre-industrial England' – a lost mythic England of beef and ale and robust farming and trading families evoked in contrast to the dark satanic mills of the new industrial landscape and the pinched pale frames of the urban poor.[19] Like her husband, she embodied the myth of the well-fed prosperous English race, contrasted with the undernourished Scots, Irish and French. The shift in focus from rural to urban family in *The English Woman's Journal* piece was facilitated by the slightly indeterminate class and location of the Bulls: earlier nineteenth-century images most commonly placed John Bull as urban shopkeeper, while from its launch in 1841 *Punch* popularised a Victorian John Bull as a gentleman, farmer with riding boots and crop. The Bulls also had the advantage for feminists of not being associated with any particular political position: they were figures mobilised by both radicals and conservatives seeking to represent their views as patriotic common sense.[20] The evocation of Mrs Bull at the launch of *The English Woman's Journal* thus not only gave the first article a nationalistic tone, but also positioned feminist calls for new employment opportunities for middle-class women not as a revolutionary demand (a break with the past), but rather as rooted in traditional English domestic womanhood (a return to the past). In a parallel way, Edwardian women's suffrage campaigners later deployed the figure of Mrs Bull as part of their attempt to redefine the 'womanly woman' along feminist lines.[21]

The use of a discourse of Anglo-Saxonism fulfilled a similar purpose. Political radicals had long drawn on the popular constitutionalist rhetoric of the freeborn Englishman and woman, figures rooted in the Anglo-Saxon past.[22] However, in this article the Anglo-Saxon is defined through an association of cultural difference with innate racial difference in a way that was characteristic of mid-nineteenth-century discourse.[23] The association of Anglo-Saxon racial heritage with English domestic femininity was also made in a very different type of contribution to the second issue of *The English Woman's Journal*. Written in response to the Indian Rebellion of 1857–8, the poem by 'I.B.', entitled *Light and Dark*, evokes a peaceful English scene of homes with babes asleep on their mothers' breasts in contrast with the chaos of an India with dying 'white-limbed girls', where 'Fair Saxon hair all dimmed with gore,/and soft pale breasts all rudely torn,/and babes whom English mothers bore,/Are brought out day by day to die'.[24] In assigning a prominent place to this poem, the feminist editors of *The English Woman's Journal* contributed to the representation in the British press of the rebellion's threat to Britain's imperial interests as a threat to white women's bodies from violent brown men, imagery that fuelled the development of increasingly racist views of colonised peoples in the mid-Victorian period.[25]

The stress on English national character in the opening article of *The English Woman's Journal* also chimed with the title of the periodical itself. As Jane Rendall has noted, the journal grew out of a Scottish-based women's periodical, the *Waverley Journal*, which Bessie Rayner Parkes took over editing in 1857, repositioning it from a domestic magazine to a 'Working Woman's Journal' addressing women of all classes engaged in paid or voluntary work. Interestingly, Parkes also specified that it was addressed at women 'at home and in the colonies', indicating that she aspired to make her project of promoting female employment and improving women's position an Empire-wide one.[26] It was when Parkes failed in her negotiations to take over the ownership of this journal that she decided to launch *The English Woman's Journal* in London, along with her friend, Barbara Leigh Smith Bodichon. The new title positioned the journal as specifically English focused, moving from a title that referenced Walter Scott's best-selling Scottish historical novels to one that echoed the title of the most widely read middle-class English women's magazine of the period, Samuel and Isabella Beaton's *Englishwoman's Domestic Magazine*, the leading example of a genre of domestic-oriented magazines for women that emerged in Britain in the 1850s.[27]

When they launched the *Englishwoman's Domestic Magazine* in 1852, the Beetons had explicitly linked English national pride to pride in the 'moral and domestic character' of Englishwomen. They aimed to help women make happy homes through combining practical advice on domestic management with cultivation of women's intellectual and moral qualities, directing themselves 'as much to the elevation as to the amusement of English Mothers, English Wives, and English Daughters' and echoing the agenda of Sarah Stickney Ellis's best-selling evangelical prescriptive tracts.[28]

In dropping the designation 'domestic', the feminist founders of *The English Woman's Journal* clearly wanted to distinguish their agenda from that of the Beetons'. As the opening article discussed above suggests, they sought to develop a new take on the relationship between Englishness and middle-class womanhood, focused around female self-fulfilment rather than dependence, but nevertheless positioned as rooted in notions of English women's domestic virtues rather than as an abrupt break with the past. Indeed, the *Englishwoman's Domestic Magazine* itself provided a vital bridge between the feminine mainstream and feminist campaigners. With sales of some 50,000 compared with some 500 to 1000 for *The English Woman's Journal*, it acted as a conduit for feminist ideas to a much wider female audience, doing this even before *The English Woman's Journal* itself was founded in 1858. The editorial preface for the *Englishwoman's Domestic Magazine* of 1856–7 signalled the editors' interest in addressing issues that they identified as intimately concerning the interests of Englishwomen: reform of the divorce laws, education of girls, and employment of women in branches of manufacture. The volume included an essay on 'the property of married women' by Langham Place feminist Maria Rye, soon to become well known as the leading feminist promoter of female emigration, which included the text of the petition for married women's property rights that marked the launch of public feminist campaigning.[29]

Alongside such essays on contemporary feminism, Maria Rye also contributed pieces on the history of women to the *Englishwoman's Domestic Magazine*. In an essay on 'Women in barbarism' she contrasts the relative equality of women in Christian and European lands with their oppression elsewhere, using the position of women as the marker of the level of civilisation in a way that drew on earlier Enlightenment thought and, as we have seen in Chapter 1, was typical of feminist writers of the period.[30] She also contributed a serialised 'Domestic History of England', a historical survey of everyday life in England addressed to the women of England. This wrote women and everyday life into the history of the nation, perhaps in conscious counterpart to Whig historian Thomas Babington Macaulay's widely read *History of England* (1848–55), which focused on men and politics in its story of the progressive development of the nation.[31] Written during a period when popular cultural nationalism was manifested in what Peter Mandler has described as a 'seemingly insatiable appetite' for specifically English histories, Rye's associates English domesticity with a history of support for women's rights, and, like the opening article in *The English Woman's Journal* discussed above, grounds contemporary feminist claims in the Anglo-Saxon past.[32] Rye claims that their husbands held Anglo-Saxon women in 'high estimation' and details the legal rights they accorded to married women. She moves on to praise the 'many and great virtues' of the Anglo-Saxons, who are credited with laying the foundation 'of nearly all that is great and honourable in the English character'.[33] Rye's 'History' also includes a paean of praise to British imperial expansion linked to the allegorical female personification for the nation: 'if the dominion of Britannia is continued as hitherto (for the greater part, at least) for the good of the whole [world] as well as the especial benefit of herself, long, long, may she retain her sovereignty as mistress of the seas!'[34]

The cover of the *Englishwoman's Domestic Magazine* featured the real woman who, since her ascension to the throne, had become even more important than the allegorical female figure of Britannia as an embodiment of the British nation, namely Queen Victoria. The cover image showed the young Queen surrounded by scenes of English women's domestic life, drawing on an established tradition of presenting the Queen as an ideal model of English bourgeois domesticity.[35] Rather than distancing themselves from this feminine role-model, members of the Langham Place Circle very successfully appropriated the figure of Queen Victoria for the feminist cause: while the figure of Mrs Bull helped link feminism to the English national past, the figure of Victoria helped link it to contemporary patriotism. Victoria, both wife and mother and ruler of nation and Empire, was for feminists an exemplary model of womanhood bridging the supposedly separate spheres of private and public, domestic and political, life. Emily Faithfull, speaking in 1860 at the annual meeting of the National Association for the Promotion of Social Science (NAPSS), an organisation that was the 'focus for social and institutional reform in mid-Victorian Britain' and the first middle-class public organisation to accord equal participation and public speaking rights to women, linked promotion of female employment both to English domesticity and to the figure of the Queen.[36] The need to find women employment, she argued, was 'a problem in which is bound up so much of the welfare and happiness of English homes during this and future generations'. Discussing the setting up of the Victoria Press, which published *The English Woman's Journal* and offered women training as compositors, she explained that it was named 'after the Sovereign to whose influence English women owe so large a debt of gratitude' and stressed the Queen's approbation of such steps to open industry to women.[37] Indeed, Faithfull had succeeded in enlisting the Queen as a patron of the Society for Promoting the Employment of Women (SPEW), formed in 1859.

The imperial associations of Victoria were also important to patriotic feminists. In 1861, *The Victoria Regia*, published by the Victoria Press to show off the skill of its female compositors, was dedicated 'by special permission' to the Queen, a sovereign 'who has known how to unite the dignified discharge of public duties with a constant regard for the cares of domestic life' with the following dedicatory poem, accompanied by an engraving of water lilies:

> When on the shining waters of the west
> An English traveller saw the queen of flowers,
> He sought a name whereby might be exprest
> The chiefest glory of this world of ours.
> Victoria Regia! – Never happier name
> A flower, a woman, or a queen could claim!
> So we this title with due reverence chose

For this our flower, which we aspire to lay
At her dear feet round whose dominion flows
The perfect light of undeclining day.
Victoria regia! May our blossom hold
In pure white leaves a loyal heart of gold.[38]

Through title and dedicatory poem, Langham Place feminists thus linked their project of promoting new employment opportunities for women to the imperial project. Purity (symbolised by the lily) is linked to whiteness, seaborne empire to the spread of enlightenment, English exploration to the naming of the world. The discovery and naming of a flower after Queen Victoria provides a prettified feminised metaphor for imperial expansion and the creation of imperial knowledge. Victoria's name was, of course, also given in the mid-nineteenth century to a number of the key geographic sites of British imperial expansion: to an Australian colony, to the capital of Vancouver Island, and to the lake at the heart of Africa 'discovered' by British explorers as the source of the Nile.

It is interesting to place the poem alongside an earlier text by one of the women whose work is included in the *Victoria Regia*, the writer Anna Jameson. As Gillian Whitlock has discussed, Jameson describes finding out about the ascension of Queen Victoria while travelling by canoe in the backwoods of Canada, at the frontiers of white settler colonisation. Tears come to her eyes when she realised that 'even here, in this new world of woods and waters, and these remote wilds, to her so utterly unknown, her power reaches and her sovereignty is acknowledged'.[39] Whitlock notes, in a passage that might also stand as a comment on the later poem, that 'the absorption of the self into the imperial, was easier to sustain ... in moments of solitary reflection in a natural world, and in a landscape emptied of 'other' people'.[40] The poem offered to English women at the bustling heart of the imperial British metropolis an opportunity to experience vicariously the thrill of this colonial moment of identification, binding together the feminist project of feminine self-actualisation with the project of expanding Victorian imperial power.

What the colonies could offer Miss Bull

Women of the Langham Place Circle, then, sought to develop a new model of independent English womanhood. Through drawing on the figures of Mr and Mrs Bull and seeking the patronage of Queen Victoria, and through promoting their agenda in the pages of the mainstream *English Women's Domestic Magazine* as well as the feminist *English Woman's Journal*, they positioned their campaigns to increase employment opportunities for educated single women as buttressing, rather than challenging, English domesticity, as rooted in the Anglo-Saxon past rather than a break with tradition, as linked to patriotism and to support for Empire rather than a radical challenge to established structures of authority. As will now be shown, promotion of female colonial emigration was rooted in this agenda, presenting the emigration of educated single English women as beneficial both to themselves and to the Empire.

Langham Place feminists first discussed female colonial emigration in terms of the potential paid employment of women as emigrators rather than emigrants. Barbara Leigh Smith, in *Women and Work* (1857), began her argument for increased employment opportunities for women in terms that echoed evangelical discourse, inaccurately describing Muslim beliefs in order to draw a contrast between progressive West and backwards East: 'women are God's children equally with men. In Britain this is admitted; because it is a Christian country: in Mahommedan countries this is denied'. However, rather than stressing British Christian women's privileges, she drew attention to the actual lack of female equality in Britain: 'We admit it as a principle, but ... in practice we deny what we affirm in theory'. A key source of this lack of equality was pinpointed as the lack of professional employment opportunities for women, and Smith proceeded to identify a number of professions that were in want of women, including nursing, medicine and work hitherto undertaken on a voluntary basis. She highlighted the voluntary work of Caroline Chisholm, whose 'careful and wise' system of organising working-class women's emigration to Australia had, she claimed, shown that women are ideally suited to become professional 'organizers of colonization, emigration, secretaries to colonies'.[41]

Similar praise of Chisholm's work in organising female emigration was offered by Langham Place activist Isa Craig, who delivered a paper to the reformatory department of the NAPSS Congress at Liverpool in October 1858 that discussed emigration as a 'preventive agency', providing unemployed working-class women with an alternative to crime.[42] Chisholm, a famous figure in Australian history who is, in contrast, now barely remembered in Britain, was one of a number of women who followed their husbands around the circuits of Empire, playing a part in consolidating settler communities and developing colonial philanthropy. The wife of an army officer employed by the East India Company, she established a school for the daughters of European soldiers in Madras in the 1830s and then spent eight years in Sydney, where she organised rescue work among single female immigrants, before returning to England in 1846 and founding her Family Colonization Loan Society. Between 1849 and 1854 this assisted thousands of skilled working-class and lower middle-class people to emigrate to Australia in family groups and also enabled some single women to emigrate under their protection. Chisholm became a public celebrity in Britain in the 1850s after Charles Dickens promoted her work, opening the first issue of *Household Words* with an article praising her efforts.[43] Kathryn Ledbetter has also drawn attention to the extensive reporting of Chisholm and female emigration in *The Lady's Newspaper*.[44]

Despite being one of the models for Mrs Jellyby in *Bleak House* (1852–3), a character through which Dickens expressed his disapproval of British philanthropists who focused on civilising Africa rather than improving the lives of the poor at home, Chisholm was publicly lauded as an example to women of the proper direction for their philanthropy at a period of growing disillusion with the results of slave emancipation and missionary efforts overseas. 'A Carol on Caroline Chisholm' published in *Punch* in August 1853 praised her for 'saving British natives' instead of 'making here and there a convert of a Turk'.[45]

While Dickens and others urged middle-class women to switch their philanthropic focus from the colonised to the poor at home, feminists were keen to concentrate on improving the lot of educated English women like themselves. Bessie Rayner Parkes, in a review of a year's efforts by the Langham Place Circle to promote women's employment delivered to the annual congress of the NAPSS in 1860, linked praise for Chisholm with advocacy of a new scheme to promote female emigration: whereas Chisholm had made herself 'mother of the female emigrant of a lower class', there was a need for women to get together to help educated women to emigrate as a partial solution to the lack of suitable employment in England.[46] This plan was promoted in *The English Woman's Journal* by Maria Rye, who, having previously reviewed current working-class female emigration, including the work of emigrant-ship matrons and the British Ladies Female Emigration Society (f. 1849), now urged 'English ladies' to raise a fund under the auspices of the feminist SPEW to inaugurate a new scheme of assisted middle-class female emigration.[47]

SPEW, despite setting up its own press to train women compositors and running its own law-copying office, headed by Maria Rye, was facing the problem of finding adequate sources of employment within the British metropole for the flood of educated single women who needed to work for a living. In turning to colonial emigration as one potential solution they were taking up an idea that had first been mooted in 1849 by the Governesses Benevolent Institution, the organisation that formed the focus of the opening article in *The English Woman's Journal* discussed above.[48] 'Miss Bull' was to be encouraged to seek her fortune in the colonies.

The first women were sent out by SPEW to positions in the white settler colonies in 1860, and in 1862 the scheme was put on a more established footing with the setting up of a separate society, the Female Middle Class Emigration Society (FMCES), under the leadership of Maria Rye. Rye and her colleagues promoted female emigration through the pages of *The English Woman's Journal*, the letter columns of *The Times*, and the annual congresses of the NAPSS. The new society numbered Lord Brougham, the founder and president of the NAPSS, among its patrons, together with other prominent philanthropists and social reformers with prior involvement in female emigration projects, including Arthur Kinnaird, treasurer of the British Ladies Female Emigration Society, and Lord Ashley, a leading patron of Chisholm's Family Colonisation Society.[49]

Though the FMCES was based in the imperial metropole, it was, like the Female Education Society discussed in Chapter 4, heavily reliant on colonial contacts. Indeed, the society was highly successful in obtaining the moral support and practical involvement of colonial elites. The Bishop of Sydney and Lady Dowling, widow of the Chief Justice of New South Wales, became patrons, and its formal network of colonial correspondents included groups of well-connected married women in Sydney and Melbourne and, in British Columbia, Governor Douglas, Bishop Hills, Archdeacon and Mrs Wright and Colonel and Mrs Moody.[50] These colonial connections were crucial in giving the society credibility and prestige in the eyes of both the British government and colonial authorities. They were invaluable to the society in practical terms, providing information on employment openings for women and reception committees to safeguard young women who arrived off ship looking for work. They also influenced the shaping of British feminist discourse on emigration.

The decision by feminists to promote emigration as one solution to the employment problems facing middle-class women in Britain can only be understood in the context of the broader enthusiasm for colonial emigration in Britain at this period. From the end of the wars with France in 1815, and influenced by the ideas of Thomas Malthus, emigration had begun to be promoted as a solution to rising population, unemployment, pressure on poor relief and social conflict within the nation. During the economic revival of the 1830s, colonial reformer Edward Gibbon Wakefield began to argue that colonies of white settlement should no longer be seen as convenient dumping grounds for British paupers and transported convicts, but rather as maturing societies moving towards responsible self-government within the Empire and needing respectable working-class emigrants. The colonies themselves were keen to attract hard-working male agricultural workers and female domestic servants and began to offer assisted passages. The Colonial Land and Emigration Commissioners were formed in 1840 and by 1848 had taken control of assisted emigration. It was at this juncture that the first voluntary societies were set up to offer practical help and protection to single female emigrants. Emigration had become tied to the project of colonisation from the mother country in order to create permanent settlement overseas in supposedly unoccupied land, and female migration began to be encouraged to redress the gender imbalance in the white settler population, particularly in the Australian colonies. Wakefield, in his *View of the Art of Colonization* (1849), asserted that 'in colonization, women have a part so important that all depends on their participation in the work. If only men emigrate, there is no colonization ... an equal colonisation of the sexes is one essential condition of the best colonization'.[51] There were persistent concerns, however, about the respectability of the single working-class women who were attracted by assisted emigration schemes.[52]

The FMCES sought to help those women who were not eligible for assisted passages to the colonies: educated single women who needed to support themselves. As Rye's co-worker in the society, Jane E. Lewin, specified: 'the large class lying between a finishing governess on the one hand, and a woman who can do little beyond teaching English correctly, on the other'. The particular qualities required of female emigrants were a combination of those traditionally expected of middle-class women and those normally expected of respectable working-class women: 'education of the hands, as well as of the head'; familiarity with household work and cooking and willingness to assist in domestic matters, plus 'good moral character'.[53] Maria Rye herself stressed the combination of physical and moral toughness required 'to form a good colonist': 'sufficient physical capability to endure the hardness of colonial life' as well as 'a moral status likely to withstand the inevitable temptations', namely 'the moral perils of a sea voyage' and 'the debaucheries of a colony'.[54] The emphasis on practical domesticity and moral sturdiness suggests a cross between the *Englishwoman's Domestic Magazine's* middle-class feminine ideal and the qualities Caroline Chisholm had looked for in the working-class women she helped to emigrate.

Whereas Chisholm saw marriage as the natural outcome of working-class female emigration and was concerned that well-paid jobs might lure women away from their proper destiny as wives and mothers, feminists presented emigration as a root to independence for middle-class women, echoing the emigration propaganda directed at male artisans.[55] The values of independence, hard work, persistence, self-help and mutual aid, argued Jessie Boucherett, were as applicable to educated single young Englishwomen as to the young male artisans addressed by Samuel Smiles in his famous book *Self Help* (1859).[56] Whereas Chisholm had articulated an Arcadian vision of Australia transformed into a country of yeoman farmers with virtuous wives – Mr and Mrs Bull transplanted to the colonies – feminists focused on Miss Bull: the single woman whom they wished to help to 'go to *work for independence*, not to marry, and be idle'.[57] They developed their own Arcadian vision of Britain's white settler colonies that, as in propaganda directed at male artisans, were presented as less class-bound societies than Victorian England, places where wages were good and hard work was rewarded. Emigration rhetoric was gendered, however: male artisans were encouraged to emigrate to acquire land and become heads of families, a masculine destiny seen as obstructed by conditions in England; feminists encouraged educated women to emigrate through claiming that self-sufficient single women were valued in the colonies. Maria Rye suggested that it was easier for middle-class women to take on jobs as shop-owners, teachers, midwives or even superior domestics in a colonial context where they were not competing with working-class women and where they would not suffer wounded self-respect because their help would be prized.[58] Other colonial and ex-colonial residents were quoted at length in *The English Woman's Journal*, backing Rye's views. One claimed that in Australia there 'is none of the English prejudice in favour of idleness to contend with', meaning that those who ran schools 'would be received as equals by all; their wish for independence would be acknowledged, as also their right'.[59] Another suggested that 'women, by courtesy called educated, to distinguish them from the labouring class, can and do become domestic servants in the colonies, when, owing to various causes it would be inconvenient and objectionable to do so in England'.[60]

Despite the reality of a population concentrated in coastal cities, which offered most openings for female employment, feminists represented an Australian Arcadia in terms of the egalitarian life 'up the country', drawing on the approach of emigration propagandist Samuel Sidney, whose ideas were popularised in Charles Dickens' *Household Words* in the 1850s.[61] In the bush, Rye claimed, governesses would be accepted as 'really, and not nominally, one of the family', their awkward position between working-class servant and middle-class family member resolved. This independent life was contrasted with the life they could expect in England: a 'dependent, spirit-wearying life', a 'lonely, careworn life with its incessant toil and inadequate payment'.[62] This pathetic representation closely resembled the image of *The Poor Teacher* pining for 'home, sweet home' in Richard Redgrave's famous painting that had been exhibited at the Royal Academy in 1843, the year of the foundation of the Governesses Benevolent Institution.[63] Rye claimed that most opportunities for female emigrants were to be found 'up-country' in 'the bush', where 'instead of the isolation to which too many governesses are doomed in this country, instead of weary hours wasted over sentimental and sickly novels, half-holidays and after lesson time would find them scampering across the plains on horseback with their young charges and companions, or busily engaged in some out-of-door cheerful occupation or amusement'.[64] Here, unhealthy confinement and unedifying leisure pursuits are contrasted with an image of freedom, invigorating exercise and wide-open spaces.

Such Arcadian visions doubtless attracted young women yearning to escape their constricted lives in England, though the mismatch with the rough reality of life in the bush laid feminists open to ridicule in the colonial press.[65] While *The English Woman's Journal* carefully selected positive letters from emigrant women and colonial correspondents for publication, in *The Times* Rye's letters promoting female emigration were counteracted by other letters warning of limited opportunities and crushed hopes.[66] Letters preserved in the archive of the FMCES in the Women's Library in London suggest that, for most educated single women, life proved as tough in the colonies as at home,[67] and this feedback doubtless influenced feminists' decisions to keep their emigration project on a small scale. Input from colonial contacts also counselled caution, with one contributor to *The English Woman's Journal* stressing the limited demand for governesses in Australia, calling for the government to get involved in training up educated women because 'the colonists have had great difficulty in obtaining the services of the right sort of women', and suggesting that emigration should be viewed as only one means of among many of improving the condition of women. The solution, she argued, lay not in 'wholesale deportation of educated women' to the antipodes, but in broadening out the range of women's job opportunities at home as well as in the colonies.[68]

Promotion of colonial emigration as part of a feminist agenda was also hampered by the appearance of William Rathbone Greg's misogynist article on 'redundant women' in the *National Review* in 1862. This called for the shipping of unmarried women like surplus goods to the colonies, so that they could fulfil their 'proper' roles of wives and mothers. Just as the Female Education Society had earlier been dogged by jibes that it was a bachelor's aid society, designed to provide wives for lonely male missionaries, so the

FMCES found it hard to shake off claims that it was sending out bride-ships. Frances Power Cobbe's vehement rebuttal of Greg's solution for 'redundant woman', while endorsing the work of the FMCES, articulated a growing feminist consensus that emigration was only a solution for a tiny number, and could not be the main way to 'improve the condition of the thirty per cent of single women in England'. A similar tack was adopted by Jessie Boucherett in *Hints on Self Help* (1863), where she pointed out that though colonies afforded a 'wide field of well-paid labour to certain classes of women' they did not want the educated women currently keen to emigrate because they were not trained in any particular trade or profession – they needed proper education and apprenticeship to trades or handicrafts.[69] Thus, education and training for jobs in both metropole and colony, rather than emigration in itself, came to be seen as the best solution. At the end of 1862, Rye herself, the leading feminist propagandist for female emigration, moved away from feminist circles to focus on developing large-scale emigration to the colonies by working-class women.[70]

What Miss Bull could offer the colonies

The feminist movement's preoccupation with colonial emigration, then, was relatively short-lived, despite the continued activity of the FMCES into the 1880s. Nevertheless, in the years when an organised women's movement was emerging in Britain, feminist discourse on emigration, as we have seen, played an important role in defining a new model Englishwoman, practical, independent and hard working. It was also significant in shaping gendered debates about colonisation, for Langham Place feminists presented female middle-class emigration not only as a solution for English women, but also as a solution for England and for its colonies. Feminist, national and colonial interests were positioned as in harmony.

Feminists articulated their vision of what educated English women could offer the colonies in the context of shifting debates in Britain and the settler colonies about the economic and political relationship between colony and metropole, and the right sort of coloniser required to consolidate settler societies. Some feminist discussion of the benefits of female emigration over the 1860–2 period generalised about the problems and needs of white settler colonies. Other propaganda focused on the two areas where the society's colonial contacts were strongest, where there was the strongest demand at the period for white female emigrants, and to which the society dispatched the majority of emigrants in its early years of operation: the Australian colony of Victoria and the North American colony of British Columbia. Victoria had seen a tripling of its population to around 1.2 million in the 1850s, attracting mainly male emigrants after the discovery of gold in the colony in 1851. By 1860 there were substantial cities at Melbourne and Sydney, and white settlers had set up farms, ranches and towns in the interior on lands appropriated from aboriginal peoples under the doctrine of *terra nullius* that failed to recognise aboriginal rights to the land on the grounds that they were not settled cultivators but primitive nomadic savages. Australian colonies had gained the right of responsible government in 1856, and the white colonial elites with whom British feminists were in close contact were keen to consolidate a settled, civilised and less male-dominated society. Australia was beginning to take over from the United States as the favoured destination of emigrants from the British Isles.[71] In British Columbia the need for respectable white female emigrants was perceived as even more urgent, as Adele Perry has highlighted. Vancouver had been founded as a British colony in 1849, but it was not until 1858, with the discovery of gold, that there was a large influx of mainly male settlers onto the mainland. Attempts to create a stable settler colony there were seen by the colonial authorities as being hampered by the lack of white women settlers, by influxes of Anglo-Americans, Chinese and African-Americans, by the continued demographic dominance of indigenous First Nation peoples, and by the custom of male fur-traders employed by the Hudson Bay Company of forming sexual partnerships with Native American women.[72] Settlers' gender, race and ethnicity were thus at the forefront of the concerns of the colonial activists with whom British feminists corresponded, and these concerns, together with mid-nineteenth-century metropolitan debates on race, ethnicity and Empire, contributed to shaping feminist emigration propaganda.

British feminist interest in female middle-class emigration did not in fact begin with the Langham Place Circle. In 1851, Harriet Martineau, feminist, abolitionist and author of popular works on political economy, had written a series of leaders on emigration to Australia for the *Daily News*, an organ of liberal reform aimed at a middle-class readership. Writing at the time of the gold rush in the colony of Victoria, she criticised the lack of forethought in sending out only working-class single women and called for assistance to single educated women such as governesses to emigrate to a new home: 'forwarding a noble intellectual and moral element to our magnificent dependency, while converting a crowd of pining daughters of England into rejoicing Australian matrons, the mothers of a new race'.[73] Martineau, who wrote extensively on imperial issues in the 1850s,[74] here linked the improvement of middle-class English women's lives both with the elevation and civilising of colonial life and with the reproduction of the imperial race.

While the option of marriage was downplayed by Langham Place feminists concerned to stress female independence and to distance themselves from misogynist calls for the export of 'surplus' women as colonial brides, and there was thus no talk of women becoming 'mothers of a new race', the conjunction Martineau stressed between the solutions to the woman question, the condition of England question and the colonial question was reiterated by Maria Rye and the FMCES. Rye lamented that England, 'a country peopled to repletion', an 'overflowing nation', and 'possessing such magnificent colonies' should be so backwards in promoting emigration and criticised colonial governments for selfishly only assisting the emigration of female domestic servants, thus excluding 'educated women of limited incomes' from seeking a 'fresh field' in which to improve their prospects and position in life.[75] In a paper to the NAPSS on 'the colonies and their requirements', she promoted female emigration as a solution for educated women unable to find jobs at home as 'not only a relief to England, but an actual benefit to the colonies themselves', since it would result in 'an elevation of morals'.[76] Writing from a colonial perspective, another contributor to *The English Woman's Journal* affirmed this picture, concluding that: 'By sending us such women, England will confer upon her colonies the greatest benefit she has ever bestowed'.[77]

Langham Place feminists promoted educated English women as ideal colonists by contrasting them with supposedly less civilised women of other ethnicities. This was partly a way of distancing their emigration project from the first attempt to send single women to the colonies in the 1830s, which had led to a public scandal, with colonial criticism of the supposedly depraved Irish women sent over.[78] It also reflected the negative stereotypes of the Irish peasantry and Highland Scots crofters current among both colonial elites and the English middle class, and the positioning of Celts below Anglo-Saxons in Victorian racial thought.[79] Feminists did not scruple to utilise and reaffirm such racial and ethnic stereotypes. An article in *The English Woman's Journal*, giving a sketch of SPEW's plan to organise the emigration of educated women, deplored the fact that the colonies were becoming 'burdened with the half-savage and wholly untaught and unskilled population of the wilds of Ireland and Scotland. Women born and bred in peat huts, who know nothing of the requirements or even decencies of civilized life, whose whole art of cooking consists in knowing how to boil a potato or mix porridge, whose skill as laundresses is confined to the wishing of their own garments in the running brook, stronger in the domestic duty of peat-cutting than house-cleaning'.[80] As Alison Twells has noted, educationalist Hannah Kilham, writing in the 1830s, set up a hierarchy of civilisation based around domestic housing that placed African 'huts' at its base, Irish 'cabins' in the middle, and British middle-class 'homes' at the top. By the 1850s the term 'cabin' was more commonly used of settler homes on the colonial frontier, and in *The English Woman's Journal* text the use of the term 'huts' presents the Celtic fringes of the United Kingdom as being below the level aspired to by colonial settlers and on a par with 'savage' Africa.[81]

These wrong sorts of women were contrasted with the 'right sort' of female emigrants: 'a body of women infinitely superior by birth, by education, and by taste, to the hordes of wild uneducated creatures we have hitherto sent abroad'.[82] Backing her argument with statements from colonial sources about the need for 'some clever, modest, and industrious women' to replace the current 'uninstructed' Irish peasant women emigrants, Rye blended together ethnic stereotypes generated in metropole and colony.[83]

Educated English women were presented as crucial for keeping up the standard of English education in the colonies. Rye, in a letter to the editor of *The Times*, reproduced a letter from one of her lady correspondents in

Melbourne asserting 'the importance at this distance from dear old England of setting good examples to our young Australians' and suggesting the need for teachers from 'the best of old England's sons and daughters' to keep up educational standards.[84] An article in *The English Woman's Journal* quoted a lady resident in New South Wales who stressed that female emigrants needed 'to speak and write correct English' in order to counteract the neglect of this in colonial families caused by 'the constant association with uneducated servants, aborigines, and Americans'.[85] In another letter to *The Times*, Rye appropriated the words from her earlier Melbourne correspondent thus: 'there are vacant situations in the colonies for many hundreds of women vastly superior to the hordes of wild Irish and fast young ladies who have hitherto started as emigrants': whether these new emigrants worked or married 'good must arise for the colonies, for our countrywomen, and for commerce'.[86] This rousing slogan, in evoking the '3 C's' of the slogan 'Christianity, civilisation and commerce', encouraged readers to connect colonial emigration of educated English women with the benevolent spread of British imperial mission. However, the final lines of the letter, in which the writer equates emigration to the colonies to emigration to Canaan, perhaps inadvertently evokes the dark side of settler and missionary imperialism. For as Rye, a devout Anglican, would no doubt have been aware, the Bible records that Moses said to the Israelites at the end of their journey in the wilderness: 'When ye are passed over the Jordan into the land of Canaan; then ye shall drive out all the inhabitants of the land from before you, and destroy all their pictures, and destroy all their molten images, and quite pluck down all their high places; and ye shall dispossess the inhabitants of the land, and dwell therein: for I have given you the land to possess it'.[87]

Concern for the indigenous peoples displaced and dispossessed of their lands by the tide of white settlement did not feature in Rye's discussion of emigration. Instead, she positioned the emigration of educated women as part of a progressive project of colonial development through the exploitation of natural resources and the consolidation of settler society: 'If we look to the resources of our colonies, to the untold wealth and powers yet to be expanded – the rapid stride they are making towards refinement, and in the elegances of life – surely we may take courage and hope that there, amidst the many homesteads of our wonderful colonial possessions, some, at least, of our many worthy, industrious, poor, young countrywomen may be safely planted'.[88] Antipodean colonies were presented as places already well on the road to civilisation. Rye lamented the difficulty of obtaining accurate information from British newspapers about social conditions there, complaining that news tended to focus on dramatic events, whether good or bad, such as the discovery of a new gold field or a Maori War. Signs of emigration by rough men seeking a quick fortune and evidence of sustained indigenous resistance to European incursion were brushed off as obscuring the reality of the steady development of civilised settlement. As well as the major cities and ports, Rye stated, there were many townships and villages in the interior – not, as one might imagine, 'a few wooden huts sparsely scattered over a vast stretch of country', but often advanced enough to support banks and newspapers. The colonies, she stressed, 'are neither the sandy deserts not the waste howling wilderness, some morbid imaginations would picture them'.[89] As another contributor to *The English Woman's Journal* stated, the colonies had grown up and were no longer willing to accept 'the left-off garments of our parents'. The roughness of colonists has been exaggerated: 'there are as true gentlemen and ladies, in the right sense of the words, to be found in the far-away bush of Australia, in the wilds of Africa, or in the backwoods of Canada, as in any London ball-room'.[90]

Feminist promoters of emigration tended to simply ignore the presence of the aboriginal population in Australia, seemingly accepting without question what Patrick Brantlinger has described as 'a mantra for the advocates of British imperial expansion': the myth that indigenous peoples were racially inferior savages who were doomed to extinction because of their own backwardness.[91] In the aftermath of the Indian Rebellion, promoters of female colonial emigration were also doubtless keen to play down potential threats to white women from black men: a letter to editor of *The Times* by the Queensland emigration commissioner in 1862 sought to allay the fears of potential emigrants following an incident in which a white man and his servants were murdered by aboriginal people, stressing that this event was an extremely rare occurrence and that female servants could be left unprotected on cattle stations without any danger of injury or intimidation by 'natives'.[92] Rather, it was the presence of Chinese migrants to which an ex-Australian resident writing in *The English Woman's Journal* drew attention, warning against uncritical use of census figures as guides to where such women were most wanted: 'in Victoria and New South Wales, the Chinese, who are *all* men, swell the returns of the male population'.[93] These census figures reflected the fact that large numbers of Chinese men had emigrated to Victoria following the discovery of gold in 1851. The assumption here that the Chinese are clearly not the right sort of male settler to associate with English women reflected the taboo on relations between white women and non-white men in the Empire. It also reflected the intense uneasiness about Chinese emigration to the Australian colonies, which had led to riots, demonstrations, physical attacks and the passing of discriminatory immigration legislation. Half a century later such concerns were to lead to the adoption of the notorious 'White Australia policy'.[94] Such alarm was not confined to colonists: liberal political economist Henry Fawcett presented a paper to the 1859 congress of the NAPSS which warned of the danger of Australia becoming 'little more than a vast Chinese colony'.[95]

In the case of emigration to British Columbia, the other main geographical focus of feminist promoters of emigration in the early years, the anxiety was less about English women associating with the wrong sort of men than English men associating with the wrong sort of women. As Adele Perry has pointed out, this included concerns about the colony's governor, James Douglas, himself: his mixed-heritage wife, Amelia Connolly Douglas, was encouraged to keep a low public profile in the colony, where she was seen as an inappropriate representative of settler society and colonial womanhood.[96] These colonial racial politics spilled over into the FMCES: while James Douglas became one of the official colonial correspondents of the feminist society, his wife did not, in contrast to the wives of other prominent colonial men. On occasion, too, British feminists uncritically replicated racist colonial attitudes. An editorial in *The English Woman's Journal* of April 1862 introduced 'stray letters on emigration' by reporting on a London meeting of the Columbian Emigration Society, which had been set up by the Anglican philanthropist Angela Burdett Coutts to recruit girls from English workhouses to send to the colony as potential wives for settlers. At the meeting, the article reported, it was asserted that 'religion and morality would be altogether ruined unless an emigration of white women from Great Britain took place'.[97] From the 1850s, colonial officials and missionaries in British Columbia, as a solution to the supposed problem of inter-racial relationships and the roughness and immorality of white male settlers, were touting emigration by white women.[98] *The English Woman's Journal* article, in linking the report with a series of letters from ladies in British colonies calling for the emigration of educated women, implicitly linked the feminist emigration project to this racialised agenda, while distinguishing it in class terms from Coutts' project. This willingness of feminists uncritically to purvey and adopt the racist attitudes of white settlers is also evident in one of the letters that Maria Rye wrote to the editor of *The Times*. Rye quotes from a letter she had received from a lady in British Columbia about the need for English female emigrants. This highlighted problem of lack of good servants in racist terms common in the colonial press at the period: 'my woman, a half-breed, is extremely insolent, and I am obliged to have her infant as well as herself in the house'. Rye ends by urging female emigration 'for the sake of a fine colony' as well as to relieve suffering at home, implicitly endorsing the letter-writer's sentiments.[99]

Race, ethnicity and migration in the early women's movement

In the early years of the organised feminist movement in Britain, then, what I have labelled a 'new model' Englishwoman was defined by the Langham Place Circle. Independent, hard working and self-supporting, she was positioned not as in opposition to mainstream models of English or middle-class womanhood, but rather as a development from them. In the opening article of *The English Woman's Journal*, she was imagined as the daughter of Mr and Mrs John Bull, archetypal Anglo-Saxons, their liberties rooted in their English heritage. In feminist Maria Rye's 'History of England' in the *Englishwoman's Domestic Magazine*, a similar idealisation of women's lives in Anglo-Saxon England is present. As Jane Rendall has noted, when the women's suffrage movement emerged in the mid-1860s campaigners presented themselves as the inheritors of an Anglo-Saxon culture that had offered women freedom and respect in contrast to southern cultures; exploring suffragist histories written by British feminists, including Millicent Garrett Fawcett in the late nineteenth century, Sandra Holton has discerned a similar attempt to legitimate the cause through appeals to notions of English national character and 'constitutionalist' claims to women's heritage as 'freeborn' members of the Anglo-Saxon race.[100] The evidence of this chapter suggests that this discourse, with its slippage between ethnicity and race, developed as the organised women's movement emerged in the late 1850s.

The 'new model' of English womanhood was most clearly defined in feminist emigration discourse. Here, the key early feminist project of opening up new job opportunities for single middle-class women was intimately discursively interlinked with the imperial project of consolidating white colonial settlement. Female emigrants' English ethnicity and, to a lesser extent, their whiteness were presented as key to the qualities of character they brought to the project of colonial settlement as a feminist take on questions of gender, emigration and colonization was articulated. Single educated English women were presented as the ideal white settler who could bring morality and cultural Englishness to the colonies, set in sharp contrast to 'wild' Irish or Scots girls and 'fast women', who were seen as having brought down the moral tone of the colonies, and to indigenous peoples, who were associated with the dangers of miscegenation. Feminist discourse focused on emigration and colonial discourse focused on white settler colonisation became mutually constitutive: an imperial feminist discourse emerged.

Presenting the 'new model' Englishwoman as an ideal emigrant, this imperial feminist discourse contrasted with the masculinist slant of much emigration propaganda of the first half of the nineteenth century, which, as John Tosh has pointed out, presented the male artisan as the ideal emigrant and positioned emigration as 'a career which calls for ... all the masculine virtues'.[101] Feminists seeking to increase employment opportunities for women suggested that some of the virtues possessed by the self-made man were also appropriate for the independent woman, and that greater freedom and improved employment opportunities were suitable emigration goals for single educated women as well as male artisans.

Feminist promoters of emigration distinguished their agenda from that of Caroline Chisholm, despite their expressed admiration of her work. Both stressed women's importance in consolidating colonial settlement. However, while Chisholm saw this in terms of respectable working-class women strengthening family life as wives and mothers, Rye emphasised educated single women's potential contribution to preserving and strengthening English culture. There was nothing in Langham Place emigration propaganda of the agenda of 'imperious maternity' that Julia Bush has identified as characteristic of the propaganda of the new female emigration societies into which the FMCES eventually merged in the 1880s, and which had earlier been mooted by Harriet Martineau in her call in the 1851 *Daily News* leader for female emigrants to Australia to become 'mothers of the race'. However, it would be wrong to postulate a sharp ideological break between the emigration discourse of Langham Place feminists and the female emigrationists, both feminist and anti-feminist, whom Julia Bush identifies as comprising a key component of the 'imperial women's movement' of the late Victorian and Edwardian period. These later organisers of emigration actually sought to combine the earlier feminist agenda of female employment opportunity with the promotion of 'imperious maternity'.[102] In addition, as we have seen, the issues of ethnicity, race and colonisation were integral to Langham Place debates on emigration, though the debate was more around English cultural ethnicity than the later debates that focused on women's bodies as bearers of the white race. The role of the first feminist periodical, *The English Woman's Journal*, in this regard is interesting. As a number of scholars have noted, the Victorian periodical press, including periodicals addressed to women, played an important role in linking together Anglo-Saxonist myths of national identity and idealised concepts of female domesticity with the promotion of cultural imperialism and female emigration.[103] *The English Woman's Journal's* approach can be seen as a feminist development of this agenda, rather than a distancing from it.

How, then, did Langham Place feminists' promotion of white English women's role in imperial colonisation relate to their associations with French colonialism in Algeria that have been identified by Deborah Cherry? Interest in Algerian women as the target of imperial social mission across the bounds of national-imperial rivalry between Britain and France had a rather different tenor to promotion of female colonial emigration, with its stress on English ethnicity, and sense of a mission to moralise English culture among white settlers rather than spread it to colonised indigenous peoples. Nevertheless, Barbara Leigh Smith Bodichon's experiences as part of a white settler community, albeit a French colony very different in form to Britain's settler colonies, probably contributed to fuelling feminist interest in, and sympathy for, the project of colonial settlement, and alignment with the perspectives of white settlers.

The stress on Anglo-Saxon roots, on English heritage and, though to a lesser extent, on whiteness in feminist discourses around the new model Englishwoman, epitomised in the figure of the ideal female emigrant, gave Langham Place feminism an ethnically and racially exclusionary tone. Other educated single women who did not fit within the boundaries of this discourse were, however, publicly modelling more inclusive new models of independent womanhood linked to migration at this time in Britain, notably the Crimean War heroine Mary Seacole and abolitionist and feminist Sarah Parker Remond.

Remond, an African-American from a prominent free black family, came to England in 1859 and succeeded in establishing a place for herself within English feminist circles as well as within the transatlantic sisterhood of radical abolitionists that had developed since the 1840s. As I have discussed elsewhere, Remond contributed to the anti-slavery cause through becoming the first woman to deliver public lectures against slavery to diverse audiences around Britain, and also came to Britain in order to escape the overt racial discrimination she had experienced in the United States to gain an education at

Bedford College, founded by feminist Elizabeth Reid. She later went to live in Italy, where she qualified and practiced as a doctor. Remond expressed a Black Atlantic perspective that implicitly challenged Anglo-Saxonism as the basis for women's trans-national organisation and articulated a black feminist politics that combined women's rights, anti-slavery and anti-racism.[104] While her main political preoccupation was with slavery in the United States of America, Remond also spoke out against racism in Britain and its colonies. Addressing the NAPSS Congress in 1861 about her fears that the racism endemic in the United States was spreading to British colonies in North America, she expressed outrage at the separate pews for people of colour set up in a church on Vancouver Island, highlighting an issue completely ignored by the white feminists whose promotion of female emigration to British Columbia and whose willingness to accept racist colonial agendas unquestioningly has been highlighted above.[105]

Remond, a well-educated woman from a well-known middle-class black abolitionist family at the heart of transatlantic reform circles, a foreign visitor to Britain rather than a colonial immigrant, was accepted within the English feminist fold and was able to gain female allies in the fight against slavery. For black colonial subjects like Mary Seacole the situation was rather different. Helen Cooper has discussed how Seacole, an African-Caribbean 'doctress' and businesswoman from Britain's plantation colony of Jamaica, used her 1857 autobiography, *The Wonderful Adventures of Mrs Seacole in Many Lands*, to position herself as a new type of middle-class Englishwoman not identified with the domestic sphere, but with paid work – a type that accords with the feminist ideal discussed in this chapter. Cooper argues that Seacole implicitly challenged the equation of Englishness with whiteness, expressing pride in her mixed Scottish and African heritage and opposition to racial prejudice within England, and positioning herself as a proud colonial who saw England as home, and as a mother to the English soldiers she had gone to tend in the Crimea.[106]

The word-picture Seacole gives of herself as a young woman – 'I was never weary of tracing upon an old map the route to England; and never followed with my gaze the stately ships homeward bound without longing to be in them, and see the blue hills of Jamaica fade into the distance' – reverses the image in Ford Maddox Brown's painting *The Last of England* (1852–5), of the English emigrant couple on a ship with the white cliffs of Dover vanishing in the distance behind them.[107] It also provides an interesting counterpoint to A.C. Hayter's portrait of Caroline Chisholm, exhibited at the Royal Academy in 1852, which shows her at her desk in England with a map of Australia, the English emigrants' promised land, on the wall behind her.[108] For Seacole, England was positioned as home as much as it was for English emigrants, but her migrant journey was towards it rather than away from it.

In her cartoon in *Punch*, Seacole was celebrated, despite her skin colour, as just that kind of 'motherly body' more usually imagined as Mrs Bull, the idealised Englishwoman of *The English Woman's Journal* article discussed in the first section of this chapter. Her joke about her companions trying to pass her off as Queen Victoria to Russian troops shows her playing with another central symbol of the nation, one also used by Langham Place feminists to lend respectability to their cause, while a bust of her by the royal sculptor shows her wearing the kind of medals normally worn by imperial war heroes, signalling her acceptance at the heart of the nation.[109] Despite this national recognition, however, and despite fulfilling many of the criteria of the feminist new model Englishwoman, Seacole was not celebrated by Langham Place feminists as an exemplar, in sharp contrast to two of her middle-class white English contemporaries, Caroline Chisholm and Florence Nightingale, that other female heroine of the Crimea. The reasons for this probably lay in a combination of her race, her ethnicity and her class position, those reasons that had earlier led to the rejection of her application to join Nightingale's band of nurses in the Crimea in 1854.

Langham Place feminists envisioned the new model Englishwoman not as the immigrant black British colonial subject, but as the emigrant white Anglo-Saxon colonial settler. In linking their feminist project to the project of white colonial settlement they chose to neglect the link between British colonisation, racism and the oppression of indigenous women and men. While Sarah Parker Remond could still find a place within the British feminist fold in the 1860s, when the anti-slavery movement remained alive, the seeds of an exclusionary Anglo-Saxonist feminism were already growing. As Sandra Holton has noted, when feminist and liberal imperialist Millicent Garrett Fawcett came to write her version of suffrage history some 20 years later, she felt able to ignore completely the contributions to the feminist cause made by Remond and other women abolitionists, both black and white.[110]

Afterword

At a conference on the history of feminism held in 1992 to commemorate the bicentenary of the publication of Mary Wollstonecraft's *Vindication of the Rights of Woman*, Himmani Bannerji offered 'a spectrum of readings' of the text charted through different biographical and political moments of her own life, from her initial enthusiastic identification when she encountered it through her English headmistress in Bengal, through the critical distance she adopted when re-encountering it as a Marxist, feminist and anti-racist living in the West, to the position of negotiation from which she revisited it in the context of her dissatisfaction with identity politics, finding that the ways in which it 'poses the particular issues of women's rights in the context of human or universal rights', including the rights of slaves, offered insights into 'the revolutionary potential of humanism or universal rights when articulated in historicised projects of political justice'.[1]

Placing Bannerji's account alongside the memories of my own childhood in Britain, and my reading of Charlotte Brontë's 'proto-feminist' novel *Jane Eyre* – alluded to in the introduction to this book – brought home to me the power of Mrinalini Sinha's assertion that 'the histories of feminism in Britain and India demonstrate not only the inadequacy of a model that merely contrasts Western and non-Western feminisms, but also the necessity of revising feminism as a whole from a 'global' perspective' that acknowledges their 'mutual constitution' within 'a single imperial social formation'.[2] This book, building on the scholarship undertaken over the 15 years since Bannerji's intervention, is intended to forward this process through its detailed historical exploration of the imperial social formation of British feminism.

Feminism and Empire will, I hope, be the subject of an 'active reading', which Bannerji defines as 'the ability to see a text as a middle space, a sort of social relationship between on the one hand a writer and her writing and on the other a reader and her context and form of reading'. As she points out, 'neither writing nor reading is a private individual activity, independent of the time and space within which it occurs'.[3] The specific contexts within which I have completed this text in London in 2007 are fraught with public contestations over the nature and extent of racism in contemporary Britain, over the alleged threat posed by Muslims to the 'British' way of life, seen as symbolised by the veiling of women, and over the legacies of Empire in the year of the bicentenary of the abolition of the slave trade. This book, while not a direct intervention into these contemporary debates, does, I hope, offer new feminist historical perspectives from which to engage with them. Dismissal and distancing are, I am convinced, no ways of coming to terms with our imperial pasts; only by understanding these pasts can we hope to shape better futures in a world of continuing massive inequalities in access to resources and power.

The women living in Europe's most powerful imperial nation who have formed the focus of this study developed their positions on the woman question through engaging with Empire in a variety of ways. This book makes no claim to be comprehensive: it deals with both supporters and opponents of women's rights whose identities as white, British and (in the main) Protestant were shaped within an imperial nation. The question of aristocratic and working-class women's relationships to the development of 'imperial feminism' over the 1790–1865 period has not been explored. To make the study manageable, I have also concentrated on women writing and acting within imperial Britain, rather than women in colonial contexts; in the process, some of the subtleties of the mutual constitution of colony and metropole have, undoubtedly, been lost. The interactions between colonising and colonised women only appear as they were represented in accounts circulated within Britain, where complexities tended to be ignored in favour of simplistic generalisations. In addition, I have said little in this book about the contribution to the development of feminism by black and Asian women who lived within imperial Britain over this period, because my aim was to study the roots of the form of feminism that became hegemonic in the West rather than to explore the early challenges to it posed by activists such as Sarah Parker Remond.

Exploring the origins of 'imperial feminism' has entailed looking beyond a label that is valuable in signalling the mutual constitution of feminism and Empire, but also carries the danger of closing rather than opening up the past to critical thought. The legacy of British women's activism in the 1790–1865 period to the development of modern Western feminism is, as I have shown, a complex one. In the name of liberating colonised women, British women played an important part in reforming Empire through helping to bring about the end of colonial slavery; at the same time, positioned at one remove from the direct assertion of coercive imperial power, women were crucial in providing justifications for the continuance of imperial rule through its re-presentation as social mission rather than exploitation and violence. British women expressed identification with and empathy for colonised and non-Western women while using their positioning at the heart of Empire to assert their 'maternalist' power to speak on behalf of 'other' women, creating distorted pictures of their lives and aspirations, and imposing their own visions of freedom. They sought to encourage ethical consumer responsibility among British women by promoting the boycott of slave-grown sugar, but some also uncritically promoted 'legitimate' forms of imperial commerce as the alternative, failing to question the exploitative nature of supposedly 'free' trade and 'free' labour within an imperial system that locked colonies into the position of suppliers of raw materials to, and markets for manufactured goods from, the metropole. Those who openly advocated women's rights at this period, in seeking to position to the emancipation of women within European Enlightenment and liberal discourses of civilisational progress, promoted the rights of black slaves alongside white women's rights, but they also circulated negative and often inaccurate stereotypes of non-Western cultures. When an organised women's movement emerged in the late 1850s, imperial social mission became linked to an advocacy of female emigration that associated new employment opportunities for women with the consolidation of white colonial settlement.

Some white middle-class British women, however, adopted forms of radical universalism that signalled an alternative to the main road leading to imperial feminism. Mary Darby Robinson, in the 1790s, wanted women to become 'citizens of the world' and urged Europeans to take heed of the example of Native Americans who gave women a share in public decision-making. Elizabeth Heyrick called for the rights of man, woman and beast, campaigned for justice and immediate emancipation for both the enslaved in the colonies and the poor at home, placed the blame for slave rebellions in the colonies and machine breaking at home on the oppressors rather than the oppressed, and mounted a principled challenge to the authority of male policy-makers in the anti-slavery movement. Fanny Parks, publishing the journals of her stay in India in the 1820s to 1840s, called into question the disinterested humanitarian motives of the British government in abolishing *sati* and linked her opposition to the victimisation of Indian women to a wider condemnation of the universal subordination of women. Such writers and activists may perhaps offer inspiration to those currently seeking to develop a radical politics of female solidarity in a world still scarred by the legacies of European imperialism and buffeted by the new US imperialism.

Notes

Introduction

1 R. Strachey, *The Cause. A Short History of the Women's Movement in Great Britain*, London, Virago, 1978, p. 5.
2 B. Blakely, 'The Society for the Oversea Settlement of British Women and the problems of Empire settlement, 1917–1936', *Albion*, 1988, vol. 20, pp. 403–19; B. Bush, '"Britain's conscience on Africa": white women, race and imperial politics in interwar Britain', in C. Midgley (ed.), *Gender and Imperialism*, Manchester, Manchester University Press, 1998, pp. 200–23; S. Pedersen, *Eleanor Rathbone and the Politics of Conscience*, Newhaven, Yale University Press, 2004, pp. 241–64; H. Adi and M. Sherwood, *Pan-African History: Political Figures from Africa and the Diaspora since 1787*, London, Routledge, 2003; D.J. Macauley, *The Life of Una Marson, 1905–65*, Manchester, Manchester University Press, 1998; R. Visram, *Ayahs, Lascars and Princes. Indians in Britain 1700–1947*, London, Pluto Press, 1986; A. Woollacott, *To Try Her Fortune in London. Australian Women, Colonialism, and Modernity*, Oxford, Oxford University Press, 2001.
3 D. Rubinstein, *A Different World for Women: The Life of Millicent Garrett Fawcett*, Columbus, Ohio State University Press, 1991, pp. 115–30.
4 C. Hall, *White, Male and Middle Class. Explorations in Feminism and History*, Cambridge, Polity Press, 1992, pp. 1–42; for an influential early attempt to bring the histories of British women and of Empire together, see Anna Davin, 'Imperialism and motherhood', *History Workshop Journal*, 1978, vol. 5, pp. 9–65.
5 Examples include M. Macmillan, *Women of the Raj*, New York, Thames and Hudson, 1988; J. Trollope, *Britannia's Daughters: Women of the British Empire*, London, Random House, 1983.
6 For discussion of the 'ruin of Empire' stereotype, see M. Strobel, *European Women and the Second British Empire*, Bloomington, Indiana University Press, 1991, pp. 1–16. For early academic attempts to combat this stereotype, see H. Callaway, *Gender, Culture and Empire: European Women in Colonial Nigeria*, Urbana, University of Illinois Press, 1987; C. Knapman, *White Women in Fiji 1835–1930: The Ruin of Empire?*, Sydney, Allen and Unwin, 1986. For an influential critique of such revisionist approaches, see Jane Haggis, 'Gendering colonialism or colonising gender? Recent women's studies approaches to white women and the history of British colonialism', *Women's Studies International Forum*, 1990, vol. 13, pp. 105–15.
7 b. hooks, *Ain't I a Woman: Black Women and Feminism*, London, Pluto Press, 1981; A. Davis, *Women, Race and Class*, London, Women's Press, 1981; V. Amos and P. Parmar, 'Challenging imperial feminism', *Feminist Review*, 1984, vol. 17, pp. 3–19; G. Spivak, 'Three women's texts and a critique of imperialism', *Critical Inquiry*, 1985, vol. 12, pp. 243–61; C.T. Mohanty, 'Under Western eyes: feminist

scholarship and colonial discourses' in C.T. Mohanty, A. Russo and L. Torres (eds), *Third World Women and the Politics of Feminism*, Bloomington, Indiana University Press, 1991, pp. 51–80.

8 N. Chaudhuri and M. Strobel, *Western Women and Imperialism: Complicity and Resistance*, Bloomington, Indiana University Press, 1992; V. Ware, *Beyond the Pale: White Women, Racism and History*, London, Verso, 1992; L.E. Donaldson, *Decolonizing Feminisms. Race, Empire and Empire-Building*, Chapel Hill, University of North Carolina Press, 1992; C. Midgley, *Women Against Slavery. The British Campaigns*, London, Routledge, 1992; M. Ferguson, *Subject to Others: British Women Writers and Colonial Slavery*, London, Routledge, 1992; A. Burton, 'History is now: feminist theory and the production of historical feminism', *Women's History Review*, 1992, vol. 1, pp. 25–38; A. Burton, *Burdens of History, British Feminists, Indian Women, and Imperial Culture, 1865–1915*, Chapel Hill, University of North Carolina Press, 1994.

9 For useful introductions to these development, see G. Prakash (ed.), *After Colonialism: Imperial Histories and Postcolonial Displacements*, Princeton, Princeton University Press, 1994; V. Chaturvedi (ed.), *Mapping Subaltern Studies and the Postcolonial*, London, Verso, 2000; K. Wilson (ed.), *A New Imperial History. Culture, Identity and Modernity in Britain and the Empire, 1660–1840*, Cambridge, Cambridge University Press, 2004, pp. 1–28; C. Hall (ed.), *Cultures of Empire. A Reader*, Manchester, Manchester University Press, 2000, pp. 1–36; A. Burton, 'Rules of thumb: British history and "imperial culture" in nineteenth- and twentieth-century Britain', *Women's History Review*, 1994, vol. 3, pp. 483–500.

10 J.M. Mackenzie, *Propaganda and Empire. The Manipulation of British Public Opinion 1880–1960*, Manchester, Manchester University Press, 1984; J.M. Mackenzie (ed.), *Imperialism and Popular Culture*, Manchester, Manchester University Press, 1986; C. Bolt, *Victorian Attitudes to Race*, London, Routledge and Kegan Paul, 1971; D. Lorimer, *Colour, Class and the Victorians*, Leicester, Leicester University Press, 1978; P. Fryer, *Staying Power. The History of Black People in Britain*, London, Pluto Press, 1984; Vizram, *Ayahs, Lascars and Princes*; J. Walvin, (ed.), *Slavery and British Society, 1776–1846*, London, Macmillan Press, 1982.

11 For a useful introduction to these new approaches, see C. Hall (ed.), *Cultures of Empire. A Reader*, Manchester, Manchester University Press, 2000, pp. 1–36.

12 C. Hall and S. Rose (eds), *At Home With the Empire*, Cambridge, Cambridge University Press, 2006. For the counter-argument, see B. Porter, *Absent-Minded Imperialists. Empire, Society, and Culture in Britain*, Oxford, Oxford University Press, 2004.

13 K. Wilson, *An Island Race: Englishness, Empire and Gender in the Eighteenth Century*, London, Routledge, 2003, pp. 4, 19. See also K. Wilson, *The Sense of the People: Politics, Culture and Imperialism in Britain, 1715–1785*, Cambridge, Cambridge University Press, 1995.

14 C. Hall, *Civilising Subjects. Metropole and Colony in the English Imagination, 1830–1867*, Cambridge, Polity Press, 2002, pp. 8, 12.

15 R.J. Young, *Postcolonialism. An Historical Introduction*, Oxford, Blackwell, 2001, p. 37. See also A. Burton, 'Recapturing Jane Eyre: reflections on historicising the colonial encounter in Victorian Britain', *Radical History Review*, 1996, vol. 64, pp. 58–72.

16 The quotes are from Spivak, 'Three Women's Texts'.

17 E.W. Said, *Out of Place. A Memoir*, London, Granta, 1999, pp. 36, 37, 39, 42.

18 Z. Eisenstein, *Against Empire. Feminism, Racism, and the West*, London, Zed Books, 2004; B. Ehrenreich and A.R. Hochschild (eds), *Global Women. Nannies, Maids and Sex Workers in the New Economy*, London, Granta Books, 2003; M.J. Alexander and C.T. Mohanty (eds), *Feminist Genealogies, Colonial Legacies, Democratic Futures*,

New York, Routledge, 1997; C.T. Mohanty, *Feminism Without Borders. Decolonizing Theory, Practicing Solidarity*, Durham, Duke University Press, 2003; I. Gedalof, *Against Purity. Rethinking Identity with Indian and Western Feminism*, London, Routledge, 1999; C. Bulbeck, *Re-Orienting Western Feminisms. Women's Diversity in a Postcolonial World*, Cambridge, Cambridge University Press, 1998; L.M. Newman, *White Women's Rights. The Racial Origins of Feminism in the United States*, New York, Oxford University Press, 1999; S.M. James and C.C. Robertson, *Genital Cutting and Transnational Sisterhood. Disputing U.S. Polemics*, Urbana, University of Illinois Press, 2002.

19　J.W. Scott, 'The imagination of Olympe de Gouges' in E.J. Yeo (ed.), *Mary Wollstonecraft and 200 Years of Feminisms*, London, Rivers Oram Press, 1997, pp. 36–49, quotes from p. 37.

20　J. Rendall, *The Origins of Modern Feminism: Women in Britain, France and the United States, 1780–1860*, Basingstoke, Macmillan, 1985.

21　C.A. Bayly, *Imperial Meridian. The British Empire and the World 1780–1830*, London, Longman, 1989; A. Porter (ed.), *The Oxford History of the British Empire Vol. III: The Nineteenth Century*, Oxford, Oxford University Press, 1999; P.J. Cain and A.G. Hopkins, *British Imperialism, Vol. 1: Innovation and Expansion, 1688–1914*, London, Longman, 1993; A.N. Porter (ed.), *Atlas of British Overseas Expansion*, London, Routledge, 1991; R. Blackburn, *The Overthrow of Colonial Slavery 1776–1848*, London, Verso, 1988.

22　For recent approaches to the study of the period, see B. Hilton, *A Mad, Bad, and Dangerous People? England 1783–1846*, Oxford, Clarendon Press, 2006; A. Burns and J. Innes (eds), *Rethinking the Age of Reform: Britain, 1780–1850*, Cambridge, Cambridge University Press, 2003.

23　B. Hilton, *The Age of Atonement: The Influence of Evangelicalism on Social and Economic Thought, 1795–1865*, Oxford, Oxford University Press, 1988.

24　A. Briggs, *The Age of Improvement, 1783–1867*, Harlow, Longman, 2000.

25　Burton, *Burdens of History*. See also A. Burton, 'The feminist quest for identity: British imperial suffragism and "global sisterhood", 1900–1915', *Journal of Women's History*, 1991, vol. 3, pp. 46–81.

26　J. Bush, *Edwardian Ladies and Imperial Power*, London, Leicester University Press, 2000. See also J. Bush, ' "The right sort of woman": female emigrators and emigration to the British Empire, 1890–1910', *Women's History Review*, 1994, vol. 3, pp. 385–410.

27　For a discussion of the origins of the term and the question of using it anachronistically, see K. Offen, *European Feminisms, 1700–1950*, Stanford, Stanford University Press, 2000, pp. 19–26.

28　Wilson, *The Island Race*, p. 2.

29　Young, *Postcolonialism*, p. 63.

30　K. Offen, 'Defining feminism: a comparative historical approach', *Signs*, 1988, vol. 14, pp. 119–57 provides a useful discussion of varieties of feminisms, but confines comparison within the borders of Europe; Mohanty, *Feminism Without Borders* offers a rethinking of definitions from a transnational perspective, stressing the importance of solidarity between women.

31　Rendall, *The Origins of Modern Feminism*, p. 1.

32　See B. Caine, *English Feminism 1780–1980*, Oxford, Oxford University Press, 1997, pp. 1–10 for a thoughtful discussion of the problem of identifying feminism and feminists historically.

33　K. Sutherland, 'Hannah More's counter-revolutionary feminism', in K. Everest (ed.), *Revolution in Writing. British Literary Responses to the French Revolution*, Milton Keynes, Open University Press, 1991, pp. 27–63; J. McDermid, 'Conservative feminism and female education in the eighteenth century', *History of Education*,

1989, vol. 18, pp. 309–22; G. Kelly, 'Revolutionary and romantic feminism: women, writing and cultural revolution', in K. Hanley and R. Selden (eds), *Revolution and English Romanticism. Politics and Rhetoric*, Hemel Hempstead, Harvester Wheatsheaf, 1990, pp. 107–30.

34 Key studies of the 'woman question' and of middle-class women's activism which cover this period include: K. Gleadle and S. Richardson (eds), *Women in British Politics, 1760–1860. The Power of the Petticoat*, Basingstoke, Macmillan, 2000; K. Gleadle, *The Early Feminists. Radical Unitarians and the Emergence of the Women's Rights Movement, 1831–51*, Basingstoke, Macmillan, 1995; H. Guest, *Small Change. Women, Learning, Patriotism, 1750–1810*, Chicago, Chicago University Press, 2000; A.K. Mellor, *Mothers of the Nation. Women's Political Writing in England, 1780–1830*, Bloomington, Indiana University Press, 2002; F. Prochaska, *Women and Philanthropy in 19th Century England*, Oxford, Clarendon Press, 1980; J. Rendall, *Equal or Different. Women's Politics 1800–1914*, Oxford, Basil Blackwell, 1987; Rendall, *The Origins of Modern Feminism*; W. Stafford, *English Feminists and Their Opponents in the 1790s. Unsex'd and Proper Females*, Manchester, Manchester University Press, 2002; A. Summers, *Female Lives, Moral States. Women, Religion and Public Life in Britain 1800–1930*, Newbury, Threshold Press, 2000; B. Taylor, *Mary Wollstonecraft and the Feminist Imagination*, Cambridge, Cambridge University Press, 2003; A. Vickery (ed.), *Women, Privilege and Power. British Politics, 1750 to the Present*, Stanford, Stanford University Press, 2003; E.J. Yeo, *Radical Femininity. Women's Self-Representation in the Public Sphere*, Manchester, Manchester University Press, 1998.

35 B. Taylor, *Eve and the New Jerusalem. Socialism and Feminism in the Nineteenth Century*, London, Virago, 1983; A. Clark, *The Struggle for the Breeches. Gender and the Making of the British Working Class*, Berkeley, University of California Press, 1995; J. Schwarzkopf, *Women in the Chartist Movement*, Basingstoke, Macmillan, 1991; H. Rogers, *Women and the People. Authority, Authorship and the Radical Tradition in Nineteenth-Century England*, Aldershot, Ashgate, 2000.

36 H.McD. Beckles, *Natural Rebels. A Social History of Enslaved Black Women in Barbados*, London, Zed Books, 1989; H.McD. Beckles, *Centering Woman, Gender Discourses in Caribbean Slave Society*, Kingston, Ian Randle, 1999; B. Bush, *Slave Women in Caribbean Society 1650–1838*, London, James Currey, 1990; V. Shepherd, B. Brereton and B. Bailey (eds), *Engendering History. Caribbean Women in Historical Perspective*, Kingston, Ian Randle Publishers, 1995.

37 J.W. Scott, *Gender and the Politics of History*, New York: Columbia University Press, 1988; D. Riley, *'Am I That Name?' Feminism and the Category of 'Women' in History*, London, Macmillan, 1988.

38 Wilson, *The Island Race*, p. 30.

39 P. Gilroy, *The Black Atlantic. Modernity and Double Consciousness*, London, Verso, 1993, p. 17.

40 For an interesting feminist perspective on the relationship between social and cultural history, discussed in relation to the 'new imperial history', see A. Burton, 'Thinking beyond the boundaries: empire, feminism and the domains of history', *Social History*, 2001, vol. 26, pp. 60–71.

1 The 'woman question' in imperial Britain

1 For useful introductory overviews of the 'woman question' in late eighteenth- and early nineteenth-century Britain see: B. Caine, *English Feminism 1780–1980*, Oxford, Oxford University Press, 1997, chapters 1 and 2; J. Rendall, *The Origins of Modern Feminism: Women in Britain, France and the United States, 1780–1860*, Basingstoke, Macmillan, 1985.

2 S. Tomaselli, 'The Enlightenment debate on women', *History Workshop*, 1985, 20, pp. 101–24; P. Bowles, 'John Millar, the four stages theory, and women's position in society', *History of Political Economy*, 1984, 16, pp. 619–38; J. Rendall, 'Clio, Mars and Minerva: the Scottish Enlightenment and the writing of women's history' in T.M. Devine and J.R. Young (eds), *Eighteenth-Century Scotland. New Perspectives*, East Linton, Tuckwell Press, 1999, pp. 134–51; M.C. Moran, ' "The commerce of the sexes". Gender and the social sphere in Scottish Enlightenment accounts of civil society' in F. Trentmann (ed.), *Paradoxes of Civil Society. New Perspectives on Modern German and British History*, New York, Berghahn Books, 2000, pp. 61–84; M.E. Burnstein, *Narrating Women's History in Britain, 1770–1902*, Aldershot, Ashgate, 2004, pp. 16–49; B. Taylor, *Mary Wollstonecraft and the Feminist Imagination*, Cambridge, Cambridge University Press, 2003, quote from p. 156.

3 For contrasting approaches to the history of the eighteenth-century British Empire see: P.J. Marshall (ed.), *The Oxford History of the British Empire. Vol. 2. The Eighteenth Century*, Oxford, Oxford University Press, 1998; K. Wilson (ed.), *A New Imperial History. Cultural. Identity and Modernity in Britain and the Empire 1660–1840*, Cambridge, Cambridge University Press, 2004.

4 L. Colley, *Britons. Forging the Nation 1707–1837*, New Haven, Yale University Press, 1992; K. Wilson, *The Island Race. Englishness, Empire and Gender in the Eighteenth Century*, London, Routledge, 2003.

5 R. Blackburn, *The Making of New World Slavery. From the Baroque to the Modern 1492–1800*, London, Verso, 1997; J. Walvin, *Black Ivory: a History of British Slavery*, London, Harper Collins, 1992.

6 E. Said, *Orientalism*, Harmonsworth, Penguin, 1985 [original ed. 1978], p. 3.

7 S. Muthu, *Enlightenment against Empire*, Princeton, Princeton University Press, 2003.

8 G.S. Rousseau and R. Porter, 'Introduction: Approaching Enlightenment exoticism' in G.S. Rousseau and R. Porter (eds), *Exoticism in the Enlightenment*, Manchester, Manchester University Press, 1990, p. 9. See also P.J. Marshall and G. Williams, *The Great Map of Mankind: British Perceptions of the World in the Age of Enlightenment*, London, J.M. Dent & Sons, 1982. For the Enlightenment origins of the idea of progress, see J.B. Bury, *The Idea of Progress*, New York, Dover Publications, 1987.

9 S. Sebastiani, 'Race, women, and progress in the late Scottish Enlightenment' in S. Knott and B. Taylor (eds), *Women, Gender and Enlightenment*, Basingstoke, Palgrave Macmillan, 2005, pp. 75–96, quotes from pp. 84, 90.

10 J. Mander, 'No woman is an island: the female figure in French Enlightenment anthropology' in Knott and Taylor (eds), *Women, Gender and Enlightenment*, pp. 97–116; L. Jordanova, *Sexual Visions: Images of Gender in Science and Medicine between the Eighteenth and Twentieth Centuries*, London, Harvester Wheatsheaf, 1989, p. 29; 'Natural facts: a historical perspective on science and sexuality', *Nature, Culture and Gender*, Cambridge, Cambridge University Press, 1980, p. 61; T. Laqueur, *Making Sex: Body and Gender from the Greeks to Freud*, Cambridge (MA), Harvard University Press, 1990; L. Schiebinger, *The Mind Has No Sex? Women in the Origins of Modern Science*, Cambridge (MA), Harvard University Press, 1989; J. Rendall, *The Origins of Modern Feminism: Women in Britain, France and the United States, 1780–1860*, Basingstoke, Macmillan, 1987, pp. 7–32.

11 J.E. Bradley, *Religion, Revolution and English Radicalism: Nonconformity in Eighteenth-Century Politics and Society*, Cambridge, Cambridge University Press, 1990; D. Geggus, 'British opinion and the emergence of Haiti, 1791–1805' in J. Walvin (ed.), *Slavery and British Society 1776–1846*, London, Macmillan, 1982,

pp. 123–49. For women and radical dissent, see: K. Gleadle, 'British women and radical politics in the late nonconformist Enlightenment, *c.* 1780–1830' in A. Vickery (ed.), *Women, Privilege and Power. British Politics, 1750 to the Present*, Stanford, Stanford University Press, 2001, pp. 123–51.

12 K. O'Brien, 'Catherine Macaulay's histories of England: a female perspective on the history of liberty' in Knott and Taylor (eds), *Women, Gender and Enlightenment*, pp. 523–37.

13 C. Macaulay Graham, *Letters on Education. With Observations on Religious and Metaphysical Subjects*, London, C. Dilly, 1790, pp. 257–8.

14 Macaulay Graham, *Letters on Education*, p. 210.

15 Macaulay Graham, *Letters on Education*, pp. 48–9.

16 Macaulay Graham, *Letters of Education*, p. 213.

17 Macaulay Graham, *Letters on Education*, p. 220.

18 J. Zonana, 'The sultan and the slave: feminist orientalism and the structure of *Jane Eyre*', *Signs*, 1993, vol. 18, pp. 592–617. See also R. Kabbani, *Europe's Myths of Orient*, London, Pandora Press, 1988.

19 M. Wollstonecraft, *A Vindication of the Rights of Woman*, C.H. Poston (ed.), New York, W.W. Norton, 1975 ed. [reprint of 2nd ed., 1792], pp. 13, 60.

20 Wollstonecraft, *A Vindication*, p. 14. Note that modern scholars would see this as a common eighteenth-century misinterpretation of Rousseau, who actually saw settled agrarian society as the ideal state – see P. Gay, *The Enlightenment: An Interpretation. The Science of Freedom*, New York, W.W. Norton, 1977, pp. 538–9.

21 Wollstonecraft, *A Vindication*, p. 15.

22 Wollstonecraft, *A Vindication*, p. 7.

23 B. Taylor, *Mary Wollstonecraft and the Feminist Imagination*, Cambridge, Cambridge University Press, 2003, p. 155.

24 Taylor, *Mary Wollstonecraft*, p. 19.

25 J. Rendall, '"The grand causes which combine to carry mankind forward": Wollstonecraft, history and revolution', *Women's Writing*, vol. 4, no. 2 (1997), pp. 155–72.

26 Wollstonecraft, *A Vindication*, p. 144–5.

27 M. Ferguson, *Colonialism and Gender Relations from Mary Wollstonecraft to Jamaica Kincaid*, New York, Columbia University Press, 1993, pp. 8–33.

28 B. Carey, *British Abolitionism and the Rhetoric of Sensibility. Writing, Sentiment and Slavery, 1760–1807*, Basingstoke, Palgrave Macmillan, 2005; Moira Ferguson, *Subject to Others: British Women Writers and Colonial Slavery 1670–1834*, London, Routledge, 1992.

29 Wollstonecraft, *A Vindication*, pp. 186–7.

30 Wollstonecraft, *A Vindication*, p. 187.

31 Wollstonecraft, *A Vindication*, pp. 188, 117.

32 Wollstonecraft, *A Vindication*, p. 194.

33 C. Tomalin, *The Life and Death of Mary Wollstonecraft*, New York, Harcourt, Brace, Jovanovich, 1974; J. Todd, *Mary Wollstoncraft: A Revolutionary Life*, London, Weidenfeld & Nicholson, 2000; L. Gordon, *Mary Wollstonecraft, a New Genus*, London, Little, Brown, 2005.

34 M. Hays, 'Memoirs of Mary Wollstonecraft', *The Annual Necrology for 1797–8*, London, R. Phillips, 1800, pp. 422–3, as quoted in G.L. Walker, 'Mary Hays (1759–1843): an enlightened quest' in Taylor and Knott (eds), *Women, Gender and Enlightenment*, p. 507.

35 *Anti-Jacobin Review*, 1 (July 1798), pp. 94–9, as quoted in C. Franklin, 'Romantic patriotism as feminist critique of empire: Helen Maria Williams, Sydney Owenson and Germaine de Stael' in Hutton and Taylor, *Women, Gender and Enlightenment*, p. 552.

36 W. Stafford, *English Feminists and Their Opponents in the 1790s. Unsex'd and Proper Females*, Manchester, Manchester University Press, 2002, pp. 22–5, 84–7, 110–11, 201–2. For Robinson's anti-slavery poetry, see M. Ferguson, *Subject to Others. British Women Writers and Colonial Slavery, 1670–1834*, London, Routledge, 1992, pp. 175–8.

37 A.F. Randall [pseud.], *A Letter to the Women of England, on the Injustice of Mental Subordination*, London, T.N. Longman & O. Rees, 1799, pp. 4, 13.

38 Randall, *A Letter*, pp. 63, 64.

39 Randall, *A Letter*, p. 69.

40 Randall, *A Letter*, p. 87, footnote on p. 89.

41 H. Guest, *Small Change. Women, Learning, Patriotism, 1750–1810*, Chicago, University of Chicago Press, 2000; A.K. Mellor, *Mothers of the Nation. Women's Political Writing in England, 1780–1830*, Bloomington, Indiana University Press, 2002.

42 Randall, *A Letter*, p. 91.

43 L. Aikin, *Epistles on Women. Exemplifying Their Character and Condition in Various Ages and Nations*, London, J. Johnson & Co., 1810, pp. v, 19.

44 Aikin, *Epistles on Women*, pp. vii, viii.

45 A. Johnston, *Missionary Writing and Empire, 1800–1860*, Cambridge, Cambridge University Press, 2003, pp. 115–66.

46 A. Fausto-Sterling, 'Gender, race and nation: the comparative anatomy of "Hottentot" women in Europe, 1815–1817' in J. Terry and J. Urla (eds), *Deviant Bodies. Critical Perspectives on Difference in Science and Popular Culture*, Bloomington, Indiana University Press, 1995, pp. 19–48; Y. Abrahams, 'Images of Sara Bartmann: sexuality, race, and gender in early-nineteenth-century Britain' in R.R. Pierson and N. Chaudhuri (eds), *Nation, Empire, Colony. Historicizing Race and Gender*, Bloomington, Indiana University Press, 1998, pp. 220–36.

47 Aikin, *Epistles on Women*, p. 53, lines 10, 11.

48 Aikin, *Epistles on Women*, p. 68, line 262; p. 69, line 281; p.78, lines 442, 452–3; p. 79, line 460.

49 For the concept of republican motherhood, see Rendall, *The Origins of Modern Feminism*, pp. 33–62.

50 Stafford, *English Feminists*, p. 213.

51 B. Taylor, *Eve and the New Jerusalem. Socialism and Feminism in the Nineteenth Century*, London, Virago, 1984; D. Dooley, *Equality in Commmunity. Sexual Equality in the Writings of William Thompson and Anna Doyle Wheeler*, Cork, Cork University Press, 1996.

52 W. Thompson, *Appeal of One Half of the Human Race, Women, Against the Pretensions of the Other Half, Men, to Retain Them in Political and Thence in Civil and Domestic Slavery*, London, Longman, Hurst Rees, Orme, Brown and Green, 1825, p. 43. See also p. 42, pp. 55–63, 66–7.

53 Thompson, *Appeal*, pp. 194, 213.

54 R. Pankhurst, *William Thompson (1775–1833). Pioneering Socialist*, London, Pluto Press, 1991, pp. 57–69; Dooley, *Equality in Community*, pp. 107–39.

55 Thompson, *Appeal*, p. 18.

56 J. Pitts, *A Turn to Empire. The Rise of Imperial Liberalism in Britain and France*, Princeton, Princeton University Press, p. 129.

57 E. Stokes, *The English Utilitarians and India*, Delhi, Oxford University Press, 1982 edition; J. Majeed, *Ungoverned Imaginings: James Mill's 'The History of British India' and Orientalism*, Oxford, Clarendon Press, 1992.

58 Thompson, *Appeal*, pp. ix, xiii.

59 Thompson, *Appeal*, pp. 184–5.

60 Thompson, *Appeal*, p. 195.

61 Thompson, *Appeal*, p. 17.
62 Stokes, *The English Utilitarians*, p. viii.
63 Thompson, *Appeal*, p. 84.
64 Thompson, *Appeal,* p. 92.
65 M. Reid, *A Plea for Woman*, Edinburgh, Polygon, 1988 edition [reprint of original ed. 1843], p. 2. Susanna Ferguson (p. v) notes in her foreword that the book went into a second edition in 1845, was produced in a cheap edition in London in 1850 and was reprinted several times in America between 1845 and 1852.
66 Reid, *A Plea*, p. ix.
67 Reid, *A Plea*, pp. 1–4; p. 47.
68 Reid, *A Plea*, pp. 56–7.
69 K. Gleadle, *The Early Feminists. Radical Unitarians and the Emergence of the Women's Rights Movement, 1831–51*, Basingstoke, Macmillan, 1995, pp. 62–70, 75–96.
70 G. Malmgreen, 'Anne Knight and the radical subculture', *Quaker History*, 1982, vol. 71, p. 108; J. Schwarzkopf, *Women in the Chartist Movement*, Basingstoke, Macmillan, 1991, pp. 248 ff; Rendall, *The Origins of Modern Feminism*, pp. 308–9.
71 Midgley, *Women Against Slavery*, chapters 6 and 7.
72 H. Taylor Mill, 'The enfranchisement of women', *Westminster Review*, July 1851, reprinted in J.S. Mill and H. Taylor Mill, *Essays on Sex Equality*, A.S. Rossi (ed.), Chicago, University of Chicago Press, 1970, pp. 95–6.
73 Taylor Mill, 'The enfranchisement', p. 120.
74 Taylor Mill, 'The enfranchisement', pp. 108–9, 110, 117.
75 Taylor Mill, 'The enfranchisement, p. 117.
76 Pitt, *A Turn to Empire*, chapter 5.
77 J. Rendall, 'John Stuart Mill, liberal politics, and the movements for women's suffrage, 1865–1873' in A. Vickery (ed.), *Women, Privilege and Power. British Politics, 1750 to the Present*, Stanford, Stanford Unviersity Press, 2001, pp. 168–95, discusses Mill's use of Enlightenment stadial theory; see also C. Midgley, 'Anti-slavery and the roots of "imperial feminism"' in C. Midgley (ed.), *Gender and Imperialism*, Manchester, Manchester University Press, pp. 161–79.
78 D.W. Bebbington, *Evangelicalism in Modern Britain: A History from the 1730 to the 1980s*, London, Unwin Hyman, 1989; B. Hilton, *The Age of Atonement: The Influence of Evangelicalism on Social and Economic Thought*, Oxford, Oxford University Press, 1988; J. Wolffe (ed.), *Evangelical Faith and Public Zeal: Evangelicals and Society in Britaiun, 1780–1980*, London, SPCK, 1995; I. Bradley, *The Call to Seriousness: The Evangelical Impact on the Victorians*, London, Jonathan Cape, 1979; E.M. Howse, *Saints in Politics. The 'Clapham Sect' and the Growth of Freedom*, London, George Allen & Unwin, 1953; L. Davidoff and C. Hall, *Family Fortunes. Men and Women of the English Middle Class 1780–1850*, Routledge, London, 2002, *Part 1: Religion and Ideology*, pp. 71–192.
79 Rendall, *The Origins of Modern Feminism*, pp. 73–107, quote from p. 73; H. Guest, *Small Change. Women, Learning and Pariotism, 1750–1810*, Chicago, University of Chicago Press, 2000, pp. 271–289; M. Myers, 'Reform or ruin: "A revolution in female manners"', *Studies in Eighteenth-Century Culture*, 1982, vol. 11, pp. 199–216; J. McDermid, 'Conservative feminism and female education in the eighteenth century', *History of Education*, 1989, vol. 18, pp. 309–322.
80 Thomas Gisborne, *An Enquiry into the Duties of the Female Sex,* London: T. Cadell jun. and W. Davies, 1797, quotes from pp. 16, 17–18, 19.
81 Gisborne, *An Enquiry*, pp. 19–21, 23, 23–4.
82 A. Stott, *Hannah More. The First Victorian*, Oxford, Oxford University Press, 2003; A.K. Mellor, *Mothers of the Nation. Women's Political Writing in England, 1780–1830*, Bloomington, Indiana University Press, 2002, pp. 13–38; M. Myers, 'Hannah More's tracts for the times. Social fiction and female ideology' in M.A. Schofield

and C. Macheski (eds), *Fetter'd or Free? British Women Novelists, 1670–1815*, Athens (OH), Ohio University Press, 1986, pp. 264–84.

83 H. More, *Strictures on the Modern System of Female Education. With a View of the Principles and Conduct Prevalent among Women of Rank and Fortune*, London, T. Cadell jun., and W. Davies, 1799, vol. 1, p. x.

84 More, *Strictures*, vol. 1, pp. 2, 3.

85 More, *Strictures*, vol. 1, pp. 6, 4.

86 More, *Strictures*, vol. 1, pp. 215, 251.

87 More, *Strictures*, vol. 2, pp. 21, 22, 25–6.

88 More, *Strictures*, vol. 2, pp. 28–9.

89 More, *Strictures*, vol. 2, p. 30.

90 F.A. Cox, *Female Scripture Biography: Including an Essay on What Christianity Has Done for Women*, London, Gale & Fenner, 1817, vol. 1, pp. i–xcix.

91 Davidoff and Hall, *Family Fortunes*, pp. 181–5. The memoir of Mary Ellis will be discussed in Chapter 4.

92 For Ellis's influence on James, see Davidoff and Hall, *Family Fortunes*, p. 181.

93 James, *Female Piety: or, the Young Woman's Friend and Guide through Life to Immortality*, London, Hamilton, Adams & Co., 1852, quotes from pp. 5, 12, 16, 7, 18, 7, 19, 21 respectively.

94 James, *Female Piety*, quotes from pp. 23, 47, 24, 49 respectively.

95 James, *Female Piety*, sermon 3: women's mission, quotes from pp. 50, 59, 65, 63 respectively.

96 For an interesting discussion of the complex agendas, gender politics and orientalist features of Montesquieu's text and of Elizabeth Wortley Montagu's accounts of her experiences as the British ambassador's wife in the Ottoman Empire (published as *Embassy Letters* in 1763), see J. de Groot, 'Oriental feminiotopias? Montagu's and Montesquieu's "seraglios" revisited' in *Gender & History*, 2006, vol. 18, pp. 66–86.

97 A.K. Mellor, 'Romantic orientalism begins at home: Elizabeth Hamilton's *Translation of the Letters of a Hindoo Rajah*', *Studies in Romanticism*, 2005, vol. 44, pp. 151, 153, 155.

98 E. Benger, *Memoirs of the Late Mrs Elizabeth Hamilton*, 2 vols, London, Longman, Hurst, Rees, Orme & Brown, 1818, vol. 1, p. 126. See also S.B. Taylor, 'Feminism and orientalism in Elizabeth Hamilton's *Translation of the Letters of a Hindoo Rajah*', *Women's Studies*, 2000, vol. 29, p. 566; Claire Grogan, 'Crossing genre, gender and race in Elizabeth Hamilton's *The Translation of the Letters of a Hindoo Rajah*', *Studies in the Novel*, 2002, vol. 34, pp. 37–8.

99 G. Kelly, *Women, Writing and Revolution 1790–1827*, Oxford, Clarendon Press, 1993, pp. 127–8. For the impact of the Hastings trial, see N.B. Dirks, *The Scandal of Empire. India and the Creation of Imperial Britain*, Cambridge, Belknap Press, 2006.

100 E. Hamilton, *Translation of the Letters of a Hindoo Rajah*, London, G.G. & J. Robinson, 1776, vol. 1, pp. i–lx, quote from p. ix.

101 Hamilton, *Translation*, vol. 1, pp. 28–30, 34.

102 Hamilton, *Translation*, vol. 1, quotes from pp. 138, 144–5, 255–6.

103 Hamilton, *Translation*, vol. 2, p. 9.

104 Hamilton, *Translation*, vol. 2, p. 253.

105 Hamilton, *Translation*, vol. 1, pp. 32–4, 46.

106 Hamilton, *Translation*, vol. 2, pp. 314, 327–9.

107 Hamilton, *Translation*, vol. 2, pp. 168–73.

108 Rendall, 'Writing history for British women', pp. 89–90. The original source of the quotation is E. Hamilton, *Memoirs of the Life of Agrippina, Wife of Germanicus*, 3 vols, Bath, R. Cruttwell, 1804, vol. 2, pp. 21–2.

109 G. Claeys (ed.), *Modern British Utopias 1700–1850*, 8 vols, London, Pickering & Chatto, 1997, vol. 1, introduction, p. xxii. For the text's influence on the poet Shelley, see *The Empire of the Nairs (1811) by James H. Lawrence*, New York, Delmar, facsimile edition, 1976, introduction, by J.M. Todd, pp. ix–xi.

110 J. Lawrence, *The Empire of the Nairs; or, the Rights of Women. An Utopian Romance, in Twelve Books*, 4 vols, London, 2nd edn, T. Hookham and Son and E.T. Hookham, 1811.

111 Todd, introduction to the facsimile edition of *The Empire of the Nairs*, pp. i–vi.

112 Lawrence, *The Empire of the Nairs*, vol. 1, pp. ii, iii, xliii.

113 Lawrence, *The Empire of the Nairs*, vol. 1, p. 41.

114 Lawrrence, *The Empire of the Nairs*, vol. 1, quotes from pp. 4, 170 respectively.

115 Lawrence, *The Empire of the Nairs*, quotes from vol. 2, pp. 84, 110; vol. 3, p. 84; vol. 4, p. 262 respectively.

116 Entry by R. Garnett and N. Leask on James Henry Lawrence in H.C.G. Matthew and B. Harrison (eds), *Oxford Dictionary of National Biography*, Oxford, Oxford University Press, 2004.

117 Hamilton, *The Empire of the Nairs*, vol. 4, pp. 119–200; vol. 2, p. 60, vol. 1, p. xliii.

2 Sweetness and power: the domestic woman and anti-slavery politics

1 C. Midgley, *Women Against Slavery. The British Campaigns, 1780–1870*, London, Routledge, 1992, pp. 154–77; C. Midgley, 'Anti-slavery and feminism in Britain', *Gender and History*, 1993, vol. 5, pp. 343–62.

2 C. Midgley, 'British abolition and feminism in transatlantic perspective', in K.K. Sklar and J.B. Stewart (eds), *Women's Rights and Transatlantic Antislavery in the Era of Abolition*, Yale, Yale University Press, 2007, pp. 144–68. See also the valuable introductions to M. Ferguson (ed.), *The History of Mary Prince, A West Indian Slave. Related by Herself*, Ann Arbor, The University of Michigan Press, 1997; S. Salih (ed.), *The History of Mary Prince. A West Indian Slave*, London, Penguin, 2004.

3 Sidney W. Mintz, *Sweetness and Power. The Place of Sugar in Modern History*, New York, Viking Penguin, 1985.

4 For an interesting discussion of 'social motherhood', see E.J. Yeo, *The Contest for Social Science. Relations and Representations of Gender and Class*, London, Rivers Oram Press, 1996.

5 T. Clarkson, *History of the Rise, Progress, and Accomplishment of the Abolition of the African Slave-Trade by the British Parliament*, 2 vols, London, Longman, Hurst, Rees, and Orme, 1808, vol. 2, pp. 347–52; see also E.G. Wilson, *Thomas Clarkson. A Biography*, Basingstoke, Macmillan, 1989, pp. 72–7.

6 For example, D. Turley, *The Culture of English Antislavery*, London, Routledge, 1992, devotes under two pages (pp. 78–9) to the sugar boycott despite his focus on anti-slavery culture. For a fuller and more positive assessment, see J.R. Oldfield, *Popular Politics and British Anti-Slavery. The Mobilisation of Public Opinion Against the Slave Trade, 1787–1807*, Manchester, Manchester University Press, 1995.

7 G.J. Barker-Benfield, *The Culture of Sensibility. Sex and Society in Eighteenth-Century Britain*, Chicago, Chicago University Press, 1992, pp. 154–214; M. Berg and H. Clifford (eds), *Consumers and Luxury. Consumer Culture in Europe 1650–1850*, Manchester, Manchester University Press, 1999; M. Berg and E. Eger (eds), *Luxury in the Eighteenth Century: Debates, Desires and Delectable Goods*, Basingstoke, Palgrave Macmillan, 2003; J. Brewer and R. Porter (eds), *Consumption and the World of Goods*, London, Routledge, 1993; E. Kowaleski-Wallace, *Consuming Subjects: Women, Shopping, and Business in the Eighteenth Century*, New York, Columbia University

Press, 1997; W.D. Smith, 'Complications of the commonplace: tea, sugar, and imperialism', *Journal of Interdisciplinary History*, 1992, vol. 23, pp. 259–78.

8 C. Sussman, 'Women and the politics of sugar, 1792', *Representations*, 1994, vol. 48, pp. 48–69; C. Sussman, *Consuming Anxieties. Consumer Protest, Gender and British Slavery, 1713–1833*, Stanford, Stanford University Press, 2000; K. Davies, 'A moral purchase: femininity, commerce and abolition, 1788–1792', in E. Eger *et al.* (eds), *Women, Writing and the Public Sphere, 1700–1830*, Cambridge, Cambridge University Press, 2001, pp. 133–62; K.F. Hall, 'Culinary spaces, colonial spaces: the gendering of sugar in the seventeenth century', in V. Traub *et al.* (eds), *Feminist Readings of Early Modern Culture: Emerging Subjects*, Cambridge, Cambridge University Press, 1996, pp. 168–90.

9 This phrase is taken from P. Langford, *A Polite and Commercial People: England 1727–1783*, Oxford, Oxford University Press, 1989.

10 N. Deerr, *The History of Sugar*, London, Chapman and Hall, 1950, vol. 2, p. 430.

11 For a discussion of the relationship between sugar, slavery and the growth of British industrial production, see David Richardson, 'The slave trade, sugar, and British economic growth, 1748–1776', in B.L. Solow and S.L. Engerman (eds), *British Capitalism and Caribbean Slavery: the Legacy of Eric Williams*, Cambridge, Cambridge University Press, 1987, pp. 103–34.

12 J.E. Wills, 'European consumption and Asian production in the seventeenth and eighteenth centuries', in Brewer and Porter (eds), *Consumption and the World of Goods*, pp. 140–3.

13 J. Burnett, *Plenty and Want: A Social History of Diet in England from 1815 to the Present Day*, London: Nelson, 1966; J. Walvin, *Fruits of Empire. Exotic Produce and British Taste, 1660–1800*, Basingstoke, Macmillan, 1997; R.B. Sheridan, *Sugar and Slavery*, Lodge Hill, Caribbean Universities Press, 1974, pp. 26, 31, 32, Table 2.3; Mintz, *Sweetness and Power*, p. 157.

14 S. Marks, 'History, the nation and empire: sniping from the periphery', *History Workshop Journal*, 1990, vol. 29, p. 116.

15 S. Nenadic, 'Middle-rank consumers and domestic culture in Edinburgh and Glasgow 1720–1840', *Past and Present*, 1994, vol. 145, pp. 122–56; Sheridan, *Sugar and Slavery*, Chapter 15 and Table 15.2 (p. 351); Carole Shammas, 'Changes in English and Anglo-American consumption from 1550 to 1880 in Brewer and Porter (eds), *Consumption and the World of Goods*, p. 183.

16 Punch-bowl, tin-glazed earthenware, made at Pennington's works, Liverpool, 1760s, Ref. no. 536, City Museum and Art Gallery, Stoke-on-Trent.

17 D. Dabydeen (ed.), *The Black Presence in English Literature*, Manchester, Manchester University Press, 1985, p. 34; Keith A. Sandiford, *The Cultural Politics of Sugar. Caribbean Slavery and Narratives of Colonialism*, Cambridge, Cambridge University Press, 2000; J. Gilmore, *The Poetics of Empire: A Study of James Grainger's 'The Sugar Cane'*, London, Athlone Press, 2000; E.A. Bohls, 'The aesthetics of colonialism: Janet Schaw in the West Indies, 1774–5', *Eighteenth-Century Studies*, 1994, vol. 27, pp. 363–90.

18 M. Craton, *Testing the Chains: Resistance to Slavery in the British West Indies*, Ithaca, Cornell University Press, 1982.

19 D. Dabydeen, *Hogarth's Blacks: Images of Blacks in Eighteenth Century Art*, Manchester: Manchester University Press, 1987, pp. 17–40. The legality of black slavery within Britain was not challenged until the 1760s and, despite the 1772 judgment by Lord Mansfield prohibiting the forcible removal of Africans from Britain to slavery in the West Indies, the freedom of black people within Britain remained insecure until the passage of the Emancipation Act in 1833.

20 Creamware coffee pot and coffee cup, National Museums and Galleries on Merseyside (Liverpool Museum), 1980.24.2 and 59.119.107, see illustrations 150

and 151 in Anthony Tibbles (ed.), *Transatlantic Slavery: Against Human Dignity*, London, HMSO, 1994. See also G. Cameron and S. Crooke, *Liverpool – Capital of the Slave Trade*, Liverpool, Picton Press, 1992; R. Anstey and P. Hair, *Liverpool, the African Slave Trade, and Abolition*, [Liverpool], Historic Society of Lancashire and Cheshire, 1989.

21 *A Lady and her Children Relieving a Cottager*, mezzotint by John Raphael Smith, 1782 (after painting by W.R. Bigg), in collection of David Alexander, reproduced in Barker-Benfield, *The Culture of Sensibility*, p. 230.

22 G. Gerzina, *Black England. Life before Emancipation*, London, John Murray, 1995, pp. 90–132.

23 Hall, 'Culinary spaces'.

24 Frederick Slare, *Observations upon Bezoar-Stones, with a Vindication of Sugars against the Charge of Dr Willis, Other Physicians, and Common Prejudices*, London, Tim Goodwin, 1715, pp. 4, 8, as quoted in Mintz, *Sweetness and Power*, pp. 106–7.

25 Sussman, 'Women and the politics of sugar', p. 49.

26 H. Glasse, *The Compleat Confectioner: or, the Whole Art of Confectionary*, Dublin, John Exshaw, 1760.

27 The 1807 inventory of household contents of a Glasgow merchant, Scottish Record Office, CS 96/686, as listed in Nenadic, 'Middle-rank consumers', Appendix 3 (p. 156); Lorna Weatherill, 'The meaning of consumer behaviour in late seventeenth- and early eighteenth-century England', in Brewer and Porter (eds), *Consumption and the World of Goods*, p. 216; M. Berg, 'New commodities, luxuries and their consumers in eighteenth-century England', in Berg and Clifford (eds), *Consumers and Luxury*, pp. 63–85; H. Clifford, 'A commerce with things: the value of precious metalwork in early modern England', in Berg and Clifford (eds), *Consumers and Luxury*, pp. 147–69; Amanda Vickery, 'Women and the world of goods: a Lancashire consumer and her possessions, 1751–81', in Brewer and Porter (eds), *Consumption and the World of Goods*, p. 283.

28 Barker-Benfield, *The Culture of Sensibility*, p. xxvi, and discussion of the genre of teatime paintings on p. 159; see also Smith, 'Complications of the commonplace'.

29 Berg and Eger (eds), *Luxury in the Eighteenth Century*, pp. 3, 18–19, 191.

30 Clifford, 'A commerce with things', p. 163; Berg and Eger (eds), *Luxury in the Eighteenth Century*, introduction, p. 2; Hall, 'Culinary spaces', p. 169.

31 B. Kowaleski-Wallace, 'Tea, gender and domesticity in eighteenth-century England', *Studies in Eighteenth-Century Culture*, 1994, vol. 23, pp. 131–45; see also Kowaleski-Wallace, *Consuming Subjects*, pp. 1–15.

32 Dabydeen, *Hogarth's Blacks*.

33 Kowaleski-Wallace, *Consuming Subjects*, p. 39.

34 J. Austen, *Mansfield Park*, Harmondsworth, Penguin, 1966 reprint, p. 213; E. Said, *Culture and Imperialism*, New York, Alfred A. Knopf, 1993, p. 96.

35 B. Carey, *British Abolitionism and the Rhetoric of Sensibility. Writing, Sentiment, and Slavery, 1760–1807*, Basingstoke, Palgrave Macmillan, 2005; M. Ellis, *The Politics of Sensibility. Race, Gender and Commerce in the Sentimental Novel*, Cambridge, Cambridge University Press, 1996.

36 For women's role in the American boycotts on the 1760s and 1770s, see M.B. Norton, *Liberty's Daughters: the Revolutionary Experience of American Women, 1750–1800*, Boston, Little, Brown and Co., 1980, pp. 155–70; Linda K. Kerber, *Women of the Republic: Intellect and Ideology in Revolutionary America*, Chapel Hill: University of North Carolina Press, 1980, pp. 8, 36–45.

37 *Chester Chronicle*, 2 December 1791; E. Heyrick, *Appeal to the Hearts and Consciences of British Women*, Leicester, A. Cockshaw, 1828, p. 6.

38 For fascinating discussions linking women's consumption of anti-slavery literature with the broader relationship between abolitionism, consumption and commerce, see Davies, 'A moral purchase'; Sussman, *Consuming Anxieties.*

39 Barker-Benfield, *The Culture of Sensibility*, pp. 213–14; Oldfield, *Popular Politics*, pp. 155–61.

40 Clarkson, *The History of the Rise*, vol. 2, p. 192; see also W. Dickson, 'Diary of a visit to Scotland on behalf of the London Abolition Committee', Temp. MSS 10/4, Friends House Library, London.

41 Sussman, 'Women and the politics of sugar', p. 62.

42 M. Wood, *Blind Memory. Visual Representations of Slavery in England and America, 1780–1865*, Manchester, Manchester University Press, 2000, especially pp. 21–3.

43 L. Walker and V. Ware, 'Political pincushions: decorating the abolitionist interior 1787–1865', in I. Blyden and J. Floyd (eds), *Domestic Space. Reading the Nineteenth-Century Interior*, Manchester, Manchester University Press, 1999, pp. 58–83, quote from p. 58.

44 T. Wright, *The Life of William Cowper*, London, T. Fisher Unwin, 1892.

45 *An Address to Her Royal Highness the Duchess of York, against the Use of Sugar*, 1792; J. Gillray, *Anti-saccharites, or John Bull and his family leaving off the use of sugar*, 1792, engraving reproduced in Mary Dorothy George, *Catalogue of political and personal satires preserved in the Department of Prints and Drawings in the British Museum*, London, British Museum Publications, 1978, vol. 6, cat. no. 8074; G. Cruikshank, *The gradual abolition of the slave trade. Or leaving off sugar by degrees*, 1792, engraving in the British Museum's collection of prints and drawings, reproduced in Oldfield, *Popular Politics*, p. 178.

46 Clarkson, *History of the Rise*, vol. 2, p. 349.

47 K. Gleadle, '"Opinions deliver'd in conversation": conversation, politics, and gender in the late eighteenth century', in J. Harris (ed.), *Civil Society in British History*, Oxford, Oxford University Press, 2003.

48 Walker and Ware, 'Political pincushions', p. 71.

49 Staffordshire jug, *c*. 1815–20 in the Willett collection, Brighton Museum, see illustration 93A in W.D. John and Warren Baker, *Old English Lustre Pottery*, Newport, R.H. Johns, 1951; L.A. Compton, 'Josiah Wedgwood and the slave trade: a wider view', *Northern Ceramic Society Newsletter* no. 100 (Dec. 1995), p. 59, Fig. 4.

50 National Museums and Galleries on Merseyside (Liverpool Museum), 54.124.5, 54.124.1, illustrations 180, 181 in Tibbles (ed.), *Transatlantic Slavery*, pp. 93, 163; Album of the Female Society for Birmingham etc., for the Relief of Negro Slaves, *c*. 1825, ms. in Birmingham Central Library.

51 National Museums and Galleries on Merseyside (Liverpool Museum), 54.171.486, illustration 182 in Tibbles (ed.), *Transatlantic Slavery*, pp. 93, 163; Compton, 'Josiah Wedgwood and the slave trade', Figs. 2 and 3, p. 58.

52 Norwich Castle Museum 37.934 and illustration 184 in Tibbles (ed.), *Transatlantic Slavery*.

53 B. Henderson, 'East India sugar basins' advertising card, reproduced as Plate 22 in Deerr, *The History of Sugar*, vol. 2.

54 Statement by J.H. Flooks in West Indian Sub-Committee Minutes, 1828–30 as quoted in Moira Ferguson, *Subject to Others: British Women Writers and Colonial Slavery, 1670–1834*, London, Routledge, 1992, p. 261.

55 For Quaker women in nineteenth-century Britain, see: S.S. Holton, *Emotional Life, Memory and Radicalism in the Lives of Women Friends, 1820–1920*, London, Routledge, 2007; E.A. O'Donnell, 'Women's rights and women's duties: Quaker women in the nineteenth century, with special reference to Newcastle monthly meeting of women friends', unpublished PhD thesis, University of

Sunderland, 2000; C.M. Johnson, 'Quaker women peace campaigners in England 1820–1915', unpublished PhD thesis, Staffordshire University, 2002. For evangelical women, see C. Hall and L. Davidoff, *Family Fortunes. Men and Women of the English Middle Class 1780–1850*, London, Routledge, 2002, especially pp. 107–92.

56 For Quaker leadership of the abstention movement in America, see R.K. Nuermberger, *The Free Produce Movement. A Quaker Protest against Slavery*, Durham, Duke University Press, 1942. For Quakers and anti-slavery, see D.B. Davis, *The Problem of Slavery in the Age of Revolution, 1770–1823*, Ithaca, Cornell University Press, 1975, pp. 213–54; J. Jennings, *The Business of Abolishing the British Slave Trade 1783–1807*, London, Frank Cass, 1997.

57 J. Walvin, *The Quakers. Manners and Morals*, London, John Murray, 1997.

58 M. Birkett, *A Poem on the African Slave Trade. Addressed to Her Own Sex*, Dublin, J. Jones, 1792.

59 J. Teakle, 'The works of Mary Birkett Card 1774–1815: originally collected by her son Nathaniel Card in 1834: an edited transcription with an introduction to her life and works in two volumes', unpublished PhD thesis, University of Gloucestershire, 2004.

60 See E.M. Howse, *Saints in Politics: the 'Clapham Sect' and the Growth of Freedom*, London, George Allen & Unwin, 1953.

61 Letter from 'C' printed in *Manchester Mercury*, 6 November 1787.

62 W. Fox, *An Address to the People of Great Britain, on the Propriety of Abstaining from West Indian Sugar and Rum*, 25th edn, London, M. Gurney, 1791. At least 35,000 copies of this pamphlet were published, in various editions under slight variations of title.

63 D. Coleman, 'Conspicuous consumption: white abolitionism and English women's protest writing in the 1790s', *ELH*, 1994, vol. 61, pp. 341–62, quote from p. 349; see also Oldfield, *Popular Politics*, pp. 172–9.

64 See discussion in T. Morton, 'Blood sugar', in T. Fulford and P.J. Kitson (eds), *Romanticism and Colonialism. Writing and Empire, 1780–1830*, Cambridge, Cambridge University Press, 1998, pp. 87–107.

65 Birkett, *A Poem on the African Slave Trade*.

66 *Sheffield Register*, 16 December 1791.

67 'An answer to the question "do you take sugar in your tea?"', *The Negro's Forget Me Not*, London, 1829.

68 For an interesting discussion of the harnessing of the eighteenth-century literary cult of sensibility to abolitionist political ends, see B. Carey, *British Abolitionism and the Rhetoric of Sensibility. Writing, Sentiment, and Slavery, 1760–1807*, Basingstoke, Palgrave Macmillan, 2005.

69 Coleman, 'Conspicuous consumption', pp. 352, 353; J. Todd and M. Butler (eds), *The Works of Mary Wollstonecraft*, 7 vols, London, William Pickering, 1989, vol. 5, p. 45; *The Works of Anna Laetitia Barbauld. With a Memoir by Lucy Aikin*, 2 vols, London, Longman, 1825, vol. 1, pp. 176–77.

70 For a chronologically based account of women's participation in the boycott of slave-grown produce, see Midgley, *Women Against Slavery*, pp. 35–40, 60–2, 137–9. For the impact on women of the Evangelical movement for moral reform, see Catherine Hall, 'The early formation of Victorian domestic ideology', in *White, Male and Middle Class: Explorations in Feminism and History*, Cambridge: Polity Press, 1992, pp. 75–93.

71 *East India Sugar*, Sheffield, J. Blackwell, n.d.

72 Minute book of the Ladies' Society for the Relief of Negro Slaves, entry for 16 November 1826, ms in Birmingham Central Library Archives Dept.; '*What Does Your Sugar Cost?*' a Cottage Conversation on the Subject of British Negro Slavery,

Birmingham, 1828; C. Townsend, *Pity the Negro; or, an Address to Children on the Subject of Slavery*, 7th edn, London, Westley and Davis, 1829. At least 14,000 copies of Townsend's pamphlet were published.

73　A. Opie, *The Black Man's Lament; or, How to Make Sugar*, London, 1826, pp. 3, 4.

74　'The negro mother's appeal' in *The Negro's Forget Me Not*, and also printed in *Anti-Slavery Scrap Book*, London, 1829. See Midgley, *Women Against Slavery*, Fig. 12, p. 101.

75　R.M. George (ed.), *Burning Down the House. Recycling Domesticity*, Boulder, Westview Press, 1998, frontispiece illustration; p. 6.

76　*The Third Report of the Female Society for Birmingham, West Bromwich, Wednesbury, Walsall, and Their Respective Neighbourhoods, for the Relief of British Negro Slaves*, Birmingham, 1828, p. 21.

77　*Rules and resolutions of the Dublin Ladies' Anti-Slavery Society*, p. 10; Minute book of the Ladies' Society for the Relief of Negro Slaves, entries for 26 November 1829; Committee on Slavery minute book, entries for 6 and 20 October 1829 (mss Brit. Emp. S.20, E2/3, Anti-Slavery Collection, Rhodes House Library, Oxford); *The Genius of Universal Emancipation*, 3rd series, vol. 2, no. 5 (Sept 1831), pp. 73–4.

78　E. Heyrick, *Immediate, Not Gradual Abolition; or, an Inquiry into the Shortest, Safest, and Most Effectual Means of Getting Rid of West Indian Slavery*, London, Harchard, 1824, p. 4.

79　Sheffield Female Anti-Slavery Society, *Appeal of the Friends of the Negro to the British People; on behalf of the slaves in their colonies*, Sheffield: J. Blackwell, 1830, pp. 6–7.

80　Fox, *An Address to the People of Great Britain*; Wilson, *Thomas Clarkson*, p. 73.

81　Heyrick, *Immediate, Not Gradual Abolition*, pp. 6, 7 (italics in original).

82　E.V. Da Costa, *Crowns of Glory, Tears of Blood, The Demerara Slave Rebellion of 1823*, New York, Oxford University Press, 1994.

83　Heyrick, *Immediate, Not Gradual Abolition*, p. 22.

84　Heyrick, *Immediate, Not Gradual Abolition*, pp. 7, 18.

85　Sheffield Female Anti-Slavery Society, *Appeal of the Friends of the Negro to the British People*, Sheffield, J. Blackwell, 1830, p. 7.

86　*Report of the Sheffield Female Anti-Slavery Society*, 1827, p. 10.

87　K. Corfield, 'Elizabeth Heyrick: radical Quaker' in G. Malmgreen (ed.), *Religion in the Lives of English Women, 1760–1930*, London, Croom Helm, 1986, p. 48; Midgley, *Women Against Slavery*, pp. 103–16.

88　Anti-Slavery Society, *Ladies' Anti-Slavery Associations*, London, Bagster & Thoms, 1828; Anti-Slavery Society, *A Picture of Colonial Slavery, in the Year 1828, Addressed Especially to the Ladies of Great Britain*, London, Bagster & Thoms, 1828.

89　[E. Heyrick], 'Apology for ladies' antislavery associations', *Genius of Universal Emancipation*, 1831–2, 3rd series, vol. 2, pp. 110–12, 133–5, 149–52, quote from p. 133.

90　For a general account of the move to immediate emancipation, D.B. Davis, 'The emergence of immediatism in British and American antislavery thought', in *From Homicide to Slavery: Studies in American Culture*, Oxford University Press, 1986, pp. 238–57.

91　E. Heyrick, *Exposition of One of the Principal Causes of the National Distress*, London, Darton, Harvey and Darton, 1817, pp. 3, 20, 21, 29 respectively (italics in original).

92　E. Heyrick, *Enquiry into the Consequences of the Present Depreciated Value of Human Labour*, London, Longman, Hurst, Rees, Orme and Brown, 1819, p. 91.

93　David Brion Davis, 'The perils of doing history by a historical abstraction: a reply to Thomas L. Haskell's AHR Forum Reply' in T. Bender (ed.), *The Antislavery Debate: Capitalism and Abolitionism as a Problem in Historical Interpretation*, Berkeley, University of California Press, 1992, p. 308.

94 H.C.G. Matthew and B. Harrison (eds), *Oxford Dictionary of National Biography*, Oxford, Oxford University Press, 2004: entry by Isobel Grundy on Elizabeth Heyrick; E. Heyrick, *A Letter of Remonstrance from an Impartial Public, to the Hosiers of Leicester*, Leicester, A. Cockshaw, 1825.

95 Midgley, 'Anti-slavery and feminism in nineteenth-century Britain'.

96 Drescher, *Capitalism and Antislavery. British Mobilization in Comparative Perspective*, Basingstoke, Macmillan, 1986, p. 79; Oldfield, *Popular Politics*, p. 57.

97 A. Franklin, 'Enterprise and advantage: the West India interest in Britain, 1774–1840', unpublished PhD thesis, University of Pennsylvania, 1992, pp. 154–66.

98 James Cropper, *Letters Addressed to William Wilberforce MP Recommending the Encouragement of the Cultivation of Sugar in our Dominions in the East Indies, as the Natural and Certain Means of Effecting the Total and General Abolition of the Slave Trade*, Liverpool, 1822, pp. 1–5.

99 Townsend, *Pity the Negro*.

100 For an interesting discussion of the rivalry between the West India and East India interests, and its relationship to the anti-slavery debate, see Franklin, 'Enterprise and Advantage', pp. 154–98. See also [Zachary Macaulay], *East and West India Sugar; or, a Refutation of the Claims of West India Colonists to a Protecting Duty on East India Sugar*, London, 1823.

101 K. Charlton, James Cropper and Liverpool's contribution to the anti-slavery movement', reprinted from *Transactions of the Historical Society of Lancashire and Cheshire*, 1972, vol. 123; *Ladies' Anti-Slavery Associations*, London, Anti-Slavery Society, 1828.

102 See T. Bender (ed.), *The Antislavery Debate*. I discuss the merits of different positions in this debate through the lens of the abstention campaign in C. Midgley, 'Slave sugar boycotts, female activism and the domestic base of British anti-slavery culture', *Slavery and Abolition*, 1996, vol. 17, pp. 137–62.

103 E. Williams, *Capitalism and Slavery*, Chapel Hill, University of North Carolina Press, 1944, pp. 186–7.

104 Davis, *From Homicide to Slavery*, p. 289.

105 Birkett, *A Poem on the African Slave Trade*, Part 1, verse 24, lines 13, 16.

106 Birkett, *A Poem on the African Slave Trade*, Part 1, verse 25, lines 1–4.

107 Davies, 'A moral purchase', pp. 138–9.

108 Birkett, *A Poem on the African Slave Trade*, Part 2, verse 11, lines 19–22.

109 C.E. Phelan, 'On the flogging of women', poem in album of the Female Society for Birmingham etc, for the Relief of British Negro Slaves, ms. In Birmingham Central Library, Archives Dept.

110 W.E.H. Lecky, *History of European Morals from Augustus to Charlemagne*, 2 vols, London, Longmans, Green & Co, 1869, vol. 1, p. 169.

111 Sussman, 'Women and the politics of sugar', p. 60.

112 W. Allen, *The Duty of Abstaining from the Use of West India Produce*, London, T.W. Hawkins, p. 22.

113 A Burton, *Burdens of History. British Feminists, Indian Women, and Imperial Culture, 1865–1915*, Chapel Hill, University of North Carolina Press, 1994.

114 Clarkson, *History of the Rise*, vol. 2, p. 349.

115 E. Heyrick, *Letters on the Necessity of a prompt extinction of British colonial slavery*, London, 1826.

3 White women saving brown women?
British women and the campaign against *sati*

1 See, for example, the text of the petition of the female inhabitants of Melbourne, *Journal of the House of Commons*, 1829, vol. 84, entry for 2 April 1829, p. 192.

The term 'suttee' rather than *sati* was used in British nineteenth-century texts. Definitions of *sati* vary in English and Indian languages: see J.S. Hawley (ed.), *Sati, the Blessing and the Curse: The Burning of Wives in India*, New York, Oxford University Press, 1994, pp. 11–15. The term *sati* can refer either to the practice of widow burning or to the woman who burns. See also: A. Sharma (ed.), *Sati. Historical and Phenomenological Essays*, Delhi, Motilal Banarsidass, 1988; A. Nandy, 'Sati: a nineteenth century tale of women, violence and protest', in V.C. Joshi (ed.), *Rammohun Roy and the Process of Modernization in India*, Delhi, Vilcas Publishing House, 1975, pp. 168–94.

2 G. Spivak, Can the subaltern speak?, in C. Nelson and L. Grossberg (eds), *Marxism and the Interpretation of Culture*, Basingstoke, Macmillan Education, 1988, p. 296. For an interesting critique of Spivak's argument that colonial discourse allows no space for subaltern women's agency, see Ania Loomba, 'Dead women tell no tales: issues of female subjectivity, subaltern agency and tradition in colonial and post-colonial writings on widow immolation in India', *History Workshop Journal*, 1993, vol. 36, pp. 209–27. For more on the use of references to the abolition of sati to justify British colonial rule, particularly in the face of nationalist agitation in the 1920s, see J. Liddle and R. Joshi, *Daughters of Independence. Gender, Caste and Class in India*, London, Zed Books, 1986, pp. 30–2; Sharma, *Sati*, pp. 9–12.

3 L. Mani, 'Contentious traditions: the debate on sati in colonial India, 1780–1833, unpublished PhD thesis, University of California, Santa Cruz, 1989, p. 11.

4 L. Mani, 'Contentious traditions: the debate on *sati* in colonial India', in K. Sangari and S. Vaid (eds), *Recasting Women: Essays in Indian Colonial History*, New Brunswick, Rutgers University Press, 1990, p. 117. See also L. Mani, 'The production of an official discourse on sati in early nineteenth-century Bengal' in Francis Barker *et al.* (eds), *Empire and its Others*, 2 vols, Colchester, University of Essex, 1985, vol. 1, pp. 107–27.

5 Mani, 'Contentious traditions' unpublished PhD thesis, pp. 169–91.

6 K. Teltscher, *India Inscribed. European and British Writing on India 1600–1800*, Delhi, Oxford University Press, 1991, pp. 8, 51, 65.

7 D.M. Figueira, 'Die flambierte Frau: sati in European culture' and R.J. Lewis, 'Comment: sati and the nineteenth-century British self' in J.S. Hawley (ed.), *Sati. The Blessing and the Curse. The Burning of Wives in India*, Oxford, Oxford University Press, 1994, pp. 55–79; T.R. Metcalf, *Ideologies of the Raj*, Cambridge, Cambridge University Press, 1995, pp. 96–9; A. Chatterjee, *Representations of India, 1740–1840. The Creation of India in the Colonial Imagination*, Basingstoke, Macmillan, 1998, pp. 111–24.

8 K.K. Dyson, *A Various Universe: A Study of the Journals and Memoirs of British Men and :Women in the Indian Subcontinent, 1765–1856*, Delhi, Oxford University Press, 1978; I. Ghose, *Women Travellers in Colonial India: The Power of the Female Gaze*, Delhi, Oxford University Press, 1998; R. Raza, *In Their Own Words. British Women Writers and India 1740–1857*, New Delhi, Oxford University Press, 2006.

9 J.W. Kindersley, *Letters from the Island of Teneriffe, Brazil, the Cape of Good Hope, and the East Indies*, London, J. Nourse, 1777, p. 125.

10 E. Fay, *Original Letters from India*, Calcutta, 1821, pp. 292–4.

11 Phebe Gibbes, *Hartly House*, Calcutta, 3 vols, London, J. Dodsley, 1789, vol. 2, pp. 140–1.

12 See discussions of the novel in F. Nussbaum, *Torrid Zoes. Maternity, Sexuality, and Empire in Eighteenth-Century English Narratives*, Baltimore, The Johns Hopkins University Press, 1995, pp. 166–91.

13 M. Starke, *The Widow of Malabar. A Tragedy, in Three Acts*, London, William Lane, 1791, pp. 9–12, 45.

14 S. Owenson (Lady Morgan), *The Missionary*, London, J.J. Stockdale, 1811; N. Leask, *British Romantic Writers and the East. Anxieties of Empire*, Cambridge, Cambridge University Press, 1992, pp. 1–12, 116.

15 The Baptist Missionary Society was formed by the Particular Baptists in 1792; the non-denominational, but predominantly Congregational, London Missionary Society was founded in 1795; Evangelical Anglicans founded the Church Missionary Society in 1799, and the Wesleyan Methodist Missionary Society was set up n 1813. See B. Stanley, *The Bible and the Flag. Protestant Missions and British Imperialism in the Nineteenth and Twentieth Centuries*, Leicester, Apollos, 1990; A. Porter, *Religion Versus Empire? British Protestant Missionaries and Overseas Expansion, 1700–1914*, Manchester, Manchester University Press, 2004; S. Thorne, *Congregational Missions and the Making of an Imperial Culture in 19th-Century England*, Stanford, Stanford University Press, 1999.

16 For the close link between 'home' and 'foreign' missions, see S. Thorne, '"The conversion of Englishmen and the conversion of the world inseparable": missionary imperialism and the language of class in early industrial Britain', in F. Cooper and L. Stoler (eds), *Tensions of Empire: Colonial Cultures in a Bourgeois World*, Berkeley, University of California Press, 1997, pp. 238–62.

17 Brian Stanley, *The Bible and the Flag*, Chapter 3.

18 C. Grant, *Observations on the State of Society among the Asiatic Subjects of Great Britain, Particularly with Respect to Morals; and on the Means of Improving It – Written Chiefly in the Year 1792*, London, House of Commons, 1813, pp. 55, 30 respectively.

19 William Wilberforce, 'Substance of the speech of William Wilberforce, Esq. on the clause of the East India Bill for promoting the religious instruction and moral improvement of the natives of the British dominions in India, on the 22nd of June, and the 1st and 12th of July, 1813', in *The Pamphleteer* 1814, vol. 3, pp. 43–113: quote from p. 70; *Parliamentary Debates*, 1st series, vol. 26, London: T.C. Hansard, 1813, pp. 860–2.

20 Lata Mani, *Contentious Traditions. The Debate on Sati in Colonial India*, Berkeley, University of California Press, 1998, p. 149. See Chapter 4 herein for a detailed account of how missionary accounts of India were reshaped as propaganda directed at British audiences, in the process becoming far more unequivocally derogatory about Indian religion and custom.

21 The quote is from leading evangelical poet William Cowper, *The Task* (1785), as quoted in Leonore Davidoff and Catherine Hall, *Men and Women of the English Middle Class 1780–1850*, London, Hutchinson, 1987, p. 165.

22 John Pollock, *Wilberforce*, Tring, Lion Publishing, 1986, p. 236.

23 Stanley, *The Bible and the Flag*, p. 98; E.M. Howse, *Saints in Politics: the 'Clapham Sect' and the Growth of Freedom*, London, George Allen and Unwin, 1953, pp. 86, 92; J. Civin, 'Slaves, sati and sugar: constructing imperial identity through Liverpool petition struggles' in J. Hoppit (ed.), *Parliaments, Nations and Identities in Britain and Ireland, 1660–1850*, Manchester, Manchester University Press, 2003, pp. 187–204, see especially p. 196; letter from Mrs H. More to Wm. Wilberforce, Barley Wood, 12 April 1813, as quoted in R.I. Wilberforce and S. Wilberforce (eds), *The Correspondence of William Wilberforce*, 2 vols, London, John Murray, 1840, vol. 2, pp. 240–1.

24 F. Prochaska, *Women and Philanthropy in Nineteenth-Century England*, Oxford, Clarendon Press, 1980, pp. 23–9; Eugene Stock, *The History of the Church Missionary Society*, 3 vols, London, Church Missionary Society, 1899, vol. 1, p. 243.

25 Ward's text became a key source of information on Hindu religion and society in Britain at this period – see Lata Mani, 'Contentious traditions', unpublished PhD thesis, p. 143.

26 *Missionary Register*, April 1814, pp. 136–40.

27 Prochaska, *Women and Philanthropy.*
28 For the links that women made between metropolitan and imperial philanthropic missions to women and children at this period, see A. Twells (1998), 'Let us begin well at home': class, ethnicity and Christian motherhood in the writing of Hannah Kilham, 1774–1832, in E.J. Yeo (ed.), *Radical Femininity. Women's Self-Representation in the Public Sphere*, Manchester, Manchester University Press, 1998, pp. 25–51; A. Twells, '"Happy English children": class, ethnicity and the making of missionary women, 1800–40', *Women's Studies International Forum*, 1998, vol. 21, pp. 235–46.
29 For the similar centrality of family and household to the British missionary project in the West Indies, see C. Hall, *White, Male and Middle Class: Explorations in Feminism and History*, Cambridge, Polity Press, 1992, pp. 205–54.
30 M.A. Laird, *Missionaries and Education in Bengal, 1793–1837*, Oxford, Clarendon Press, 1972, p. xii; K. Ingham, *Reformers in India, 1793–1833: An Account of the Work of Christian Missionaries on Behalf of Social Reform*, Cambridge, Cambridge University Press, 1956, p. 55; K.P. Sen Gupta, *The Christian Missionaries in Bengal, 1793–1833*, Calcutta, Firma K.L. Mukhopadhyay, 1971, p. 97.
31 For the lives of the early Baptist missionaries and their wives in India, see J.C. Marshman, *The Life and Times of Carey, Marshman, and Ward. Embracing a History of the Serampore Mission*, 2 vols, London, Longman, Brown, Green, Longmans, and Roberts, 1859; E.D. Potts, *British Baptist Missionaries in India 1793–1837. The History of Serampore and its Missions*, Cambridge, Cambridge University Press, 1967.
32 Stock, *The History of the Church Missionary Society*, vol. 1, pp. 124–5; for similar problems faced by a single woman who wished to undertake Christian educational work in West Africa in the 1820s, see Twells, 'Let Us Begin Well at Home'.
33 For brief overviews of development of girls' schools between 1793 and 1833, see Laird, *Missionaries and Education*, pp. 133–54; Ingham, *Reformers in India*, pp. 84–95; Sen Gupta, *The Christian Missionaries*, pp. 108–11.
34 Entries by E.D. Potts on William Ward and Hannah Marshman, in D.M. Lewis (ed.), *The Blackwell Dictionary of Evangelical Biography, 1730–1860*, 2 vols, Oxford, Blackwell, 1995.
35 W. Ward, *A View of the History, Literature and Religion of the Hindoos*, 2 vols, London, Baptist Missionary Society, 3rd edn, 1817, vol. 1, preface; W. Ward, 'Letter to the ladies of Liverpool, and of the United Kingdom', *The Times*, 3 January 1821, p. 3; W. Ward, *Farewell Letters to a Few Friends in Britain and America, on Returning to Bengal in 1821*, London, Black, Kingsbury, Oarbury and Allen, 1821, letter to Miss Hope of Liverpool, pp. 62–85. For information on Ward's visit to Britain, see Marshman, *The Life and Times*, pp. 199, 242.
36 Ward, *Farewell Letters*, p. 73
37 Ward, *A View*, vol. 1, preface, p. xvii.
38 Ward, *A View*, vol. 1, preface, p. l.
39 Stanley, *The Bible and the Flag*, p. 68.
40 Ward, *A View*, vol. 1, preface, p. l.
41 Ward, 'Letter to the ladies'.
42 Ward, *Farewell Letters*, p. 83.
43 Entry on W. Ward by D. Potts in *Blackwell's Dictionary of Evangelical Biography*; Ward, *A View*, p. 1.
44 Ward, 'Letter to the ladies'.
45 Ward, *Farewell Letters*, p. 84.
46 Ward, 'Letter to the ladies'.
47 Ward, 'Letter to the ladies'.
48 Ward, *Farewell Letters*, p. 82.

49 *Missionary Register*, Oct 1820, p. 434.

50 *Missionary Register*, Oct 1820, p. 435.

51 *Missionary Register*, May 1821, p. 197–8.

52 *Missionary Register*, Nov. 1822, p. 481.

53 *Missionary Register*, June 1825, p. 245.

54 *Missionary Register*, Nov. 1822, pp. 509–10; June 1826, pp. 346–50. Cooke's activities had initially been placed by the British and Foreign School Society under the direction of the Calcutta School Society (set up in 1818 mainly to improve indigenous elementary schools for boys), but Hindu members of the society were unhappy about the Christian curriculum in her schools, and control was soon shifted to the Church Missionary Society.

55 It was on these grounds that the Governor-General Lord Amherst in 1825 over-ruled his council and refused a government grant to the Ladies' Society for Native-Female Education – see Bengal General Letter, 30 September 1825, paragraphs 54–7, India Office Records E/4/116, British Library.

56 *Missionary Register*, March 1825, pp. 124–5; April 1825, pp. 192–3, June 1825, pp. 244–6.

57 *Missionary Register*, Sept. 1829, p. 392.

58 *Missionary Register*, Nov. 1822, p. 485.

59 *Missionary Register*, June 1825, p. 246. David Savage has argued that there was a shift in the nature of missionary education for Indian women between the 1830s and the 1850s, from a focus on the moral rescue of degraded and oppressed women to a focus on training women to be mothers and moral reformers (D. Savage, 'Missionaries and the development of a colonial ideology of female education in India', *Gender and History*, 1997, vol. 9, pp. 201–21). However, the writings of Cooke and Ward suggest that, in the 1820s, missionary education for girls combined both objectives.

60 'A scholar of the native-female schools in Calcutta', Church Missionary Society, *Missionary Papers*, 1828, no. 49; 'School of Hindoo girls at Calcutta', *Missionary Register*, March 1826; 'A suttee: or, the burning of a Hindoo widow with the body of her husband', frontispiece illustration in James Peggs, *India's Cries to British Humanity*, 2nd edn, London, Seeley & Son, 1830. All these images are reproduced in C. Midgley, 'Female emancipation in an imperial frame: English women and the campaign against sati (widow-burning) in India, 1813–30', *Women's History Review*, 2000, vol. 9, pp. 95–121.

61 Church Missionary Society, *The Quarterly Papers*, Missionary Papers nos. 26 (1822), 32 (1823), 34 (1824), 41 (1826), 49 (1828).

62 *The General Baptist Repository and Missonary Observer*, 1827, p. 258.

63 T.S. Grimshawe, *An Earnest Appeal to British Humanity in Behalf of Hindoo Widows; in Which the Abolition of the Barbarous Rite of Burning Alive, is Proved to be Both Safe and Practicable*, London, J. Hatchard and L.B. Seeley, 1825, pp. 42–3.

64 M. Mainwaring, *The Suttee; or, the Hindoo Converts*, 3 vols, London, A.K. Newman & Co., 1830.

65 J. Thompson, *Memoir of British Female Missionaries with a Survey of Women in Heathen Countries*, London, William Smith, 1841.

66 *The Children's Missonary Meeting in Exeter Hall, on Easter Tuesday, 1842*, p. 14, as quoted in F. Prochaska, *Women and Philanthropy in 19th Century England*, Oxford, Clarendon Press, 1980, pp. 92–3. Prochaska also notes a tale of 'Suttee' in *A Quarterly Token for Juvenile Subscribers*, January 1866, pp. 6–8, indicating the persistence of sati in juvenile missionary literature into the second half of the nineteenth century.

67 W. Johns, *A Collection of Facts and Opinions Relative to the Burning of Widows with the Dead Bodies of Their Husbands*, Birmingham, W. Pearce, 1816, quote from p. vi;

E.D. Potts, *British Baptist Missionaries in India 1793–1837. The History of Serampore and its Missions*, Cambridge, Cambridge University Press, 1967, p. 65; Lata Mani, 'Contentious traditions: the debate on sati in colonial India, 1780–1833', unpublished PhD thesis, p. 244.

68 There is an extensive literature on Roy. A useful starting point is V.C. Joshi (ed.), *Rammohun Roy and the Process of Modernisation in India*, Delhi, Vikas, 1975. For the English text of Roy's tracts on *sati* see 'Translation of a conference between an advocate for and an opponent of the practice of burning widows alive, Calcutta, 1818', and 'A second conference between an advocate for and an opponent of the practice of burning widows alive', Calcutta, 1820, reproduced in J.C. Ghose (ed.), *The English Works of Raja Rammohun Roy*, New Delhi, Cosmo, 1982, vol. 2.

69 *The Parliamentary Debates*, London, Hansard, 1822, new series, vol. 5, entry for 20 June 1821, col. 1217.

70 'A Petition of the Gentry, Clergy and other Inhabitants of the County of Bedford', *Journal of the House of Commons*, 1823, vol. 78, p. 404, entry for 18 June.

71 J. Peggs, *The Suttees' Cry to Britain*, London, Seeley & Co., 1827.

72 *The General Baptist Repository and Missionary Observer*, 1827, pp. 152, 312; 1828, pp. 77–80, 120, 239–40.

73 For reports of the society's formation, see, for example, *General Baptist Repository*, 1829 p. 37; *Baptist Magazine*, 1829, p. 33; *Missionary Register*, 1829, p. 146; *Monthly Repository*, 1829, p. 71.

74 First report of the Coventry Society for the Abolition of Human Sacrifices in India. February 1, 1830', *The General Baptist Repository and Missionary Observer*, 1830, pp. 113–18.

75 *Journal of the House of Commons*, 1823, vol. 78, p. 404; 1824–5, vol. 79, p. 144; 1826–7, vol. 82, pp. 234, 334, 340, 462, 472, 478, 486, 491, 505, 511, 567, 567, 571, 575; 1828, vol. 83, pp. 6, 313, 409, 443, 467, 477, 491, 494, 525, 555; 1829, vol. 84, pp. 28, 192, 370, 384, 406; 1830, vol. 85, pp. 69, 148, 160, 184, 190, 214, 235, 242, 255, 282, 402, 590, 603.

76 Joshua Civin includes a brief discussion of Liverpool anti-sati petitions in Joshua Civin, 'Slaves, sati and sugar: constructing imperial identity through Liverpool petition struggles', in Julian Hoppit (ed.), *Parliaments, Nations and Identities in Britain and Ireland, 1660–1850*, Manchester, Manchester University Press, 2003, pp. 187–205, see especially pp. 197–8. I am, however, not entirely convinced by his suggestion that these were stimulated by East India merchants keen to put a humanitarian gloss on the campaign to abolish the commercial monopoly of the East India Company.

77 J. Peggs, *The Suttees' Cry to Britain*, 2nd edn, London, Seeley and Co., 1828, p. 81.

78 Peggs, *The Suttees' Cry*, p. 91, footnote.

79 Peggs, *The Suttees' Cry*, p. 97.

80 *Baptist Magazine*, 1829, vol. 21, p. 475.

81 *Baptist Magazine*, 1830, vol. 22, pp. 74–5.

82 *Journal of the House of Commons*, 1829, vol. 84, pp. 28, 192, 370, 375, 406; 1830, vol. 85, pp. 69, 148, 184, 235; *Journal of the House of Lords*, 1829, vol. 61, p. 591; 1830, vol. 62, pp. 45, 74, 136, 183.

83 *The Times*, 3 April 1829, p. 4, col. B: 'House of Commons, Thursday, April 2'.

84 *The General Baptist Repository and Missionary Observer*, 1827, p. 471.

85 L. Colley, *Britons, Forging the Nation 1707–1837*, New Haven, Yale University Press, 1992, pp. 278–9; for parliamentary reception of these petitions in 1829, see *Parliamentary Debates*, London, Hansard, 1829, new series vol. 20, pp. 570–2, 372–3; 1322–7.

86 *Parliamentary Debates*, London, Hansard, 1829, n.s. vol. 20, pp. 570–2.

87 *Parliamentary Debates*, London, Hansard, 1829, n.s. vol. 20, pp. 372–3. See also W. Hinde, *Catholic Emancipation. A Shake to Men's Minds*, Oxford, Blackwell, 1992, pp. 138–42.

88 *Parliamentary Debates*, London, Hansard, 1829, n.s. vol. 20, pp. 1322–4.

89 Midgley, *Women Against Slavery*, pp. 23–5.

90 *The Times*, Friday, 3 April 1829, p. 4, col. B: 'House of Commons, Thursday, April 2'.

91 Midgley, *Women Against Slavery*, pp. 62–71.

92 *Appendix to the Votes and Proceedings of the House of Commons*, 1830, pp. 52, 285; *Journal of the House of Lords*, 1830, vol. 62, p. 183.

93 *Baptist Magazine*, 1829, vol. 21, p. 475.

94 *Appendix to the Votes and Proceedings of the House of Commons*, 1829, p. 1515.

95 *Baptist Magazine*, 1830, vol. 22, p. 116.

96 S. Zaeske, *Signatures of Citizenship. Petitioning, Antislavery, and Women's Political Identity*, Chapel Hill, University of North Carolina Press, 2003, p. 12.

97 *Appendix to the Votes and Proceedings of the House of Commons*, 1830, pp. 52, 285.

98 Zaeske, *Signatures of Citizenship*, pp. 23–7.

99 Midgley, *Women Against Slavery*, pp. 127–32.

100 J.R. Jeffrey, *The Great Silent Army of Abolitionism. Ordinary Women in the Antislavery Movement*, Chapel Hill, University of North Carolina Press, 1998, p. 38.

101 For a pioneering study of transatlantic links between women activists in the early nineteenth century, see B.S. Anderson, *Joyous Greetings. The First International Women's Movement 1830–1860*, Oxford, Oxford University Press, 2000.

102 Zaeske, *Signatures of Citizenship*, pp. 7–8.

103 J. Rosselli, *Lord William Bentinck. The Making of a Liberal Imperialist 1774–1839*, Delhi, Thompson Press, 1974. Rosselli notes that Bentinck was a supporter of anti-slavery, a friend of Charles Grant, an active member of the British and Foreign Bible Society and an associate of the Clapham Sect.

104 C.H. Philips, *The Correspondence of Lord William Cavendish Bentinck*, 2 vols, Oxford, Oxford University Press, 1977, vol. 1, pp. xxvi–xxviii, 94, 191–5, 335–45, 360–2 (text of the regulation). For Bombay and Madras, see K. Ballhatchet, *Social Policy and Social Change in Western India*, London, Oxford University Press, 1957, pp. 304–5.

105 For Roy's stay in Britain (he died and was buried in Bristol in 1833) and his influence here as described by three nineteenth-century English Unitarian feminists, see: P.H. le Breton (ed.), *Memoirs, Miscellanies and Letters of the Late Lucy Aikin*, London, Longmans and Co., 1824, pp. 226, 230–1, 248, 257–9, 282, 289–90, 297–8; M. Carpenter, *The Last Days in England of the Rajah Rammohun Roy*, London, Tubner and Co., 1866; S.D. Collett (ed.), *The Life and Letters of Raja Rammohun Roy*, London, Harold Collett, 1900.

106 C.A. Bayly, *Indian Society and the Making of the British Empire*, Cambridge, Cambridge University Press, 1988, Chapter 4.

107 Arvind Sharma highlights the contest between Indian and British scholars over assigning credit for the abolition of sati – see A. Sharma (ed.), *Sati. Historical and Phenomenological Essays*, Delhi, Motilal Banarsidass, 1988, pp. 10–14.

108 Peggs, *India's Cries to British Humanity*, frontispiece engraving.

109 M. Busco, *Sir Richard Westmacott, Sculptor*, Cambridge, Cambridge University Press, 1994, pp. 82–5; A.S. Das Gupta, *A Brief Guide to the Victoria Memorial, Calcutta*, Calcutta, 1967; entry on 'Lord William Cavendish Bentinck', *The Dictionary of National Biography*, London, Smith, Elder and Co., 1885, vol. 4; B. Cohn, *Colonialism and its Forms of Knowledge. The British in India*, Princeton, Princeton University Press, 1996, pp. 5–6; B. Groseclose, 'Imag(in)ing Indians', *Art History*, 1990, vol. 13, pp. 488–515.

110 Mrs Phelps, 'The suttee', in *The Suttee, and Other Poems*, Thame, H. Bradford, 1831, pp. 1–22, quote from p. 21, verse 31, lines 4–6.

111 R. Heber, *Narrative of a Journey Through the Upper Provinces of India*, 2 vols, London, John Murray, 3rd edn, 1828, vol. 1, pp. 71–2.

112 For the evangelical ideal of sensitive manhood, see Davidoff and Hall, *Family Fortunes*, pp. 110–13.

113 R.S. Rajan, *Real and Imagined Women. Gender, Culture and Postcolonialism*, London, Routledge, 1993, p. 42; G. Spivak, 'Can the subaltern speak?', p. 296.

114 Fanny Parks, *Wanderings of a Pilgrim, in Search of the Picturesque, During Four-and-Twenty Years in the East*, 2 vols, London, Pelham Richardson, 1850, pp. 91–5, 162; see also entry on Fanny Parks by R. Raza in H.C.G. Matthew and B. Harrison (eds), *Oxford Dictionary of National Biography*, Oxford, Oxford University Press, 2004.

115 Liddle and Joshi, *Daughters of Independence*, p. 7.

116 For women anti-slavery campaigners' perspectives, see Midgley, *Women Against Slavery*, Chapter 5.

117 P. H. le Breton (ed.), *Memoirs, Miscellanies and Letters of the Late Lucy Aikin*, London, Longman, Green, 1864, pp. 230–1; see also pp. 248, 258–82, 289–90, 297–8 for further praise of Roy in Aikin's letters to the leading American Unitarian divine, the Rev. Dr Channing.

118 J.E. Carpenter, *The Life and Work of Mary Carpenter*, London, Macmillan, 1879, pp. 31, 42.

119 M. Carpenter (ed.), *The Last Days in England of the Rajah Rammohun Roy*; M. Carpenter, *Six Months in India*, 2 vols, London, Longmans, Green, 1868, vol. 1 frontispiece and dedication.

120 Burton, *Burdens of History*, especially pp. 111–13, 122–3, quote from p. 122.

121 Collett (ed.), *The Life and Letters of Raja Rammahun Roy*.

122 C.T. Mohanty, Under western eyes: feminist scholarship and colonial discourse' in C.T. Mohanty, A. Russo and L. Torres (eds), *Third World Women and the Politics of Feminism*, Bloomington, Indiana University Press, 1991, pp. 51–80. See also V. Amos and P. Parmar, 'Challenging imperial feminism, *Feminist Review*, 1984, vol. 17, pp. 3–19.

123 G. Spivak, 'Three women's texts and a critique of imperialism', *Critical Inquiry*, 1985, vol. 12, pp. 243–61. See also A. Burton, 'Recapturing Jane Eyre: reflections on historicizing the colonial encounter in Victorian Britain', *Radical History Review*, 1996, vol. 64, pp. 58–72. The quote is from Charlotte Brontë, *Jane Eyre*, Harmondsworth, Penguin, 1966, p. 301.

4 Can women be missionaries?
Imperial philanthropy, female agency and feminism

1 C. Brontë, *Jane Eyre* (original edn 1847), Penguin, Harmondsworth, 1966, pp. 424–34.

2 G.C. Spivak, 'Three women's texts and a critique of imperialism', in R. Lewis and S. Mills (eds), *Feminist Postcolonial Theory. A Reader*, Edinburgh, Edinburgh University Press, 2003, pp. 306–23, quote from p. 311.

3 V. Cunningham, '"God and nature intended you for a missionary wife": Mary Hill, Jane Eyre and other missionary women in the 1840s', in F. Bowie, D. Kirkwood and S. Ardener (eds), *Women and Missions: Past and Present. Anthropological and Historical Perceptions*, Oxford, Berg, 1993, pp. 85–108, quotes from pp. 89, 97.

4 For works that focus on the later nineteenth century, see: M.T. Huber and N.C. Lutkehaus (eds), *Gendered Missions*, Ann Arbor, University of Michigan Press, 1999; R.A. Semple, *Missionary Women, Gender, Imperialism and the Victorian Idea*

of Christian Mission, Woodbridge, Boydell, 2003; S.S. Maughan, 'Civic culture, women's foreign missions, and the British imperial imagination, 1860–1914', in F. Trentmann (ed.), *Paradoxes of Civil Society. New Perspectives on Modern German and British History*, New York, Berghahn, 2000, pp. 199–219; J. Rowbotham, '"Hear an Indian Sister's plea": reporting the work of 19th-century British female missionaries', *Women's Studies International Forum*, 1998, vol. 21, pp. 247–61; S. Gill, 'Heroines of missionary adventure: the portrayal of Victorian women missionaries in popular fiction and biography', in A. Hogan and A. Bradstock (eds), *Women of Faith in Victorian Culture. Reassessing the Angel in the House*, Basingstoke, Macmillan, 1998, pp. 172–85.

5 Key studies include: E.F. Kent, *Converting Women. Gender and Protestant Christianity in Colonial South India*, Oxford, Oxford University Press, 2004; A. Twells, '"Let us begin well at home": class, ethnicity and Christian motherhood in the writing of Hannah Kilham, 1774–1832', in E.J. Yeo (ed.), *Radical Femininity. Women's Self-Representation in the Public Sphere*, Manchester, Manchester University Press, 1998, pp. 25–51; J. Goodman, 'Languages of female colonial authority: the educational network of the ladies committee of the British and Foreign School Society, 1813–1837', *Compare*, 2000, vol. 30, pp. 7–19; S. Morgan (ed.), *Women, Religion and Feminism in Britain, 1750–1900*, Basingstoke, Palgrave Macmillan, 2002.

6 C. Hall, *Civilising Subjects. Metropole and Colony in the English Imagination 1830–1867*, Cambridge, Polity Press, 2002; A. Twells, '"Happy English children:" class, ethnicity, and the making of missionary women in the early nineteenth century', *Women's Studies International Forum*, 1998, vol. 21, pp. 235–40; S. Thorne, *Congregational Missions and the Making of an Imperial Culture in 19th-Century England*, Stanford, Stanford University Press, 1999.

7 M.E. Gibson, 'Henry Martyn and England's Christian Empire: rereading *Jane Eyre* through Missionary Biography' *Victorian Literature and Culture*, 1999, vol. 27, pp. 419–42; L. Peterson, '"The feeling and claims of little people": heroic missionary memoirs, domestic(ated) spiritual autobiography, and *Jane Eyre: An Autobiography*', in L.H. Peterson, *Traditions of Victorian Women's Autobiography*, Charlottsville, University Press of Virginia, 1999, pp. 80–108; M. Lamonaca, 'Jane's crown of thorns: feminism and Christianity in Jane Eyre', *Studies in the Novel*, 2002, vol. 34, pp. 245–63. For a useful overview of earlier scholarship, see A. Burton, 'Recapturing Jane Eyre: reflections on historicizing the colonial encounter in Victorian Britain, *Radical History Review*, 1996, vol. 64, pp. 58–72.

8 F.K. Prochaska, 'Women in English philanthropy, 1790–1830', *International Review of Social History*, 1974, vol. 19, pp. 426–45; F.K. Prochaska, *Women and Philanthropy in Nineteenth-Century England*, Oxford, Clarendon Press, 1980, especially pp. 24, 31, note 41; A.S. Swan, *Seed Time and Harvest. The Story of the Hundred Years' Work of the Women's Foreign Mission of the Church of Scotland*, London, T. Nelson & Sons, 1937, p. 102; L.A.O. Macdonald, *A Unique and Glorious Mission. Women and Presbyterianism in Scotland 1830–1930*, Edinburgh, John Donald, 2000, p. 112; *Missionary Herald*, August 1820, p. 59; E. Stock, *The History of the Church Missionary Society*, 2 vols, London, Church Missionary Society, 1899, vol. 1, p. 243.

9 For specific societies, see: The Women's Auxiliary of the Wesleyan Methodist Missionary Society, *The Story of the Women's Auxiliary 1858–1922*, London, Wesleyan Methodist Missionary Society, 1923; B. Stanley, *The History of the Baptist Missionary Society, 1792–1992*, Edinburgh, T. & T. Clark, 1992, pp. 228–32; R. Lovett, *The History of the London Missionary Society, 1795–1895*, 2 vols, London, Henry Frowde, 1899, vol. 2, pp. 714–16; *Is It Nothing to You? A Record of the Work among Women in Connection with the London Missionary Society*, London, London Missionary Society, 1899; Macdonald, *A Unique and Glorious Mission*, p. 115. For the Church Missionary Society and a general overview of these developments, see: S.S. Maughan, 'Regions

beyond and the national church: domestic support for the foreign missions of the Church of England in the high imperial age, 1870–1914', unpublished PhD thesis, Harvard University, 1995, pp. 259–327.

10 Founding constitution of the Baptist Missionary Society as quoted in Stanley, *The History of the Baptist Missionary Society, 1792–1992*, p. 233.

11 J. Murray, 'Gender attitudes and the contribution of women to evangelism and ministry in the nineteenth century' in J. Wolffe (ed.), *Evangelical Faith and Public Zeal. Evangelicals and Society in Britain 1780–1980*, London, SPCK, 1995, pp. 97–116; D.M. Valence, *Prophetic Sons and Daughters*, Princeton, Princeton University Press, 1985; D.C. Dews, 'Ann Carr and the female revivalists of Leeds' in G. Malmgreen (ed.), *Religion in the Lives of English Women 1760–1930*, London, Croom Helm, 1986, pp. 68–87; O. Anderson, 'Women preachers in mid-Victorian Britain: some reflections on feminism, popular religion and social change', *The Historical Journal*, vol. 12, no. 3, 1969, pp. 467–84; B.M. Kenzle and P.J. Walker (eds), *Women Preachers and Prophets through Two Millennia of Christianity*, Berkeley, University of California Press, 1998, especially Preface and Chapter 15.

12 S. Piggin, *Making Evangelical Missionaries, 1789–1858. The Social Background, Motives and Training of British Protestant Missionaries to India*, London, Sutton Courtney Press, 1984.

13 C. Hall, *White, Male and Middle Class. Explorations in Feminism and History*, Oxford, Polity Press, 1992, pp. 205–55; C. Hall, *Civilising Subjects*.

14 Cunningham, 'God and nature', p. 93.

15 *Missionary Herald*, Sept. 1820, no. 21, pp. 71–2; Mar. 1821, no. 27, p. 23; Apr. 1821, no. 28, p. 31; May 1821, no. 29, p. 39; Jun. 1821, no. 30, p. 47; Aug. 1821, no. 32, p. 64; Dec. 1821, no. 34, p. 96.

16 W.M. Harvard, *Memoirs of Mrs Elizabeth Harvard, Late of the Wesleyan Mission to Ceylon and India. With Extracts from Her Diary and Correspondence*, London, 1825, p. 157.

17 The Women's Auxiliary of the Wesleyan Methodist Missionary Society, *The Story of the Women's Auxiliary*, pp. 3, 4, 6.

18 'Address of the ladies' committee', in *Report of the British and Foreign School Society, 1815*, London, British and Foreign School Society, 1815, pp. viii–ix (emphasis in original).

19 *16th to 32nd Reports of the British and Foreign School Society*, London, British and Foreign School Society, 1821–37. See also G. Bartle, 'The role of the British and Foreign School Society in elementary education in India and the East Indies 1813–75', *History of Education*, 1994, vol. 23, pp. 17–33; Goodman, 'Languages of female colonial authority', p. 9.

20 D. Abeel, 'An appeal to Christian ladies in behalf of female education in China and the adjacent countries', in *History of the Society for Promoting Female Education in the East. Established in the Year 1834*, London, Edward Suter, 1847, Appendix A, pp. 261–5.

21 Prochaska, *Women and Philanthropy*, p. 32; Prochaska, 'Women in English philanthropy'; Brian Stanley, *The Bible and the Flag: Protestant Missions and British Imperialism in the Nineteenth and Twentieth Centuries*, Leicester, Apollos, 1990, p. 78.

22 Noel (1799–1873) was a clergyman in the Church of England until 1848, when he became a Baptist minister. He was an influential reformist Whig who opposed the Corn Laws and led pan-evangelical initiatives to evangelise the urban poor. See Grayson Carter, entry on Noel in H.C.G. Matthew and B. Harrison (eds), *The Oxford Dictionary of National Biography*, Oxford, Oxford University Press, 2004.

23 The archive of the FES now forms part of the archive of the Church Missionary Society which is held at Interserve, the Church Missionary Society Headquarters

in London, and in the University of Birmingham Library, UK. It is available on microfilm: *CMS Archive. Section II, Missions to Women, Parts 1–3*, Chippenham, Adam Matthews Publications, 1997, Part 1. For a useful overview of the activities of the society, see Margaret Donaldson, 'The cultivation of the heart and the moulding of the will …'. The missionary contribution of the Society for Promoting Female Education in China, India, and the East' in W.J. Shiels and D. Wood (eds), *Women in the Church*, Oxford, 1990, pp. 429–42.

24 *Society for Promoting Female Education in China, India, and the East*, London, Edward Suter, n.d., pp. 5, 13; *History of the Society for Promoting Female Education*, Appendix D; B.W. Noel, *Duty of Christians Towards the Female Children of India and the East*, London, Society for Promoting Female Education in China, India, and the East, 1836, p. 14.

25 *Missionary Register*, November 1822, p. 483.

26 For the difficult position of the governess, see M. Jeanne Peterson, 'The Victorian governess: status incongruence in family and society', in Martha Vicinus (ed.), *Suffer and be Still: Women in the Victorian Age*, London, Methuen, 1980 edition, pp. 3–19.

27 *History of the Society for Promoting Female Education in the East; The Twenty-Fourth Annual Report of the Society for Promoting Female Education in the East*, London, Suter & Alexander, 1858; *Female Agency among the Heathen, as Recorded in the History and Correspondence of the Society for Promoting Female Education in the East*, London, Edward Suter, 1850; Donaldson, 'The cultivation of the heart'.

28 Orr Macdonald, *A Unique and Glorious Mission*, pp. 104–66; Swan, *Seed Time and Harvest; Eighth Annual Report of the Scottish Ladies' Association for the Advancement of Female Education in India, under the Superintendence of the General Assembly's Committee on Foreign Missions*, Edinburgh, 1846; Rev. Alexander Duff, *More Fruits from India*, Edinburgh, 1848; *The Eastern Females' Friend*, n.s. 1857, no. 1, p. 1; no. 3, p. 34.

29 Stock, *The History of the Church Missionary Society*, vol. 1, p. 128.

30 P. Chapman, *Hindoo Female Education*, London, R.B. Seeley & W. Burnside, 1839.

31 Peterson, 'The Feeling and Claims of Little People'.

32 J. Philip, *Memoir of Mrs Matilda Smith, late of Cape Town, Cape of Good Hope*, London, F. Westley, 1824, preface, pp. vii–xvi.

33 E. Elbourne, *Blood Ground. Colonialism, Mission, and the Contest for Christianity in the Cape Colony and Britain, 1799–1853*, Montreal, McGill-Queen's University Press, 2002, pp. 113–15.

34 For a fascinating account of one African-Caribbean woman's missionary work in the mid 18th century, see J.F. Sensbach, *Rebecca's Revival. Creating Black Christianity in the Atlantic World*, Cambridge, Harvard University Press, 2005.

35 *Memoirs of Mrs Harriet Newell, wife of the Rev. Samuel Newell, American Missionary to India*, London, Booth & Co., 1815.

36 A.H. Judson, *An Account of the American Baptist Mission to the Burman Empire*, 2nd edn, London, 1827; J.D. Knowles, *Memoir of Mrs Ann H. Judson, Wife of the Rev. Adoniram Judson, Missionary to Burmah*, 9th edition, London, G. Wightman, 1838, pp. 34, 35.

37 M. Winslow, *A Memoir of Mrs Harriet W. Winslow, Combining a Sketch of the Ceylon Mission; with an Introductory Essay, by James Harrington Evans, Minister of John Street Chapel*, London, 1838, pp. x, xi.

38 [Rev. A.G. Fairchild, comp.], *Memoir of Mrs Louisa A. Lowrie, of the Northern India Mission: with Introductory Notices by the Rev. E.P. Swift, the Rev. W.H. Pearce, and the Rev. A. Reed, D.D.*, London, 1838, pp. 1, 4–5.

39 Harvard, *Memoirs of Mrs Elizabeth Harvard*, quotes from dedication, p. iii; pp. 22, 52, 55, 57.

40 *Extracts from the Journal and Correspondence of the Late Mrs M.M. Clough, Wife of the Rev. Benjamin Clough, Missionary in Ceylon*, London, J. Mason, 1829, quotes from pp. xxxv, 37.

41 W. Ellis, *Memoir of Mary M. Ellis, Wife of the Rev. William Ellis, Missionary to the South Seas, and Foreign Secretary of the London Missionary Society*, London, 1835, pp. 56, 80 respectively; A. Johnston, *Missionary Writing and Empire, 1800–1860*, Cambridge, Cambridge University Press, 2003, pp. 147–55.

42 Ellis, *Memoir of Mary M. Ellis*, p. vi, see also pp. 11–12. Ellis's second wife was Sarah Stickney Ellis, a highly successful author whose literary career he supported. She was the author of best-selling prescriptive tracts for women that combined an acceptance of women's social subordination with a stress on their moral authority in the domestic sphere.

43 Rev. T. Middleditch, *The Youthful Female Missionary. A Memoir of Mary Ann Hutchins, Wife of the Rev. John Hutchins, Baptist Missionary, Savanna-la-Mar, Jamaica; and Daughter of the Rev. T. Middleditch, of Ipswich; Compiled Chiefly from Her Own Correspondence*, 2nd edn, London, G. Wightman, 1840, pp. 63, 69–72. See also C. Hall, 'Missionary stories: gender and ethnicity in England in the 1830s and 1840s', in *White, Male and Middle Class. Explorations in Feminism and History*, Cambridge, Polity Press, 1992, pp. 205–54.

44 J. Wilson, *A Memoir of Mrs Margaret Wilson of the Scottish Mission, Bombay*, 3rd edn, Edinburgh, John Johnstone, 1840.

45 *Memoirs of Female Labourers in the Missionary Cause*, Bath, 1839, pp. 25–6. Catherine Hall discusses a rather similar account relating to a woman who married a missionary to Jamaica – see Hall, 'Missionary Stories', p. 223.

46 *Memoirs of Female Labourers*; J. Thompson, *Memoirs of British Female Missionaries*, London, William Smith, 1841, quote from preface, p. ix; J. Morison, *The Fathers and Founders of the London Missionary Society*, 2 vols, London, 1840.

47 S. Biller (ed.), *Memoir of the Late Hannah Kilham*, London, 1837. For a fuller discussion of Kilham, see Twells, 'Let us begin well at home'.

48 Thompson, *Memoirs*, Preface, p. xxvi.

49 Brontë, *Jane Eyre*, p. 434.

50 E.R. Pitman, *Heroines of the Mission Field. Biographical Sketches of Female Missionaries Who Have Laboured in Various Lands among the Heathen*, London, Cassell & Co., 1880.

51 J. Luke, *Early Years of My Life*, London, Hodder & Stoughton, 1900, p. 116.

52 Brontë, *Jane Eyre*, p. 477.

53 Luke, *Early Years*, pp. 72, 85.

54 Goodman, 'Languages of female colonial authority'; Twells, 'Happy English children'.

55 Luke, *Early Years*, pp. 106–7.

56 Luke, *Early Years*, p. 108.

57 *33rd to 38th Reports of the London Missionary Society*, London, 1827–1832 record these developments.

58 J. Schwarzkopf, *Women in the Chartist Movement*, Basingstoke, Macmillan, 1991; C. Midgley, *Women Against Slavery. The British Campaigns, 1780–1870*, London, Routledge, 1992, pp. 155–67; K.K. Sklar, *Women's Rights Emerges within the Antislavery Movement 1830–1870*, Boston: Bedford/St Martins, 2000, especially pp. 118–21.

59 Luke, *Early Years*, pp. 115–23.

60 For women's important contributions to hymn writing over the previous decades, see M. Maison, '"Thine, only thine!" Women hymn writers in Britain, 1760–1835', in G. Malmgreen (ed.), *Religion in the Lives of English Women*, London, Croom Helm, 1986, pp. 11–40.

61 Thompson, *Memoirs of British Female Missionaries*, preface, pp. xxv–xxvi.

62 Entry for Mrs Jemima Luke, in S. Lee (ed.), *Dictionary of National Biography Supplement, 1901–1911*, Oxford, Oxford University Press, 1920, vol. 2; Luke, *Early Years*, pp. 148–50.

63 L. Davidoff and C. Hall, *Family Fortunes. Men and Women of the English Middle Class 1780–1850*, 2nd edn, London, Routledge, 2002, Part I: Religion and Ideology.

64 Prockaska, *Women and Philanthropy*, p. 1.

65 S. Lewis, *Woman's Mission*, 2nd edn, London, John W. Parker, 1839, quotes from pp. 12, 20, 128, 48, 11–12 respectively.

66 Amanda Vickery has suggested that such prescriptive tracts can be read not as evidence of the constriction of women's lives, but as a defensive reaction against women's public activities: Amanda Vickery, 'From golden age to separate spheres? A review of the categories and chronology of English women's history', *Historical Journal*, 1993, vol. 36, pp. 383–414.

67 Thompson, *Memoirs*, preface, p. xx.

68 Thompson, *Memoirs*, preface, p. xx.

69 J.A. James, *Female Piety: or the Young Woman's Friend and Guide through Life to Immortality*, London, 1852. This consisted of ten sermons, the first of which was entitled 'the influence of Christianity on the condition of women'. This work had run into ten editions by 1864. See note on p. 6 acknowledging its indebtedness to Cox's essay.

70 *Society for Promoting Female Education in China, India, and the East*, London, n.d., p. 14 (the text of this appeal was also published as Appendix B to *The History of the Society for Promoting Female Education*, where its author is named as the Rev. Baptist W. Noel – see pp. 266–75).

71 Thompson, *Memoirs*, pp. xv, lxxviii.

72 Thompson, *Memoirs*, p. v.

73 *Society for Promoting Female Education*, p. 13.

74 *Report of the Glasgow Association for Promoting Female Education in the East*, Glasgow, 1840, p. 7.

75 Chapman, *Hindoo Female Education*, London, p. 130, engraving p. 128; Noel, *Duty of Christians*, p. 32; *Missionary Register*, 1838, p. 328.

76 *Eighth Annual Report of the Scottish Ladies' Association*, p. 10.

77 *Eighth Annual Report of the Scottish Ladies' Association*, pp. 13, 10.

78 Noel, *Duty of Christians*, p. 12.

79 J. Luke (ed.), *Missionary Stories*, London, John Snow, 1842–3.

80 A. Duff, *More Fruits from India; or, the Outcast Safe in Christ: the Life and Happy Death of Charlotte Green a Poor Orphan*, Edinburgh, John Johnstone, n.d.

81 Mrs Weitbrecht, *An Indian Blossom Which Bore Fruit. A Memoir of Rabee, Who Died at Burdwan, December, 1848*, London, Edward Suter, 1849.

82 Weitbrecht, *An Indian Blossom*, pp. 15–17.

83 Weitbrecht, *An Indian Blossom*, pp. 21–22, 24.

84 The Home and Foreign Missionary Record for the Free Church of Scotland, 1845–6, vol. 2, p. 356.

85 *The Home and Foreign*, 1845–6, vol. 2, p. 356.

86 *The Home and Foreign*, 1846–7, vol. 3, pp. 344, 512.

87 P. Anagol, 'Indian Christian women and indigenous feminism, c1850–c1920', in C. Midgley, *Gender and Imperialism*, Manchester, Manchester University Press, 1998, pp. 79–103; E.C. Kent, *Converting Women. Gender and Protestant Christianity in Colonial South India*, Oxford, Oxford University Press, 2004.

88 Swan, *Seed Time and Harvest*, pp. 77–9.

89 *Eastern Females' Friend*, 1848, new series, vol. 8, pp. 53–4.

90 *The Female Missionary Intelligencer*, 1856, vol. 29, cover illustration.

91 *Missionary Register*, 1815, pp. 396–400.

92 Harvard, *Memoirs of Mrs Elizabeth Harvard*, p. 94.
93 B.W. Noel, *Duty of Christians*, p. 43.
94 Kenzle and Walker, *Women Preachers and Prophets*, Preface, p. xix.
95 See entry on Charlotte Elizabeth Tonna by Mary Lenard, in H.C.G. Matthew and B. Harrison (eds), *Oxford Dictionary of National Biography*, Oxford, Oxford University Press, 2004.
96 C.E., 'China, India and the East', *Christian Lady's Magazine*, 1835, vol. 3, pp. 540–42, quote from p. 542.
97 Lydia, 'China, India, and the East', *Christian Lady's Magazine*, 1836, vol. 6, pp. 498–502.
98 G.H.G., letter to the editor, *Christian Lady's Magazine*, 1837, vol. 7, pp. 241–3.
99 G.H.G., letter to the editor, p. 242.
100 J.S., letter to the editor, *Christian Lady's Magazine*, 1837, vol. 7, pp. 540–3.
101 S. Thorne, 'Missionary-imperial feminism', in Huber and Lutkehaus (eds), *Gendered Missions*, pp. 39–66.
102 H. Mathers, 'The Evangelical spirituality of a Victorian feminist. Josephine Butler 1828–1906', *Journal of Ecclesiastical History*, 2001, vol. 52, pp. 281–312; A. Summers, *Female Lives, Moral States*, Newbury, Threshold Press, 2000; A. Burton, 'The white woman's burden: Josephine Butler and the Indian campaign, 1886–1915', in A. Burton, *Burdens of History. British Feminists, Indian Women, and Imperial Culture, 1865–1915*, Chapel Hill, University of North Carolina Press, 1994, Chapter 5, pp. 127–70. For broader discussions of the relationship between feminism and religion, see Morgan, *Women, Religion and Feminism in Britain*; J. deVries, 'Rediscovering Christianity after the postmodern turn', *Feminist Studies*, 2005, vol. 31, pp. 135–55.

5 Feminism, colonial emigration and the new model Englishwoman

1 P. Levine, *Victorian Feminism 1850–1900*, London, Century Hutchinson, 1987; B. Caine, *English Feminism 1780–1980*, Oxford, Oxford University Press, 1997; pp. 88–130; J. Rendall, '"A moral engine?" Feminism, liberalism and the *English Woman's Journal*', in J. Rendall (ed.), *Equal or Different: Women's Politics 1800–1914*, Oxford, Blackwell, 1987, pp. 112–40; C. Lacey (ed.), *Barbara Leigh Smith and the Langham Place Circle*, London, Routledge and Kegan Paul, 1987; J. Rendall, 'Friendship and politics: Barbara Leigh Smith (1827–91) and Bessie Rayner Parkes (1829–1925)', in S. Mendus and J. Rendall (eds), *Sexuality and Subordination*, London, Routledge, 1989, pp. 136–70; P. Hirsch, *Barbara Leigh Smith Bodichon. Feminist, Artist and Rebel*, London, Pimlico, 1999, pp. 184–206; S.R. Herstein, *A Mid-Victorian Feminist, Barbara Leigh Smith Bodichon*, New Haven, Yale University Press, 1985.
2 A. Burton, *Burdens of History. British Feminists, Indian Women, and Imperial Culture, 1865–1915*, Chapel Hill, University of North Carolina Press, 1994.
3 K. Gleadle, *The Early Feminists. Radical Unitarians and the emergence of the Women's Rights Movement, 1831–51*, Basingstoke, Macmillan, 1995, pp. 171–83.
4 C. Midgley, *Women Against Slavery. The British Campaigns 1780–1870*, London, Routledge, 1992, pp. 154–77.
5 D. Cherry, 'Shuttling and soul making: tracing the links between Algeria and egalitarian feminism in the 1850s', in S. West (ed.), *The Victorians and Race*, Aldershot, Scolar Press, 1996, pp. 156–70, quotes from p. 168; D. Cherry, *Beyond the Frame. Feminism and Visual Culture. Britain 1850–1900*, London, Routledge, 2000, pp. 59–100.
6 A.J. Hammerton, 'Gender and migration', in P. Levine (ed.), *Gender and Empire*, Oxford, Oxford University Press, 2004, pp. 156–80, quote from p. 156.

7 A.J. Hammerton, *Emigrant Gentlewomen: Genteel Poverty and Female Emigration, 1830–1914*, London, Croom Helm, 1979; S.J. Hammerton, 'Feminism and female emigration, 1861–1886', in M. Vicinus (ed.), *A Widening Sphere. Changing Roles of Victorian Women*, London, Methuen, 1980, pp. 52–71; M. Diamond, *Emigration and Empire. The Life of Maria S. Rye*, New York, Garland, 1999.

8 Key works include: J. Gothard, *Blue China. Single Female Migration to Colonial America*, Melbourne, Melbourne University Press, 2001; C. Macdonald, *A Woman of Good Character. Single Women as Immigrant Settlers in Nineteenth-Century New Zealand*, New Zealand, Allen and Unwin, 1990; C. Swaisland, *Servants and Gentlewomen to the Golden Land. The Emigration of Single Women from Britain to Southern Africa, 1820–1939*, Oxford, Berg, 1993.

9 R.S. Kranidis, *The Victorian Spinster and Colonial Emigration*, Basingstoke, Macmillan, 1999; R.S. Kranidis (ed.), *Imperial Objects. Essays on Victorian Women's Emigration and the Unauthorized Imperial Experience*, New York, Twayne, 1998.

10 J. Bush, *Edwardian Ladies and Imperial Power*, London, Leicester University Press, 2000. See also J. Bush, ' "The right sort of woman": female emigrators and emigration to the British Empire, 1890–1910', *Women's History Review*, 1994, vol. 3, pp. 385–409.

11 Hammerton, *Emigrant Gentlewomen*, p. 125 gives the figure of 302 for those sent out by FMES between 1862 and 1886.

12 P. Clarke, *The Governesses. Letters from the Colonies 1862–1882*, London, Hutchinson, 1985; 'Records of the Female Middle Class Emigration Society', archive in the Women's Library, London, ref. GB 0106 1/FME; P. Hamilton and J. Gothard, '"The other half": sources on British female emigration at the Fawcett Library, with special reference to Australia', *Women's Studies International Forum*, 1987, vol. 10, pp. 305–9. Bush, 'The right sort of woman', p. 387.

13 A. Porter (ed.), *Atlas of British Overseas Expansion*, London, Routledge, 1991, pp. 84–6; D. Baines, *Migration in a Mature Economy. Emigration and Internal Migration in England and Wales, 1861–1900*, Cambridge, Cambridge University Press, 1985, Appendix 4, p. 301.

14 E. Jordan, *The Women's Movement and Women's Employment in Nineteenth Century Britain*, London, Routledge, 1999; Levine, *Victorian Feminism*, pp. 82–104; Herstein, *A Mid-Victorian Feminist*, pp. 125–48.

15 'The profession of the teacher. The annual reports of the Governess' Benevolent Institution, from 1843–1857', *The English Woman's Journal*, 1858, vol. 1, pp. 1–13.

16 M.J. Peterson, 'The Victorian governess: status incongruence in family and society', in M. Vicinus (ed.), *Suffer and Be Still. Women in the Victorian Age*, London, Methuen & Co., 1980, pp. 3–19; K. Hughes, *The Victorian Governess*, London, The Hambledon Press, 1993.

17 'The profession of the teacher', pp. 9–10.

18 'The profession of the teacher', p. 10.

19 M. Dresser, 'Britannia', in R. Samuel (ed.), *Patriotism. The Making and Unmaking of British National Identity, Vol. 3: National Fictions*, London, Routledge, 1989, pp. 26–49, quote from p. 41.

20 J. Surel, 'John Bull', in Samuel (ed.), *Patriotism*, pp. 3–25; M. Taylor, 'John Bull and the iconography of public opinion in England c. 1712–1929', *Past and Present*, 1992, vol. 134, pp. 93–128. The origins of John Bull and Mrs Bull as cartoon symbols of the English people lay in a 1712 political allegory: see J. Arbuthnot, *The History of John Bull*, A.W. Bower and R.A. Erickson (eds), Oxford, Clarendon Press, 1976. See also T.L. Hunt, *Defining John Bull. Political Caricature and National Identity in Late Georgian England*, Aldershot, Ashgate, 2003.

21 L. Tickner, *The Spectacle of Women. Imagery of the Suffrage Campaign 1907–14*, London, Chatto and Windus, 1987, pp. 30–42, 213–26 and figs. 3, 10, 20, 113.

22 J.A. Epstein, *Radical Expression. Political Language, Ritual and Symbol in England 1790–1850*, Oxford, Oxford University Press, 1994; H. Rogers, *Women and the People. Authority, Authorship and the Radical Tradition in Nineteenth-Century England*, Aldershot, Ashgate, 2000, especially pp. 1–47.

23 R. Horsman, 'Origins of racial Anglo-Saxonism in Great Britain before 1850', *Journal of the History of Ideas*, 1976, vol. 37, pp. 387–410; C. Hall, *Civilising Subjects. Metropole and Colony in the English Imagination 1830–1867*, Cambridge, Polity Press, 2002, pp. 338–79. The linking of physiognomy to national character in *The English Woman's Journal* article calls into question Peter Mandler's claim that ideas about the racial basis of English national character were not widely accepted at this period (see P. Mandler, ' "Race" and "nation" in mid-Victorian thought', in S. Collini, R. Whatmore and B. Young (eds), *History, Religion, and Culture. British Intellectual History, 1750–1950*, Cambridge, Cambridge University Press, 2000; P. Mandler, *The English National Character. The History of an Idea from Edmund Burke to Tony Blair*, New Haven, Yale University Press, 2006, pp. 59–105, especially pp. 100–1).

24 'Light and dark', *The English Woman's Journal*, 1858, vol. 1, pp. 163–4. Penny Tuson identifies the author as Isabella Blagden, a friend of Robert and Elizabeth Browning and acquaintance of Bessie Rayner Parkes who lived in Florence and was rumoured to be the illegitimate daughter of an English father and Indian mother – see P. Tuson, *The Queen's Daughters. An Anthology of Victorian Feminist Writings on India 1857–1900*, Reading, Ithaca Press, 1995, p. 25.

25 J. Sharpe, *Allegories of Empire. The Figure of the Woman in the Colonial Text*, Minneapolis, University of Minnesota Press, 1993, pp. 56–84.

26 Rendall, 'A moral engine', quote from p. 115.

27 M. Beetham, *A Magazine of Her Own? Domesticity and Desire in the Woman's Magazine, 1800–1914*, London, Routledge, 1996.

28 'Our address', *Englishwoman's Domestic Magazine*, 1852, 1st series, vol. 1, p. 5; 1853–4, 1st series, vol. 2, preface. For a discussion of Ellis's tracts, see L. Davidoff and C. Hall, *Family Fortunes. Men and Women of the English Middle Class 1780–1850*, 2nd edn, London, Routledge, 2002, pp. 180–5.

29 *Englishwoman's Domestic Magazine*, 1856–7, 1st series, vol. 5, 'Preface' and 'Property of married women' pp. 234ff. See also: M. Diamond, 'Maria Rye and *The Englishwoman's Domestic Magazine*', *Victorian Periodicals Review*, 1997, vol. 30, pp. 5–16.

30 'Women in barbarism', *Englishwoman's Domestic Magazine*, 1856–7, 1st series, vol. 5, pp. 23–27.

31 C. Hall, 'At home with history: Macaulay and the *History of England*', in C. Hall and S. Rose (eds), *At Home with the Empire*, pp. 32–52.

32 Peter Mandler, *History and National Life*, London, Profile, 2002, p. 20. See also Peter Mandler, '"In the olden time": romantic history and English national identity, 1820–1850', in L. Brockliss and D. Eastwood (eds), *A Union of Multiple Identities: The British Isles, c. 1750–c. 1850*, Manchester: Manchester University Press, 1997, pp. 78–92.

33 'The domestic history of England. Ancient Britons and Anglo-Saxons', *Englishwoman's Domestic Magazine*, 1860, new series, vol. 1, pp. 12–20, quotes from pp. 19, 20.

34 *Englishwoman's Domestic Magazine*, 1861, new series, vol. 2, p. 20.

35 M. Homans and A. Munich (eds), *Remaking Queen Victoria*, Cambridge, Cambridge Univesity Press, 1997; M. Homans, *Royal Representations: Queen Victoria and British Culture, 1837–1876*, Chicago, University of Chicago Press, 1998;

Elizabeth Langland, *Telling Tales: Gender and Narrative Form in Victorian Literature and Culture*, Columbus, The Ohio State University Press, 2002, pp. 111–29; D. Thompson, *Queen Victoria. Gender and Power*, London, Virago, 1990.

36 L. Goldman, *Science Reform and Politics in Victorian Britain. The Social Science Association, 1857–1886*, Cambridge, Cambridge University Press, 2002, quote from p. 1.

37 E. Faithfull, 'The Victoria Press', *Transactions of the National Association for the Promotion of Social Science. 1860,* London, John W. Parker & Son, 1861, pp. 819–20.

38 A.A. Procter (ed.), *The Victoria Regia: a Volume of Original Contributions in Poetry and Prose*, London, Emily Faithfull and Co., Victoria Press (for the Employment of Women), 1861. My thanks to my former colleagues at London Metropolitan University and the Women's Library who presented me with this book as a leaving present.

39 A. Jameson, *Winter Studies and Summer Rambles in Canada*, London, Saunders and Otley, 1838, vol. 3, p. 262, as quoted in G. Whitlock, *The Intimate Empire. Reading Women's Autobiography*, London, Cassell, p. 76.

40 Whitlock, *The Intimate Empire*, pp. 76–7.

41 Barbara Leigh Smith, *Women and Work*, London, Bosworth & Harrison, 1857, quotes from pp. 6, 20.

42 Isa Craig, 'Emigration as preventative agency. Read in the reformatory department of the National Association for the Promotion of Social Science, at Liverpool, October 13th, 1858', *The English Woman's Journal*, 1858–9, vol. 2, pp. 289–97.

43 M. Kiddle, *Caroline Chisholm*, Melbourne, Melbourne University Press, 1950; C. Lansbury, *Arcady in Australia. The Evocation of Australia in Nineteenth-Century English Literature*, Carlton, Melbourne University Press, 1970, see Chapter 5, p. 69 and Chapter 7 for Chisholm, Dickens and *Household Words*.

44 K. Ledbetter, 'Bonnets and Rebellions: imperialism in *The Lady's Newspaper*, *Victorian Periodicals Review*, 2004, vol. 34, pp. 252–72.

45 Kiddle, *Caroline Chisholm*, pp. 163–7. The full text of the *Punch* poem from which the quotes are taken is given on pp. 163–4.

46 Bessie R. Parkes, 'A year's experience in woman's work', *Transactions of the National Association for the Promotion of Social Science, 1860*, London, John W. Parker & Son, 1861, pp. 811–19, see especially pp. 817–18.

47 M.S.R., 'Emigrant-ship matrons', *The English Woman's Journal*, 1860, vol. 5, pp. 24–36; M.S.R., 'On assisted emigration', *The English Woman's Journal*, 1860, vol. 5, pp. 235–40.

48 Hammerton, *Emigrant Gentlewomen*, p. 94.

49 The records of the Female Middle Class Emigration Society are in the Women's Library, London, ref: GB 0106 1/FME. They comprise reports, letter-books and pamphlets. For the patrons and original officers of the society and its rules and foundation, see *Female Middle Class Emigration Society* [First Report], London, Emily Faithfull [1861].

50 *Female Middle Class Emigration Society* [First Report], p. 1.

51 Edward Gibbon Wakefield (ed.), *A View of the Art of Colonization, with Present Reference to the British Empire; in Letters Between a Statesman and a Colonist*, London, John W. Parker, 1849, p. 155.

52 M. Harper, 'British migration and the peopling of empire', in A. Porter (ed.), *The Oxford History of the British Empire. Vol. 3. The Nineteenth Century*, Oxford, Oxford University Press, 1999, pp. 75–87.

53 J.E. Lewin, 'Female middle-class emigration. A paper read at the Social Science Congress', *The English Woman's Journal*, 1863–4, vol. 12, pp. 313–18, quotes from p. 315.

54 Maria S. Rye, 'Female middle class emigration. A paper read at the meeting of the Association for the Promotion of Social Science, London, 1862', *The English Woman's Journal*, 1862–3, vol. 10, pp. 20–30, quotes from pp. 22–23.

55 Kiddle, *Caroline Chisholm*, pp. 72–3; J. Tosh, '"All the masculine virtues": English emigration to the colonies, 1815–1852', in J. Tosh, *Manliness and Masculinities in Nineteenth-Century Britain. Essays on Gender, Family and Empire*, Harlow, Pearson Education, 2005, pp. 173–91.

56 Jessie Boucherett, *Hints on Self Help: A Book for Young Women*, London, S.W. Partridge, 1863.

57 Lansbury, *Arcady in Australia*, p. 64; S.C., 'Emigration for educated women', *The English Woman's Journal*, 1861, vol. 7, pp. 1–9, quote from p. 8 (italics in original).

58 M.S.R., 'On assisted emigration'.

59 S.C., 'Emigration for educated women', p. 8.

60 C.E.C., 'Middle-class female emigration impartially considered', *The English Woman's Journal*, 1862–3, vol. 10, pp. 73–85, quote from p. 82.

61 Lansbury, *Arcady in Australia*, pp. 60–78.

62 Rye, 'Female middle-class emigration', p. 25; M.S.R., 'On assisted emigration', p. 237.

63 H.E. Roberts, 'Marriage, redundancy or sin: the painter's view of women in the first twenty-five years of Victoria's reign', in Vicinus (ed.), *Suffer and Be Still*, pp. 45–76 and Plate 4 (which reproduces the later 1844 version of the painting). For discussion of the various other versions of this painting, see S.P. Casteras and R. Parkinson (eds), *Richard Redgrave 1804–1888*, New Haven, Yale University Press, 1988, pp. 18–19, 111–14.

64 Rye, 'Female middle-class emigration', pp. 24–5.

65 See the cartoon from *Melbourne Punch* of 2 March 1861 reproduced in A.J. Hammerton, 'Feminism and female emigration, 1861–1886', in M. Vicinus (ed.), *A Widening Sphere. Changing Roles of Victorian Women*, London, Methuen, 1980, pp. 52–71, illustration on p. 65.

66 Compare letters published in *The English Woman's Journal*, 1860, vol. 5, pp. 326–35; 1861–2, vol. 8, pp. 237–44; 1862, vol. 9, pp. 109–19, 407 with letters published in *The Times* 23 April 1862, p. 6; 24 April 1862, p. 12; 26 April 1862, p. 12.

67 A selection of these letters is reproduced and discussed in Clarke, *The Governesses*.

68 C.E.C., 'Female middle-class emigration impartially considered', quotes from pp. 82, 83.

69 [William Rathbone Greg], 'Why are women redundant?', *The National Review*, vol. 14, 1862, pp. 434–60; Frances Power Cobbe, 'What shall we do with our old maids', *Fraser's Magazine*, vol. 66, November 1862, pp. 594–610, quote from p. 600; Boucherett, *Hints on Self Help*, pp. 23–48, quote from p. 42.

70 Diamond, *Emigration and Empire*.

71 D. Denoon and M. Wyndham, 'Australia and the Western Pacific', in A. Porter (ed.), *The Oxford History of the British Empire, Vol. 3: The Nineteenth Century*, pp. 549–72; H. Reynolds, *Frontier: Aborigines, Settlers, and Land*, Sydney, Allen and Unwin, 1987; C. Lansbury, *Arcady in Australia*, especially Chapter 8.

72 A. Perry, *On the Edge of Empire. Gender, Race and the Making of British Colombia, 1849–1871*, Toronto, University of Toronto Press, 2001.

73 H. Martineau, article in *Daily News*, 8 June 1852, as reproduced in E.S. Arbuckle (ed.), *Harriet Martineau in the London Daily News. Selected Contributions, 1852–1866*, New York, Garland Publishing, p. 8.

74 D. Logan (ed.), *Harriet Martineau's Writing on the British Empire*, 4 vols, London, Pickering & Chatto, 2004; C. Hall, 'Imperial careering at home: Harriet Martineau

on empire', in A. Lester and D. Lambert (eds), *Colonial Lives Across the British Empire*, Cambridge, Cambridge University Press, 2006.

75 M.S.R., 'On assisted emigration', pp. 235, 240.

76 Maria S. Rye, 'The colonies and their requirements. A paper read at the meeting of the Association for the Promotion of Social Science, held at Dublin, August, 1861', *The English Woman's Journal*, 1861–2, vol. 8, pp. 167–71, quotes from p. 168.

77 C.E.C., 'Middle-class female emigration impartially considered', p. 80.

78 Hammerton, *Emigrant Gentlewomen*, Chapter 2.

79 L.P. Curtis, *Apes and Angels: The Irishmen in Victorian Caricature*, Newton Abbot, David and Charles, 1971.

80 S.C., 'Emigration for educated women', p. 2.

81 A. Twells, '"Let us begin well at home": class, ethnicity and Christian motherhood in the writing of Hanhah Kilham, 1774–1832', in E.J. Yeo, *Radical Femininity. Women's Self-Representation in the Public Sphere*, Manchester, Manchester University Press, 1998, pp. 25–51.

82 C.E.C., 'Middle-class female emigration impartially considered', p. 82; Rye, 'The colonies and their requirements', p. 170.

83 Rye, 'Female middle class emigration', p. 28.

84 Maria S. Rye, letter to the editor of *The Times*, 25 April 1862, p. 5.

85 S.C., 'Emigration for educated women', p. 5.

86 Maria S. Rye, letter to the editor of *The Times*, 29 April 1862, p. 14.

87 *The Holy Bible*, Numbers 33: 51–3.

88 Rye, 'The colonies and their requirements', p. 171.

89 Rye, 'Female middle class emigration', p. 25.

90 C.E.C., 'Middle-class female emigration impartially considered', p. 74.

91 P. Brantlinger, *Dark Vanishings. Discourse on the Extinction of Primitive Races, 1800–1930*, Ithaca, Cornell University Press, 2003, p. 6.

92 Henry Jordan, letter to the editor of *The Times*, 20 January 1862, p. 9.

93 C.E.C., 'Middle-class female emigration impartially considered', p. 77.

94 R.A., Huttenback, *Racism and Empire, White Settlers and Colored Immigrants in the British Self-Governing Colonies, 1830–1910*, Ithaca, Cornell University Press, 1976, especially pp. 59–71.

95 Henry Fawcett, 'Protection of labour against immigration. The Chinese coolie traffic', *Transactions of the National Association for the Promotion of Social Science, 1859*, pp. 704–06, quote from p. 705. A few years later Fawcett was to become Professor of Political Economy at Cambridge and a Liberal MP and to marry feminist activist Millicent Garrett Fawcett.

96 See Perry, *On the Edge of Empire*, Chapter 2 for attitudes to mixed-race relationships in general and pp. 174–5 and 182 for attitudes to the Douglas's relationship.

97 'Stray letters on emigration', *The English Woman's Journal*, 1862, vol. 9, pp. 109–19, quote from p. 109.

98 Perry, *On the Edge of Empire*, pp. 138–46.

99 M.S. Rye, letter to the editor, *The Times*, 21 June 1862, p. 12; see also Perry, *At the Edge of Empire*, p. 14.

100 J. Rendall, 'Citizenship, culture and civilisation: the languages of British suffragists, 1866–1874', in C. Daley and M. Nolan (eds), *Suffrage and Beyond: International Feminist Perspectives*, Auckland, Auckland University Press, 1994, pp. 127–50; S.S. Holton, 'British freewomen: national identity, constitutionalism and languages of race in early suffrage histories', in E.J. Yeo (ed.), *Radical Femininity. Women's Self-Representation in the Public Sphere*, Manchester, Manchester University Press, 1998, pp. 149–71.

101 C. Hursthouse, *New Zealand or Zealandia, the Britain of the South*, London, 1857, p. 637, as quoted in Tosh, *Manliness and Masculinities*, p. 180.

102 Bush, 'The right sort of woman'; Bush, *Edwardian Ladies and Imperial Power*, especially pp. 146–69.

103 H. Fraser, S. Green and J. Johnston, *Gender and the Victorian Periodical, Cambridge*, Cambridge University Press, 2003, pp. 121–42; Ledbetter, 'Bonnets and rebellions'; N. Chaudhuri, 'Issues of race, gender and nation in *Englishwomen's Domestic Magazine* and *Queen*, 1850–1900'; D.P. Quirk, '"True Englishwomen" and "Anglo-Indians": gender, national identity, and feminism in the Victorian women's periodical press', in J.F. Codell (ed.), *Imperial Co-Histories. National Identities and the British and Colonial Press*, London, Associated University Press, 2003.

104 C. Midgley, *Women Against Slavery. The British Campaigns, 1780–1870*, London, Routledge, 1992, pp. 143–5. For women and the Black Atlantic, see D.G. White, 'Nationalism and feminism in the Black Atlantic', in P. Grimshaw, K. Holmes and M. Lake (eds), *Women's Rights and Human Rights. International Historical Perspectives*, Basingstoke, Palgrave, 2001, pp. 231–42.

105 G. Hastings (ed.), *Transactions of the National Association for the Promotion of Social Science. 1861*, London, John W. Parker, Son, and Bourne, 1862, pp. 689–91; report of paper read by Sarah P. Remond on 'American slavery and its influence in Great Britain'.

106 H.M. Cooper, '"Tracing the route to England": nineteenth-century Caribbean interventions in in English debates on race and slavery', in S. West (ed.), *The Victorians and Race*, Aldershot, Scolar Press, 1996, pp. 194–212. See also: L. Paravisini-Gebert, 'Mrs Seacole's *Wonderful Adventures in Many Lands* and the consciousness of transit', in G.H. Gerzina (ed.), *Black Victorians, Black Victoriana*, New Brunswick, Rutgers University Press, 2003, pp. 71–87.

107 Z. Alexander and A. Dewjee (eds), *The Wonderful Adventures of Mrs Seacole in Many Lands*, Bristol, Falling Wall Press, 1984, p. 57.

108 Kiddle, *Caroline Chisholm*, p. 162.

109 Alexander and Dewjee (eds), *The Wonderful Adventures*, Plate 10 (reproduction of engraving from *Punch*, 30 May 1857), pp. 224–5; Plate 15 (photograph of bust of Mary Seacole by Count Gleichen, 1871).

110 Holton, 'British freewomen', p. 155. For the shifting perspectives on race and racism among women activists from the 1880s, see also S.S. Holton, 'Segregation, racism and white women reformers: a transnational analysis, 1840–1912', *Women's History Review*, 2001, vol. 10, pp. 5–25.

Afterword

1 H. Bannerji, 'Mary Wollstonecraft, feminism and humanism. A spectrum of reading', in E.J. Yeo (ed.), *Mary Wollstonecraft and 200 Years of Feminisms*, London, Rivers Oram Press, 2007, pp. 222–42, quotes from pp. 236, 237.

2 M. Sinha, 'How history matters. Complicating the categories of "Western" and "non-Western" feminisms', The Social Justice Group at the Center for Advanced Feminist Studies, University of Minnesota (ed.), *Is Academic Feminism Dead? Theory in Practice*, New York, New York University Press, 2000, Chapter 6, pp. 168–86, quotes from pp. 170, 182.

3 Bannerji, p. 241.

Bibliography

Note: This bibliography lists published secondary sources (published in 1920 or later); for full references to primary sources and to unpublished PhD theses consulted, see the endnotes.

Abrahams, Y., 'Images of Sara Bartmann: sexuality, race and gender in early-nineteenth-century Britain', in R.R. Pierson and N. Chaudhuri (eds), *Nation, Empire, Colony. Historicizing Race and Gender*, Bloomington, Indiana University Press, 1998, pp. 220–36.

Adi, H., and Sherwood, M., *Pan-African History: Political Figures from Africa and the Diaspora since 1787*, London, Routledge, 2003.

Alexander, M.J., and Mohanty, C.T. (eds), *Feminist Genealogies, Colonial Legacies, Democratic Futures*, New York, Routledge, 1997.

Alexander, Z., and Dewjee, A. (eds), *The Wonderful Adventures of Mrs Seacole in Many Lands*, Bristol, Falling Wall Press, 1984.

Amos, V., and Parmar, P., 'Challenging imperial feminism', *Feminist Review*, 1984, vol. 17, pp. 3–19.

Anagol, P., 'Indian Christian women and indigenous feminism, c1850–c1920' in C. Midgley, *Gender and Imperialism*, Manchester, Manchester University Press, 1998, pp. 79–103.

Anderson, B.S., *Joyous Greetings. The First International Women's Movement 1830–1860*, Oxford, Oxford University Press, 2000.

Anderson, O., 'Women preachers in mid-Victorian Britain: some reflections on feminism, popular religion and social change', *The Historical Journal*, 1969, vol. 12, pp. 467–84.

Anstey, R., and Hair, P., *Liverpool, the African Slave Trade, and Abolition*, [Liverpool] Historic Society of Lancashire and Cheshire, 1989.

Arbuckle, E.S. (ed.), *Harriet Martineau in the London Daily News. Selected Contributions, 1852–1866*, New York, Garland Publishing, 1994.

Arbuthnot, J., *The History of John Bull*, edited by A.W. Bower and R.A. Erickson, Oxford, Clarendon Press, 1976.

Austen, J., *Mansfield Park*, Harmondsworth, Penguin, 1966 reprint.

Baines, D., *Migration in a Mature Economy. Emigration and Internal Migration in England and Wales, 1861–1900*, Cambridge, Cambridge University Press, 1985.

Ballhatchet, K., *Social Policy and Social Change in Western India*, London, Oxford University Press, 1957.

Bannerji, H., 'Mary Wollstonecraft, feminism and humanism. A spectrum of reading' in E.J. Yeo (ed.), *Mary Wollstonecraft and 200 Years of Feminisms*, London, Rivers Oram Press, 1997, pp. 222–42.

Barker-Benfield, G.J., *The Culture of Sensibility. Sex and Society in Eighteenth-Century Britain*, Chicago, Chicago University Press, 1992.

Bartle, G., 'The role of the British and Foreign School Society in elementary education in India and the East Indies 1813–75', *History of Education*, 1994, vol. 23, pp. 17–33.

Bayly, C.A., *Indian Society and the Making of the British Empire*, Cambridge, Cambridge University Press, 1988.

Bayly, C.A., *Imperial Meridian. The British Empire and the World 1780–1830*, London, Longman, 1989.

Beckles, H.McD., *Natural Rebels. A Social History of Enslaved Black Women in Barbados*, London, Zed Books, 1989.

Beckles, H.McD., *Centering Woman, Gender Discourses in Caribbean Slave Society*, Kingston, Ian Randle, 1999.

Beetham, M., *A Magazine of Her Own? Domesticity and Desire in the Woman's Magazine, 1800–1914*, London, Routledge, 1996.

Bender, T. (ed.), *The Antislavery Debate: Capitalism and Abolitionism as a Problem in Historical Interpretation*, Berkeley, University of California Press, 1992.

Berg, M., and Clifford, H. (eds), *Consumers and Luxury, Consumer Culture in Europe 1650–1850*, Manchester, Manchester University Press, 1999.

Berg, M., and Eger, E. (eds), *Luxury in the Eighteenth Century: Debates, Desires and Delectable Goods*, Basingstoke, Palgrave Macmillan, 2003.

Blackburn, R., *The Overthrow of Colonial Slavery 1776–1848*, London, Verso, 1988.

Bohls, E.A., 'The aesthetics of colonialism: Janet Schaw in the West Indies, 1774–5', *Eighteenth-Century Studies*, 1994, vol. 27, pp. 363–90.

Bolt, C., *Victorian Attitudes to Race*, London, Routledge and Kegan Paul, 1971.

Brantlinger, P., *Dark Vanishings. Discourse on the Extinction of Primitive Races, 1800–1930*, Ithaca, Cornell University Press, 2003.

Brewer, J., and Porter, R. (eds), *Consumption and the World of Goods*, London, Routledge, 1993.

Briggs, A., *The Age of Improvement, 1783–1867*, Harlow, Longman, 2000.

Brontë, C., *Jane Eyre,* Harmondsworth, Penguin, 1966 edition.

Bulbeck, C., *Re-Orienting Western Feminisms. Women's Diversity in a Postcolonial World*, Cambridge, Cambridge University Press, 1998.

Burnett, J., *Plenty and Want: a Social History of Diet in England from 1815 to the Present Day*, London, Nelson, 1966.

Burns, A., and Innes, J. (eds), *Rethinking the Age of Reform: Britain, 1780–1850*, Cambridge, Cambridge University Press, 2003.

Burton, A., 'The feminist quest for identity: British imperial suffragism and "global sisterhood", 1900–1915', *Journal of Women's History*, 1991, vol. 3, pp. 46–81.

Burton, A., 'History is now: feminist theory and the production of historical feminisms', *Women's History Review*, 1992, vol. 1, pp. 25–38.

Burton, A., *Burdens of History, British Feminists, Indian women, and Imperial Culture, 1865–1915*, Chapel Hill, University of North Carolina Press, 1994.

Burton, A., 'Rules of thumb: British history and "imperial culture" in nineteenth- and twentieth-century Britain', *Women's History Review*, 1994, vol. 3, pp. 483–500.

Burton, A., 'Recapturing Jane Eyre: reflections on historicising the colonial encounter in Victorian Britain', *Radical History Review*, 1996, vol. 64, pp. 58–72.

Burton, A., 'Thinking beyond the boundaries: empire, feminism and the domains of history', *Social History*, 2001, vol. 26, pp. 60–71.

Busco, M., *Sir Richard Westmacott, Sculptor*, Cambridge, Cambridge University Press, 1994.

Bush, B., *Slave Women in Caribbean Society 1650–1838*, London, James Currey, 1990.

Bush, B., '"Britain's Conscience on Africa": White Women, Race and Imperial Politics in Interwar Britain', in C. Midgley (ed.), *Gender and Imperialism*, Manchester, Manchester University Press, 1998, pp. 200–23.

Bush, J., '"The right sort of woman": female emigrators and emigration to the British Empire, 1890–1910', *Women's History Review*, 1994, vol. 3, pp. 385–410.

Bush, J., *Edwardian Ladies and Imperial Power*, London, Leicester University Press, 2000.

Cain, P.J., and Hopkins, A.G., *British Imperialism, Volume One: Innovation and Expansion, 1688–1914*, London, Longman, 1993.

Caine, B., *English Feminism 1780–1980*, Oxford, Oxford University Press, 1997.

Cameron, G., and Crooke, S., *Liverpool – Capital of the Slave Trade*, Liverpool, Picton Press, 1992.

Carey, B., *British Abolitionism and the Rhetoric of Sensibility. Writing, Sentiment, and Slavery, 1760–1807*, Basingstoke, Palgrave Macmillan, 2005.

Casteras, S.P., and Parkinson, R. (eds), *Richard Redgrave 1804–1888*, New Haven, Yale University Press, 1988.

Charlton, K., 'James Cropper and Liverpool's contribution to the anti-slavery movement', reprinted from *Transactions of the Historical Society of Lancashire and Cheshire*, 1972, vol. 123.

Chatterjee, A., *Representations of India, 1740–1840. The Creation of India in the Colonial Imagination*, Basingstoke, Macmillan, 1998.

Chaudhuri, N., 'Issues of race, gender and nation in Englishwomen's Domestic Magazine and Queen, 1850–1900', in D. Finkelstein and D.M. Peers (eds), *Negotiating India in the Nineteenth-Century Media*, Basingstoke, Macmillan, 2000, pp. 51–62.

Cherry, D., 'Shuttling and soul making: tracing the links between Algeria and egalitarian feminism in the 1850s', in S. West (ed.), *The Victorians and Race*, Aldershot, Scolar Press, 1996.

Cherry, D., *Beyond the Frame. Feminism and Visual Culture. Britain 1850–1900*, London, Routledge, 2000.

Civin, J., 'Slaves, sati and sugar: constructing imperial identity through Liverpool petition struggles', in J. Hoppit (ed.), *Parliaments, Nations and Identities in Britain and Ireland, 1660–1850*, Manchester, Manchester University Press, 2003.

Clark, A., *The Struggle for the Breeches. Gender and the Making of the British Working Class*, Berkeley, University of California Press, 1995.

Claeys, G. (ed.), *Modern British Utopias 1700–1850*, 8 vols, London, Pickering & Chatto, 1997.

Clarke, P., *The Governesses. Letters from the Colonies 1862–1882*, London, Hutchinson, 1985.

Cohn, B., *Colonialism and its Forms of Knowledge. The British in India,* Princeton, Princeton University Press, 1996.

Coleman, D., 'Conspicuous consumption: white abolitionism and English women's protest writing in the 1790s', *ELH*, 1994, vol. 61, pp. 341–62.

Colley, L., *Britons Forging the Nation 1707–1837*, New Haven, Yale University Press, 1992.

Compton, L.A., 'Josiah Wedgwood and the slave trade: a wider view', *Northern Ceramic Society Newsletter,* Dec. 1995, no. 100.

Cooper, F., and Stoler, L. (eds), *Tensions of Empire: Colonial Cultures in a Bourgeois World*, Berkeley, University of California Press, 1997.

Cooper, H.M., '"Tracing the route to England": nineteenth-century Caribbean interventions in English debates on race and slavery', in S. West (ed.), *The Victorians and Race*, Aldershot, Scolar Press, 1996.

Corfield, K., 'Elizabeth Heyrick: Radical Quaker', in G. Malmgreen (ed.), *Religion in the Lives of English Women, 1760–1930*, London, Croom Helm, 1986.

Craton, M., *Testing the Chains: Resistance to Slavery in the British West Indies*, Ithaca, Cornell University Press, 1982.

Cunningham, V., '"God and nature intended you for a missionary wife": Mary Hill, Jane Eyre and other missionary women in the 1840s', in F. Bowie, D. Kirkwood and S. Ardener (eds), *Women and Missions: Past and Present. Anthropological and Historical Perceptions,* Oxford, Berg, 1993.

Curtis, L.P., *Apes and Angels: The Irishmen in Victorian Caricature*, Newton Abbot, David and Charles, 1971.

Dabydeen, D. (ed.), *The Black Presence in English Literature*, Manchester, Manchester University Press, 1985.

Dabydeen, D., *Hogarth's Blacks. Images of Blacks in Eighteenth Century Art*, Manchester, Manchester University Press, 1987.

Da Costa, E.V., *Crowns of Glory, Tears of Blood, The Demerara Slave Rebellion of 1823*, New York, Oxford University Press, 1994.

Das Gupta, A.S., *A Brief Guide to the Victoria Memorial,* Calcutta, 1967.

Davidoff, L., and Hall, C., *Family Fortunes. Men and Women of the English Middle Class 1780–1850*, 2nd edn, London, Routledge, 2002.

Davies, K., 'A moral purchase: femininity, commerce and abolition, 1788–1792', in E. Eger *et al.* (eds), *Women, Writing and the Public Sphere, 1700–1830*, Cambridge, Cambridge University Press, 2001, pp. 133–62.

Davin, A., 'Imperialism and motherhood', *History Workshop Journal*, 1978, vol. 5, pp. 9–65.

Davis, A., *Women, Race and Class*, London, Women's Press, 1981.

Davis, D.B., *The Problem of Slavery in the Age of Revolution, 1770–1823*, Ithaca, Cornell University Press, 1975.

Davis, D.B., *From Homicide to Slavery: Studies in American Culture*, Oxford, Oxford University Press, 1986.

Davis, D.B., 'The perils of doing history by a historical abstraction: a reply to Thomas L. Haskell's AHR Forum Reply', in T. Bender (ed.), *The Antislavery Debate. Capitalism and Abolitionism as a Problem in Historical Interpretation*, Berkeley, University of California Press, 1992.

Davis, D.B., *From Homicide to Slavery: Studies in American Culture*, Oxford, Oxford University Press, 1986, pp. 238–57.

Deerr, N., *The History of Sugar*, vol. 2, London, Chapman and Hall, 1950.

Denoon, D., and Wyndham, M., 'Australia and the Western Pacific', in A. Porter (ed.), *The Oxford History of the British Empire, Volume 3: The Nineteenth Century*, Oxford, Oxford University Press, 1999, pp. 549–72.

DeVries, J., 'Rediscovering Christianity after the Postmodern turn', *Feminist Studies*, 2005, vol. 31, pp. 135–55.

Dews, D.C., 'Ann Carr and the female revivalists of Leeds', in G. Malmgreen (ed.), *Religion in the Lives of English Women 1760–1930*, London, Croom Helm, 1986.

Diamond, M., 'Maria Rye and *The Englishwoman's Domestic Magazine*', *Victorian Periodicals Review*, 1997, vol. 30, pp. 5–16.

Diamond, M., *Emigration and Empire. The Life of Maria S. Rye*, New York, Garland, 1999.

Donaldson, L.E., *Decolonizing Feminisms. Race, Empire and Empire-Building*, Chapel Hill, University of North Carolina Press, 1992.

Donaldson, M., '"The cultivation of the heart and the moulding of the will ...": the missionary contribution of the Society for Promoting Female Education in China, India, and the East', in W.J. Shiels and D. Wood (eds), *Women in the Church*, Oxford, Basil Blackwell, 1990.

Drescher, S., *Capitalism and Antislavery: British Mobilization in Comparative Perspective*, Basingstoke, Macmillan, 1986.

Dresser, M., 'Britannia', in R. Samuel (ed.), *Patriotism. The Making and Unmaking of British National Identity, Volume 3: National Fictions*, London, Routledge, 1989, pp. 26–49.

Drummond, J.C., and Wilbraham, A., *The Englishman's Food: a History of Five Centuries of English Diet*, London, Jonathan Cape, 1957.

Dyson, K.K., *A Various Universe: A Study of the Journals and Memoirs of British Men and Women in the Indian Subcontinent, 1765–1856*, Delhi, Oxford University Press, 1978.

Ehrenreich, B., and Hochschild, A.R. (eds), *Global Women. Nannies, Maids and Sex Workers in the New Economy*, London, Granta Books, 2003.

Eisenstein, Z., *Against Empire. Feminism, Racism, and the West*, London, Zed Books, 2004.

Elbourne, E., *Blood Ground. Colonialism, Mission, and the Contest for Christianity in the Cape Colony and Britain, 1799–1853*, Montreal, McGill-Queen's University Press, 2002.

Ellis, M., *The Politics of Sensibility. Race, Gender and Commerce in the Sentimental Novel*, Cambridge, Cambridge University Press, 1996.

Epstein, J.A., *Radical Expression. Political Language, Ritual and Symbol in England 1790–1850*, Oxford, Oxford University Press, 1994.

Ferguson, M., *Subject to Others: British Women Writers and Colonial Slavery, 1670–1834*, London, Routledge, 1992.

Ferguson, M., *The History of Mary Prince, A West Indian Slave. Related by Herself*, revised edn, Ann Arbor, The University of Michigan Press, 1997.

Figueira, D.M., 'Die flambierte Frau: sati in European culture', in J.S. Hawley (ed.), *Sati. The Blessing and the Curse. The Burning of Wives in India*, Oxford, Oxford University Press, 1994.

Fraser, H., Green, S., and Johnston, J., *Gender and the Victorian Periodical*, Cambridge, Cambridge University Press, 2003.

Fryer, P. *Staying Power. The History of Black People in Britain*, London, Pluto Press, 1984.

Gedalof, I., *Against Purity. Rethinking Identity with Indian and Western Feminism*, London, Routledge, 1999.

Geggus, D., 'British opinion and the emergence of Haiti, 1791–1805', in J. Walvin (ed.), *Slavery and British Society, 1776–1846*, London, Macmillan, 1982, pp. 123, 125.

George, M.D., *Catalogue of political and personal satires preserved in the Department of Prints and Drawings in the British Museum*, London, British Museum Publications, 1978, vol. 6, cat. no. 8074.

George, R.M. (ed.), *Burning Down the House. Recycling Domesticity*, Boulder, Westview Press, 1998, frontispiece illustration, p. 6.

Gerzina, G., *Black England. Life before Emancipation*, London, John Murray, 1995.

Ghose, J.C. (ed.), *The English Works of Raja Rammohun Roy*, vol. 2, New Delhi, Cosmo, 1982.

Ghose, I., *Women Travellers in Colonial India: the Power of the Female Gaze*, Delhi, Oxford University Press, 1998.

Gibson, M.E., 'Henry Martyn and England's Christian Empire: rereading *Jane Eyre* through Missionary Biography', *Victorian Literature and Culture*, 1999, vol. 27, pp. 419–42.

Gill, S., 'Heroines of missionary adventure: the portrayal of Victorian women missionaries in popular fiction and biography', in A. Hogan and A. Bradstock (eds), *Women of Faith in Victorian Culture. Reassessing the Angel in the House*, Basingstoke, Basingstoke, Macmillan, 1998, pp. 172–85.

Gilmore, J., *The Poetics of Empire: A Study of James Grainger's 'The Sugar Cane'*, London, Athlone Press, 2000.

Gilroy, P., *The Black Atlantic. Modernity and Double Consciousness*, London, Verso, 1993.

Gleadle, K., *The Early Feminists. Radical Unitarians and the Emergence of the Women's Rights Movement, 1831–51*, Basingstoke, Macmillan, 1995.

Gleadle, K., 'Opinions deliver'd in conversation': conversation, politics, and gender in the late eighteenth century', in J. Harris (ed.), *Civil Society in British History. Ideas, Identities, Institutions*, Oxford, Oxford University Press, 2003, pp. 61–78.

Gleadle, K., and Richardson, S. (eds), *Women in British Politics, 1760–1860. The Power of the Petticoat*, Basingstoke, Macmillan, 2000.

Goldman, L., *Science, Reform and Politics in Victorian Britain. The Social Science Association, 1857–1886*, Cambridge, Cambridge University Press, 2002.

Goodman, J., 'Languages of female colonial authority: the educational network of the ladies committee of the British and Foreign School Society, 1813–1837', *Compare*, 2000, vol. 30, pp. 7–19.

Gothard, J., *Blue China. Single Female Migration to Colonial America*, Melbourne, Melbourne University Press, 2001.

Groseclose, B., 'Imag(in)ing Indians', *Art History*, 1990, vol. 13.

Guest, H., *Small Change. Women, Learning, Patriotism, 1750–1810*, Chicago, Chicago University Press, 2000.

Haggis, J., 'Gendering colonialism or colonising gender? Recent women's studies approaches to white women and the history of British colonialism', *Women's Studies International Forum*, 1990, vol. 13, pp. 105–15.

Hall, C., *White, Male and Middle Class. Explorations in Feminism and History*, Cambridge, Polity Press, 1992.

Hall, C. (ed.), *Cultures of Empire. A Reader*, Manchester, Manchester University Press, 2000.

Hall, C., *Civilising Subjects. Metropole and Colony in the English Imagination 1830–1867*, Cambridge, Polity Press, 2002.

Hall, C., 'Imperial careering at home: Harriet Martineau on Empire' in A. Lester and D. Lambert (eds), *Colonial Lives Across the British Empire*, Cambridge, Cambridge University Press, 2006.

Hall, C., 'At home with history: Macaulay and the *History of England*', in C. Hall and S. Rose (eds), *At Home with the Empire*, Cambridge, Cambridge University Press, 2006, pp. 32–52.

Hall, C. and Rose, S. (eds), *At Home With the Empire*, Cambridge, Cambridge University Press, 2006.

Hall, K.F., 'Culinary spaces, colonial spaces: the gendering of sugar in the seventeenth century', in V. Traub *et al.* (eds), *Feminist Readings of Early Modern Culture. Emerging Subjects*, Cambridge, Cambridge University Press, 1996, pp. 168–90.

Hamilton, P., and Gothard, J., '"The other half": sources on British female emigration at the Fawcett Library, with special reference to Australia', *Women's Studies International Forum*, 1987, vol. 10, pp. 305–9.

Hammerton, A.J., *Emigrant Gentlewomen: Genteel Poverty and Female Emigration, 1830–1914*, London, Croom Helm, 1979.

Hammerton, A.J., 'Feminism and female emigration, 1861–1886', in M. Vicinus (ed.), *A Widening Sphere. Changing Roles of Victorian Women*, London, Methuen, 1980, pp. 52–71.

Hammerton, A.J., 'Gender and migration', in P. Levine (ed.), *Gender and Empire*, Oxford, Oxford University Press, 2004.

Harper, M., 'British migration and the peopling of Empire', in A. Porter (ed.), *The Oxford History of the British Empire. Volume Three: The Nineteenth Century*, Oxford, Oxford University Press, 1999, pp. 75–87.

Hawley, J.S. (ed.), *Sati, the Blessing and the Curse: the Burning of Wives in India*, New York, Oxford University Press, 1994.

Herstein, S.R., *A Mid-Victorian Feminist, Barbara Leigh Smith Bodichon*, New Haven, Yale University Press, 1985.

Hilton, B., *The Age of Atonement: The Influence of Evangelicalism on Social and Economic Thought, 1795–1865*, Oxford, Oxford University Press, 1988.

Hilton, B., *A Mad, Bad, and Dangerous People? England 1783–1846*, Oxford, Clarendon Press, 2006.

Hinde, W. *Catholic Emancipation. A Shake to Men's Minds*, Oxford, Blackwell, 1992.

Hirsch, P., *Barbara Leigh Smith Bodichon. Feminist, Artist and Rebel*, London, Pimlico, 1999.

Holton, S.S., 'British freewomen – national identity, constitutionalism and languages of race in early suffragist histories', in E.J. Yeo (ed.), *Radical Femininity. Women's Self-Representation in the Public Sphere*, Manchester, Manchester University Press, 1998, pp. 149–72.

Holton, S.S., 'Segregation, racism and white women reformers: a transnational analysis, 1840–1912', *Women's History Review*, 2001, vol. 10, pp. 5–25.

Homans, M., and Munich, A. (eds), *Remaking Queen Victoria*, Cambridge, Cambridge University Press, 1997.

Holton, S.S., *Emotional Life, Memory and Radicalism in the Lives of Women Friends, 1800–1920*, London, Routledge, 2007.

Homans, M., *Royal Representations: Queen Victoria and British Culture, 1837–1876*, Chicago, University of Chicago Press, 1998.

Hooks, B., *Ain't I a Woman?: Black Women and Feminism*, London, Pluto Press, 1981.

Horsman, R., 'Origins of racial Anglo-Saxonism in Great Britain before 1850', *Journal of the History of Ideas*, 1976, vol. 37, pp. 387–410.

Howse, E.M., *Saints in Politics: the 'Clapham Sect' and the Growth of Freedom*, London, George Allen & Unwin, 1953.

Huber, M.T. and Lutkehaus, N.C. (eds), *Gendered Missions*, Ann Arbor, University of Michigan Press, 1999.

Hughes, K., *The Victorian Governess*, London, The Hambledon Press, 1993.

Hunt, T.L., *Defining John Bull. Political Caricature and National Identity in Late Georgian England*, Aldershot, Ashgate, 2003.

Huttenback, R.A., *Racism and Empire, White Settlers and Colored Immigrants in the British Self-Governing Colonies, 1830–1910*, Ithaca, Cornell University Press, 1976.

Ingham, K., *Reformers in India, 1793–1833: An Account of the Work of Christian Missionaries on Behalf of Social Reform*, Cambridge, Cambridge University Press, 1956.

James, S.M., and Robertson, C.C., *Genital Cutting and Transnational Sisterhood. Disputing U.S. Polemics*, Urbana, University of Illinois Press, 2002.

Jeffrey, J.R., *The Great Silent Army of Abolitionism. Ordinary Women in the Antislavery Movement*, Chapel Hill, University of North Carolina Press, 1998.

John, W.D., and Baker, W., *Old English Lustre Pottery*, Newport, R.H. Johns, 1951.

Johnston, A., *Missionary Writing and Empire, 1800–1860*, Cambridge, Cambridge University Press, 2003.

Jordan, E., *The Women's Movement and Women's Employment in Nineteenth Century Britain*, London, Routledge, 1999.

Joshi, V.C. (ed.), *Rammohun Roy and the Process of Modernisation in India*, Delhi, Vikas, 1975.

Kelly, G., 'Revolutionary and romantic feminism: women, writing and cultural revolution', in K. Hanley and R. Selden (eds), *Revolution and English Romanticism. Politics and Rhetoric*, Hemel Hempstead, Harvester Wheatsheaf, 1990, pp. 107–30.

Kent, E.F., *Converting Women. Gender and Protestant Christianity in Colonial South India*, Oxford, Oxford University Press, 2004.

Kenzle, B.M., and Walker, P.J. (eds), *Women Preachers and Prophets through Two Millennia of Christianity*, Berkeley, University of California Press, 1998.

Kerber, L.K., *Women of the Republic: Intellect and Ideology in Revolutionary America*, Chapel Hill, University of North Carolina Press, 1980.

Ketring Nuermberger, R., *The Free Produce Movement. A Quaker Protest against Slavery*, Durham, Duke University Press, 1942.

Kiddle, M., *Caroline Chisholm*, Melbourne, Melbourne University Press, 1950.

Knapman, C., *White Women in Fiji 1835–1930: The Ruin of Empire?*, Sydney, Allen and Unwin, 1986.

Kowaleski-Wallace, B. 'Tea, gender and domesticity in eighteenth-century England', *Studies in Eighteenth-Century Culture*, 1994, vol. 23, pp. 131–45.

Kowaleski-Wallace, E., *Consuming Subjects. Women, Shopping, and Business in the Eighteenth Century*, New York, Columbia University Press, 1997.

Kranidis, R.S. (ed.), *Imperial Objects. Essays on Victorian Women's Emigration and the Unauthorized Imperial Experience*, New York, Twayne, 1998.

Kranidis, R.S., *The Victorian Spinster and Colonial Emigration*, Basingstoke, Macmillan, 1999.

Lacey, C. (ed.), *Barbara Leigh Smith and the Langham Place Circle*, London, Routledge & Kegan Paul, 1987.

Laird, M.A., *Missionaries and Education in Bengal, 1793–1837*, Oxford, Clarendon Press, 1972.

Lamonaca, M., 'Jane's crown of thorns: feminism and Christianity in Jane Eyre', *Studies in the Novel*, 2002, vol. 34, pp. 245–63.

Langford, P., *A Polite and Commercial People: England 1727–1783*, Oxford, Oxford University Press, 1989.

Langland, E., *Telling Tales: Gender and Narrative Form in Victorian Literature and Culture*, Columbus, The Ohio State University Press, 2002.

Lansbury, C., *Arcady in Australia. The Evocation of Australia in Nineteenth-Century English Literature*, Carlton, Melbourne University Press, 1970.

Leask, N., *British Romantic Writers and the East. Anxieties of Empire*, Cambridge, Cambridge University Press, 1992.

Ledbetter, K., 'Bonnets and Rebellions: imperialism in *The Lady's Newspaper*', *Victorian Periodicals Review*, 2004, vol. 37, pp. 252–72.

Levine, P., *Victorian Feminism 1850–1900*, London, Century Hutchinson, 1987.

Lewis, D.M. (ed.), *The Blackwell Dictionary of Evangelical Biography, 1730–1860*, 2 vols, Oxford, Blackwell, 1995.

Lewis, R.J., 'Comment: sati and the nineteenth-century British self', in J.S. Hawley (ed.), *Sati. The Blessing and the Curse. The Burning of Wives in India*, Oxford, Oxford University Press, 1994.

Liddle, J., and Joshi, R., *Daughters of Independence. Gender, Caste and Class in India*, London, Zed Books, 1986.

Logan, D. (ed.), *Harriet Martineau's Writing on the British Empire*, 4 vols, London, Pickering & Chatto, 2004.

Loomba, A., 'Dead women tell no tales: issues of female subjectivity, subaltern agency and tradition in colonial and post-colonial writings on widow immolation in India', *History Workshop Journal*, 1993, vol. 36, pp. 209–27.

Lorimer, D., *Colour, Class and the Victorians*, Leicester, Leicester University Press, 1978.

Macauley, D.J., *The Life of Una Marson, 1905–65*, Manchester, Manchester University Press, 1998.

McDermid, J., 'Conservative feminism and female education in the eighteenth century', *History of Education*, 1989, vol. 18, pp. 309–22.

Macdonald, C., *A Woman of Good Character. Single Women as Immigrant Settlers in Nineteenth-Century New Zealand*, New Zealand, Allen and Unwin, 1990.

Macdonald, L.A.O., *A Unique and Glorious Mission. Women and Presbyterianism in Scotland 1830–1930*, Edinburgh, John Donald, 2000.

Mackenzie, J.M., *Propaganda and Empire. The Manipulation of British Public Opinion 1880–1960*, Manchester, Manchester University Press, 1984.

Mackenzie, J.M. (ed.), *Imperialism and Popular Culture*, Manchester, Manchester University Press, 1986.

Macmillan, M., *Women of the Raj*, New York, Thames and Hudson, 1988.

Maison, M., '"Thine, only thine!" Women hymn writers in Britain, 1760–1835', in G. Malmgreen (ed.), *Religion in the Lives of English Women,* London, Croom Helm, 1986.

Majeed, J., *Ungoverned Imaginings: James Mill's 'The History of British India'*, Oxford, Clarendon Press, 1992.

Mandler, P., '"In the olden time": romantic history and English national identity, 1820–1850', in L. Brockliss and D. Eastwood (eds), *A Union of Multiple Identities. The British Isles, c. 1750–c. 1850,* Manchester, Manchester University Press, 1997, pp. 78–92.

Mandler, P., '"Race" and "nation" in mid-Victorian thought' in S. Collini, R. Whatmore and B. Young (eds), *History, Religion, and Culture. British Intellectual History. 1750–1950*, Cambridge, Cambridge University Press, 2000.

Mandler, P., *The English National Character. The History of an Idea from Edmund Burke to Tony Blair*, New Haven, Yale University Press, 2006.

Mandler, P., *History and National Life*, London, Profile, 2002.

Mani, L., 'The production of an official discourse on sati in early nineteenth-century Bengal', in F. Barker *et al.* (eds), *Empire and its Others*, 2 vols, Colchester, University of Essex, 1985, vol. 1.

Mani, L., 'Contentious traditions: the debate on *sati* in colonial India', in K. Sangari and S. Vaid (eds), *Recasting Women: Essays in Indian Colonial History*, New Brunswick, Rutgers University Press, 1990.

Mani, L., *Contentious Traditions: the Debate on Sati in Colonial India*, Berkeley, University of California Press, 1998.

Marks, S., 'History, the nation and empire: sniping from the periphery', *History Workshop Journal*, 1990, vol. 29, p. 116.

Mathers, H., 'The Evangelical spirituality of a Victorian feminist. Josephine Butler 1828–1900', *Journal of Ecclesiastical History*, 2001, vol. 52, pp. 281–312.

Matthew, H.C.G., and Harrison, B. (eds), *Oxford Dictionary of National Biography*, Oxford, Oxford University Press, 2004.

Maughan, S.S., 'Civic culture, women's foreign missions, and the British imperial imagination, 1860–1914', in F. Trentmann (ed.), *Paradoxes of Civil Society. New Perspectives on Modern German and British History*, New York, Berghahn, 2000, pp. 199–219.

Mellor, A.K., *Mothers of the Nation. Women's Political Writing in England, 1780–1830*, Bloomington, Indiana University Press, 2002.

Metcalf, T.R., *Ideologies of the Raj*, Cambridge, Cambridge University Press, 1995.

Midgley, C., *Women against Slavery. The British Campaigns, 1780–1870*, London, Routledge, 1992.

Midgley, C., 'Anti-slavery and feminism in nineteenth-century Britain', *Gender and History*, 1993, vol. 5, pp. 343–62.

Midgley, C., 'Slave sugar boycotts, female activism and the domestic base of British anti-slavery culture', *Slavery & Abolition*, 1996, vol. 17, pp. 137–62.

Midgley, C. (ed.), *Gender and Imperialism*, Manchester, Manchester University Press, 1998.

Midgley, C., 'Female emancipation in an imperial frame: English women and the campaign against sati (widow-burning) in India, 1813–30', *Women's History Review*, 2000, vol. 9, pp. 95–121.

Midgley, C., 'British abolition and feminism in transatlantic perspective', in K.K. Sklar and J.B. Stewart (eds), *Women's Rights and Transatlantic Antislavery in the Era of Abolition*, Yale, Yale University Press, 2007, pp. 144–68.

Mintz, S.W., *Sweetness and Power. The Place of Sugar in Modern History*, New York, Viking Penguin, 1985.

Mohanty, C.T., 'Under Western eyes: feminist scholarship and colonial discourses', in C.T. Mohanty, A. Russo and L. Torres (eds), *Third World Women and the Politics of Feminism*, Bloomington, Indiana University Press, 1991, pp. 51–80.

Mohanty, C.T., *Feminism Without Borders. Decolonizing Theory, Practicing Solidarity*, Durham, Duke University Press, 2003.

Morgan, S. (ed.), *Women, Religion and Feminism in Britain, 1750–1900*, Basingstoke, Palgrave Macmillan, 2002.

Morton, T., 'Blood sugar' in T. Fulford and P.J. Kitson (eds), *Romanticism and Colonialism. Writing and Empire, 1780–1830*, Cambridge, Cambridge University Press, 1998, pp. 87–107.

Murray, J., 'Gender attitudes and the contribution of women to evangelism and ministry in the nineteenth century', in J. Wolffe (ed.), *Evangelical Faith and Public Zeal. Evangelicals and Society in Britain 1780–1980*, London, SPCK, 1995.

Muthu, S., *Enlightenment Against Empire*, Princeton, Princeton University Press, 2003.

Myers, S.H., *The Bluestocking Circle. Women, Friendship and the Life of the Mind in Eighteenth-Century England*, Oxford, Clarendon Press, 1990.

Nandy, A., 'Sati: a nineteenth-century tale of women, violence and protest', in V.C. Joshi (ed.), *Rammohun Roy and the Process of Modernization in India*, Delhi, Vilcas Publishing House, 1975.

Nenadic, S., 'Middle-rank consumers and domestic culture in Edinburgh and Glasgow 1720–1840', *Past and Present*, 1994, vol. 145, pp. 122–56.

Newman, L.M., *White Women's Rights. The Racial Origins of Feminism in the United States*, New York, Oxford University Press, 1999.

Norton, M.B., *Liberty's Daughters. The Revolutionary Experience of American Women, 1750–1800*, Boston, Little, Brown and Co., 1980.

Nussbaum, F.A., *Torrid Zones. Maternity, Sexuality, and Empire in Eighteenth-Century English Narratives*, Baltimore, The Johns Hopkins University Press, 1995.

Offen, K., 'Defining feminism: a comparative historical approach', *Signs*, 1988, vol. 14, pp. 119–57.

Offen, K., *European Feminisms, 1700–1950*, Stanford, Stanford University Press, 2000.

Oldfield, J.R., *Popular Politics and British Anti-Slavery. The Mobilisation of Public Opinion Against the Slave Trade, 1787–1807*, Manchester, Manchester University Press, 1995.

Paravisini-Gebert, L., 'Mrs Seacole's *Wonderful Adventures in Many Lands* and the consciousness of transit', in G.H. Gerzina (ed.), *Black Victorians, Black Victoriana*, New Brunswick, Rutgers University Press, 2003, pp. 71–87.

Paxton, N., *Writing Under the Raj: Gender, Race and Rape in the British Imagination 1830–1857*, New Brunswick, Rutgers University Press, 1999.

Pedersen, S., *Eleanor Rathbone and the Politics of Conscience*, Newhaven, Yale University Press, 2004.

Perry, A., *On the Edge of Empire. Gender, Race and the Making of British Colombia, 1849–1871*, Toronto, University of Toronto Press, 2001.

Peterson, L., '"The feeling and claims of little people": heroic missionary memoirs, domestic(ated) spiritual autobiography, and *Jane Eyre: An Autobiography*', in L. Peterson, *Traditions of Victorian Women's Autobiography: the Poetics and Politics of Life Writing*, Charlottesville, University of Virginia Press, 1999, pp. 80–108.

Peterson, M.J., 'The Victorian governess: status incongruence in family and society', in M. Vicinus (ed.), *Suffer and be Still: Women in the Victorian Age*, London, Methuen, 1980 edition, pp. 3–19.

Philips, C.H., *The Correspondence of Lord William Cavendish Bentinck*, 2 vols, Oxford, Oxford University Press, 1977.

Piggin, S., *Making Evangelical Missionaries, 1789–1858. The Social Background, Motives and Training of British Protestant Missionaries to India*, London, Sutton Courtney Press, 1984.

Pitts, J., *A Turn to Empire. The Rise of Imperial Liberalism in Britain and France*, Princeton, Princeton University Press, 2005.

Pollock, J., *Wilberforce*, Tring, Lion Publishing, 1986.

Porter, A. (ed.), *Atlas of British Overseas Expansion*, London, Routledge, 1991.

Porter, A. (ed.), *The Oxford History of the British Empire Volume III: The Nineteenth Century*, Oxford, Oxford University Press, 1999.

Porter, B., *Absent-Minded Imperialists. Empire, Society, and Culture in Britain*, Oxford, Oxford University Press, 2004.

Potts, E.D., *British Baptist Missionaries in India 1793–1837. The History of Serampore and its Missions*, Cambridge, Cambridge University Press, 1967.

Prakash, G. (ed.), *After Colonialism: Imperial Histories and Postcolonial Displacements*, Princeton, Princeton University Press, 1994.

Prochaska, F., 'Women in English philanthropy, 1790–1830', *International Review of Social History*, 1974, vol. 19, pp. 426–45.

Prochaska, F., *Women and Philanthropy in Nineteenth-Century England*, Oxford, Clarendon Press, 1980.

Quirk, D.P., '"True Englishwomen" and "Anglo-Indians": gender, national identity, and feminism in the Victorian women's periodical press', in J.F. Codell (ed.), *Imperial Co-Histories. National Identities and the British and Colonial Press*, London, Associated University Press, 2003, pp. 167–87.

Rajan, R.S., *Real and Imagined Women. Gender, Culture and Postcolonialism*, London, Routledge, 1993.

Raza, R., *In Their Own Words. British Women Writers and India 1740–1857*, New Delhi, Oxford University Press, 2006.

Rendall, J., *The Origins of Modern Feminism. Women in Britain, France and the United States, 1780–1860*, Basingstoke, Macmillan, 1985.

Rendall, J., *Equal or Different. Women's Politics 1800–1914*, Oxford, Basil Blackwell, 1987.

Rendall, J., '"A moral engine?" Feminism, liberalism and the *English Woman's Journal*', in J. Rendall (ed.), *Equal or Different: Women's Politics 1800–1914*, Oxford, Blackwell, 1987.

Rendall, J., 'Friendship and politics: Barbara Leigh Smith (1827–91) and Bessie Rayner Parkes (1829–1925)', in S. Mendus and J. Rendall (eds), *Sexuality and Subordination*, London, Routledge, 1989.

Rendall, J., 'Citizenship, culture and civilisation: the languages of British suffragists 1899–1914', in M. Nolan and C. Daley (eds), *Suffrage and Beyond: International Feminist Perspectives*, Auckland, Auckland University Press, 1994.

Rendall, J., 'John Stuart Mill, liberal politics, and the movements for women's suffrage, 1865–1873' in A. Vickery (ed.), *Women, Privilege and Power. British Politics, 1750 to the Present*, Stanford, Stanford University Press, 2001, pp. 168–200.

Rendall, J., 'The condition of women, women's writing and the Empire in nineteenth-century Britain', in C. Hall and S.O. Rose (eds), *At Home with the Empire. Metropolitan Culture and the Imperial World*, Cambridge, Cambridge University Press, 2006, pp. 101–21.

Reynolds, H., *Frontier: Aborigines, Settlers, and Land*, Sydney, Allen and Unwin, 1987.

Richardson, D., 'The slave trade, sugar, and British economic growth, 1748–1776', in B.L. Solow and S.L. Engerman (eds), *British Capitalism and Caribbean Slavery. The Legacy of Eric Williams,* Cambridge, Cambridge University Press, 1987, pp. 103–34.

Riley, D., *'Am I That Name?' Feminism and the Category of 'Women' in History*, London, Macmillan, 1988.

Roberts, H.E., 'Marriage, redundancy or sin: the painter's view of women in the first twenty-five years of Victoria's reign', in M. Vicinus (ed.), *Suffer and Be Still*, London, Methuen & Co., 1980, pp. 45–76 and Plate 4.

Rogers, H., *Women and the People. Authority, Authorship and the Radical Tradition in Nineteenth-Century England*, Aldershot, Ashgate, 2000.

Rosselli, J., *Lord William Bentinck. The Making of a Liberal Imperialist 1774–1839*, Delhi, Thompson Press, 1974.

Rowbotham, J., '"Hear an Indian Sister's plea": reporting the work of nineteenth-century British female missionaries', *Women's Studies International Forum*, 1998, vol. 21, pp. 247–61.

Rubinstein, D., *A Different World for Women: The Life of Millicent Garrett Fawcett*, Columbus, Ohio State University Press, 1991.

Said, E.W., *Culture and Imperialism*, New York, Alfred A. Knopf, 1993.

Said, E.W., *Out of Place. A Memoir*, London, Granta, 1999.

Salih, S. (ed.), *The History of Mary Prince. A West Indian Slave*, London, Penguin, revised edition, 2004.

Sandiford, K., *The Cultural Politics of Sugar. Caribbean Slavery and Narratives of Colonialism*, Cambridge, Cambridge University Press, 2000.

Savage, D., 'Missionaries and the development of a colonial ideology of female education in India', *Gender and History*, 1997, vol. 9, pp. 201–21.

Schwarzkopf, J., *Women in the Chartist Movement*, Basingstoke, Macmillan, 1991.

Scott, J.W., *Gender and the Politics of History*, New York, Columbia University Press, 1988.

Scott, J.W., 'The imagination of Olympe de Gouges', in E.J. Yeo (ed.), *Mary Wollstonecraft and 200 Years of Feminisms*, London, Rivers Oram Press, 1997, pp. 36–49.

Semple, R.A., *Missionary Women, Gender, Imperialism and the Victorian Idea of Christian Mission*, Woodbridge, Boydell, 2003.

Sen Gupta, K.P., *The Christian Missionaries in Bengal, 1793–1833*, Calcutta, Firma K.L. Mukhopadhyay, 1971.

Sensbach, J.F., *Rebecca's Revival. Creating Black Christianity in the Atlantic World,* Cambridge, Harvard University Press, 2005.

Shammas, C., 'Changes in English and Anglo-American consumption from 1550 to 1880', in J. Brewer and R. Porter (eds), *Consumption and the World of Goods*, London, Routledge, p. 183.

Sharma, A. (ed.), *Sati. Historical and Phenomenological Essays*, Delhi, Motilal Banarsidass, 1988.

Sharpe, J., *Allegories of Empire. The Figure of the Woman in the Colonial Text*, Minneapolis, University of Minnesota Press, 1993.

Shepherd, V., Brereton, B., and Bailey, B. (eds), *Engendering History. Caribbean Women in Historical Perspective*, Kingston, Ian Randle Publishers, 1995.

Sheridan, R.B., *Sugar and Slavery*, Lodge Hill, Caribbean Universities Press, 1974.

Sinha, M., 'How history matters. Complicating the categories of "western" and "non-western" feminisms', in The Social Justice Group at the Center for Advanced Feminist Studies, University of Minnesota (ed.), *Is Academic Feminism Dead? Theory in Practice*, New York, New York University Press, 2000, pp. 168–86.

Sklar, K.K., *Women's Rights Emerges within the Antislavery Movement 1830–1870*, Boston, Bedford/St Martins, 2000.

Smith, W.D., 'Complications of the commonplace: tea, sugar, and imperialism', *Journal of Interdisciplinary History*, 1992, vol. 23, pp. 259–78.

Spivak, G., 'Three women's texts and a critique of imperialism', *Critical Inquiry*, 1985, vol. 12, pp. 243–61.

Spivak, G., 'Can the subaltern speak?', in C. Nelson and L. Grossberg (eds), *Marxism and the Interpretation of Culture*, Basingstoke, Macmillan Education, 1988.

Spivak, G., 'Three women's texts and a critique of imperialism', in R. Lewis and S. Mills (eds), *Feminist Postcolonial Theory. A Reader*, Edinburgh, Edinburgh University Press, 2003, pp. 306–23.

Stafford, W., *English Feminists and Their Opponents in the 1790s. Unsex'd and Proper Females*, Manchester, Manchester University Press, 2002.

Stanley, B., *The Bible and the Flag: Protestant Missions and British Imperialism in the Nineteenth and Twentieth Centuries*, Leicester, Apollos, 1990.

Stanley, B., *The History of the Baptist Missionary Society, 1792–1992*, Edinburgh, T. & T. Clark, 1992.

Strachey, R., *The Cause. A Short History of the Women's Movement in Great Britain*, London, Virago, 1978.

Strobel, M., *European Women and the Second British Empire*, Bloomington, Indiana University Press, 1991.

Summers, A., *Female Lives, Moral States. Women, Religion and Public Life in Britain 1800–1930*, Newbury, Threshold Press, 2000.

Surel, J., 'John Bull', in R. Samuel (ed.), *Patriotism: the Making and Unmaking of British National Identity*, London, Routledge, 1989, vol. 3, pp. 3–25.

Sussman, C., 'Women and the politics of sugar, 1792', *Representations*, 1994, vol. 48, pp. 48–69.

Sussman, C., *Consuming Anxieties. Consumer Protest, Gender and British Slavery, 1713–1833*, Stanford, Stanford University Press, 2000.

Sutherland, K., 'Hannah More's counter-revolutionary feminism', in K. Everest (ed.), *Revolution in Writing. British Literary Responses to the French Revolution*, Milton Keynes, Open University Press, 1991, pp. 27–63.

Swaisland, C., *Servants and Gentlewomen to the Golden Land. The Emigration of Single Women from Britain to Southern Africa, 1820–1939*, Oxford, Berg, 1993.

Swan, A.S., *Seed Time and Harvest. The Story of the Hundred Years' Work of the Women's Foreign Mission of the Church of Scotland*, London, T. Nelson & Sons, 1937.

Taylor, B., *Eve and the New Jerusalem. Socialism and Feminism in the Nineteenth Century*, London, Virago, 1983.

Taylor, B., *Mary Wollstonecraft and the Feminist Imagination*, Cambridge, Cambridge University Press, 2003.

Taylor, M., 'John Bull and the iconography of public opinion in England –. 1712–1929', *Past and Present*, 1992, vol. 134, pp. 93–128.

Teltscher, K., *India Inscribed. European and British Writing on India 1600–1800*, Delhi, Oxford University Press, 1995.

Thompson, D., *Queen Victoria. Gender and Power*, London, Virago, 1990.

Thorne, S., '"The conversion of Englishmen and the conversion of the world insepara-ble": missionary imperialism and the language of class in early industrial Britain', in F. Cooper and L. Stoler (eds), *Tensions of Empire: Colonial Cultures in a Bourgeois World*, Berkeley, University of California Press, 1997, pp. 238–62.

Thorne, S., *Congregational Missions and the Making of an Imperial Culture in Nineteenth-Century England*, Stanford, Stanford University Press, 1999.

Thorne, S., 'Missionary-imperial feminism', in M.T. Huber and N.C. Lutkehaus (eds), *Gendered Missions*, Ann Arbor, University of Michigan Press, pp. 39–66.

Thorne, S., 'Religion and empire at home', in C. Hall and S. Rose (eds), *At Home with the Empire. Metropolitan Culture and the Imperial World*, Cambridge, Cambridge University Press, 2006, pp. 143–65.

Tibbles, A. (ed.), *Transatlantic Slavery: Against Human Dignity*, London, HMSO, 1994.

Tickner, L., *The Spectacle of Women. Imagery of the Suffrage Campaign 1907–14*, London, Chatto and Windus, 1987.

Tosh, J., '"All the masculine virtues": English emigration to the colonies, 1815–1852', in J. Tosh, *Manliness and Masculinities in Nineteenth-Century Britain. Essays on Gender, Family and Empire*, Harlow, Pearson Education, 2005, pp. 173–91.

Trollope, J., *Britannia's Daughters: Women of the British Empire*, London, Random House, 1983.

Turley, D., *The Culture of English Antislavery*, London, Routledge, 1992.

Tuson, P., *The Queen's Daughters. An Anthology of Victorian Feminist Writings on India 1857–1900*, Reading, Ithaca Press, 1995.

Twells, A., '"Let us begin well at home": class, ethnicity and Christian motherhood in the writing of Hanhah Kilham, 1774–1832', in E. J. Yeo, *Radical Femininity. Women's Self-Representation in the Public Sphere*, Manchester, Manchester University Press, 1998, pp. 25–51.

Twells, A., '"Happy English children": class, ethnicity and the making of mis-sionary women, 1800–40', *Women's Studies International Forum*, 1998, vol. 21, pp. 235–46.

Valence, D.M., *Prophetic Sons and Daughters*, Princeton, Princeton University Press, 1985.

Vickery, A., 'From golden age to separate spheres? A review of the categories and chronology of English women's history', *Historical Journal*, 1993, vol. 36, pp. 383–414.

Vickery, A. (ed.), *Women, Privilege and Power. British Politics, 1750 to the Present*, Stanford, Stanford University Press, 2003.

Visram, R., *Ayahs, Lascars and Princes. Indians in Britain 1700–1947*, London, Pluto Press, 1986.

Walker, L., and Ware, V., 'Political pincushions: decorating the abolitionist inte-rior 1787–1865', in I. Blyden and J. Floyd (eds), *Domestic Space. Reading the Nineteenth-Century Interior*, Manchester, Manchester University Press, 1999, pp. 58–83.

Walvin, J. (ed.), *Slavery and British Society, 1776–1846*, London, Macmillan Press, 1982.

Walvin, J., *Black Ivory: A History of British Slavery*, London, Harper Collins, 1992.

Walvin, J., *The Quakers. Manners and Morals*, London, John Murray, 1997.

Walvin, J., *Fruits of Empire. Exotic Produce and British Taste, 1660–1800*, Basingstoke, Macmillan, 1997.

Ware, V., *Beyond the Pale. White Women, Racism and History*, London, Verso, 1992.

White, D.G., 'Nationalism and feminism in the Black Atlantic', in P. Grimshaw, K. Holmes and M. Lake (eds), *Women's Rights and Human Rights. International Historical Perspectives*, Basingstoke, Palgrave, 2001, pp. 231–42.

Whitlock, G., *The Intimate Empire. Reading Women's Autobiography*, London, Cassell, 2000.

Williams, E., *Capitalism and Slavery*, Chapel Hill, University of North Carolina Press, 1944.

Wilson, E.G., *Thomas Clarkson. A Biography*, Basingstoke, Macmillan, 1989.

Wilson, K., *The Sense of the People: Politics, Culture and Imperialism in Britain, 1715–1785*, Cambridge, Cambridge University Press, 1995.

Wilson, K., *An Island Race: Englishness, Empire and Gender in the Eighteenth Century*, London, Routledge, 2003.

Wilson, K. (ed.), *A New Imperial History. Culture, Identity and Modernity in Britain and the Empire, 1660–1840*, Cambridge, Cambridge University Press, 2004.

Women's Auxiliary of the Wesleyan Methodist Missionary Society, *The Story of the Women's Auxiliary 1858–1922*, London, Wesleyan Methodist Missionary Society, 1923.

Wood, M., *Blind Memory. Visual Representations of Slavery in England and America, 1780–1865*, Manchester, Manchester University Press, 2000.

Woollacott, A., *To Try Her Fortune in London. Australian Women, Colonialism, and Modernity*, Oxford, Oxford University Press, 2001.

Yeo, E.J., *The Contest for Social Science. Relations and Representations of Gender and Class*, London, Rivers Oram Press, 1996.

Yeo, E.J., *Radical Femininity. Women's Self-Representation in the Public Sphere*, Manchester, Manchester University Press, 1998.

Young, R.J., *Postcolonialism. An Historical Introduction*, Oxford, Blackwell, 2001.

Zaeske, S., *Signatures of Citizenship. Petitioning, Antislavery, and Women's Political Identity*, Chapel Hill, University of North Carolina Press, 2003.

Index

Feminist History Reader

Edited by Sue Morgan

The Feminist History Reader gathers together key articles, from some of the very best writers in the field, that have shaped the dynamic historiography of the past thirty years, and introduces students to the major shifts and turning points in this dialogue.

The *Reader* is divided into four sections:

- early feminist historians' writings following the move from reclaiming women's past through to the development of gender history
- the interaction of feminist history with 'the linguistic turn' and the challenges made by post-structuralism and the responses it provoked
- the work of lesbian historians and queer theorists in their challenge of the heterosexism of feminist history writing
- the work of black feminists and postcolonial critics/Third World scholars and how they have laid bare the ethnocentric and imperialist tendencies of feminist theory.

Each reading has a comprehensive and clearly structured introduction with a guide to further reading, this wide-ranging guide to developments in feminist history is essential reading for all students of history.

978-0-415-31809-9 (Hardback)
978-0-415-31810-5 (Paperback)

Available at all good bookshops
For ordering and further information please visit:

www.routledge.com

Women's History, Britain 1700–1850

Hannah Barker and Elaine Chalus

Here for the first time is a comprehensive history of the women of Britain during a period of dramatic change. Placing women's experiences in the context of these major social, economic and cultural shifts that accompanied the industrial and commercial transformations, Hannah Barker and Elaine Chalus paint a fascinating picture of the change, revolution, and continuity that were encountered by women of this time.

A thorough and well-balanced selection of individual chapters by leading field experts and dynamic new scholars, combine original research with a discussion of current secondary literature, and the contributors examine areas as diverse as enlightenment, politics, religion, education, sexuality, family, work, poverty, and consumption.

Providing a captivating overview of women and their lives, this book is an essential purchase for the study of women's history, and, providing delightful little gems of knowledge and insight, it will also appeal to any reader with an interest in this fascinating topic.

978-0-415-29176-7 (hardback)
978-0-415-29177-4 (paperback)

Available at all good bookshops
For ordering and further information please visit:

www.routledge.com

Women's History, Britain 1850-1945: An Introduction
Edited by June Purvis

This edited collection includes chapters, written by experts in their field, on the suffrage movement, race and empire, industrialisation, the impact of war and women's literature, health, the family, education, sexuality, work and politics. Each contribution provides an overview of the main issues and debates within each area and offers suggestions for further reading. This book not only provides an invaluable introduction to every aspect of women's participation in the political, social and economic history of Britain, but also brings the reader up to date with current historical thinking on the study of women's history itself. This is an invaluable and concise overview of an essential area of historical and contemporary study.

978-1-85728-319-8 (hardback)
978-0-415-23889-2 (paperback)

Available at all good bookshops
For ordering and further information please visit:
www.routledge.com